THE ESSENTIAL
LOUISE HAY
COLLECTION

ALSO BY LOUISE HAY

The Power Is Within You (audio book)
The Power of Your Spoken Word
Receiving Prosperity
Self-Esteem Affirmations (subliminal)
Self-Healing
Stress-Free (subliminal)
Totality of Possibilities
What I Believe and Deep Relaxation
You Can Heal Your Life (audio book)
You Can Heal Your Life Study Course
Your Thoughts Create Your Life

DVDs
Dissolving Barriers
Receiving Prosperity
You Can Heal Your Life Study Course
You Can Heal Your Life, The Movie (also available in an expanded edition)
You Can Trust Your Life (with Cheryl Richardson)

CARD DECKS
Healthy Body Cards
I Can Do It® Cards
I Can Do It® Cards . . . for Creativity, Forgiveness, Health, Job Success, Wealth, Romance
Power Thought Cards
Power Thoughts for Teens
Power Thought Sticky Cards
Wisdom Cards

CALENDAR
I Can Do It® Calendar (for each individual year)

and

THE LOUISE L. HAY BOOK COLLECTION
(comprising the gift versions of *Meditations to Heal Your Life, You Can Heal Your Life,* and *You Can Heal Your Life Companion Book*)

All of the above are available at your local
bookstore, or may be ordered by visiting:

Hay House USA: www.hayhouse.com®
Hay House Australia: www.hayhouse.com.au
Hay House UK: www.hayhouse.co.uk
Hay House South Africa: www.hayhouse.co.za
Hay House India: www.hayhouse.co.in

Louise's Websites: www.LouiseHay.com® and www.HealYourLife.com®

THE ESSENTIAL
LOUISE HAY
COLLECTION

Includes the all-time international bestsellers

YOU CAN HEAL YOUR LIFE
HEAL YOUR BODY AND
THE POWER IS WITHIN YOU

HAY HOUSE, INC.
Carlsbad, California • New York City
London • Sydney • Johannesburg
Vancouver • Hong Kong • New Delhi

Published and distributed in the United States by: Hay House, Inc.: www.hay house.com® • *Published and distributed in Australia by:* Hay House Australia Pty. Ltd.: www.hayhouse.com.au • *Published and distributed in the United Kingdom by:* Hay House UK, Ltd.: www.hayhouse.co.uk • *Published and distributed in the Republic of South Africa by:* Hay House SA (Pty), Ltd.: www.hayhouse.co.za • *Distributed in Canada by:* Raincoast: www.raincoast.com • *Published in India by:* Hay House Publishers India: www.hayhouse.co.in

Cover design: Aeshna Roy

Library of Congress Control Number: 2013942780

Hardcover ISBN: 978-1-4019-4419-3

16 15 14 13   4 3 2 1
1st edition, September 2013

Printed in the United States of America

CONTENTS

HEAL YOUR BODY 185

THE POWER IS WITHIN YOU 277

Part I: Becoming Conscious

Part II: Dissolving the Barriers

Part III: Loving Yourself

Part IV: Applying Your Inner Wisdom

Part V: Letting Go of the Past

You Can Heal
Your Life

Dedication

May this offering help you find the place within where you know your own self-worth, the part of you that is pure love and self-acceptance.

Acknowledgments

I acknowledge with joy and pleasure:

My many students and clients who taught me so much and who first encouraged me to put my ideas down on paper.

My dedicated staff at Hay House, who share my dream of disseminating books, audios, and videos that help to heal the planet spiritually, emotionally, and physically.

My wonderful readers and listeners, who have shown their loving support for my work and who continue to be a source of inspiration for me.

All those whose hearts are opening more and more each day.

My dear friends throughout the world, who surround me with unconditional love, laughter, and just plain fun!

Foreword

If I were cast away on a desert island and could have only one book with me there, I might well choose Louise L. Hay's *You Can Heal Your Life*.

Not only is it the essence of a great teacher, it is also the powerful and very personal statement of a great lady.

Louise shares some of her journey to where she is in her evolvement now in this wonderful new book. I resonated in admiration and in compassion to her story — too briefly sketched here, in my view, but perhaps that's another book.

It's all here, is my point. All you need to know about life, its lessons and how to do the work on yourself is right here. And this includes Louise's reference guide to probable mental patterns behind dis-ease, which is truly remarkable and unique — in my experience. A person on a desert island who found this manuscript in a bottle could learn all he or she needs to know to make this life be the one that gets the job done.

Desert island or not, if *you* have found your way to Louise Hay, perhaps even "accidentally," you're well on your way. Louise's books, her remarkable healing tapes, and her inspired workshops are wonderful gifts to a troubled world.

It was my own deep investment in working with persons with aids that led me to meeting Louise and utilizing concepts from her healing work.

Each aids person I worked with and for whom I played Louise's tape, *A Positive Approach to AIDS*, got Louise's message on the first hearing — and many made playing this tape part of their daily healing ritual. One man named Andrew told me, "I go to bed with Louise, and I get up to her every day!"

My respect and love for Louise grew as I observed my beloved aids people make their transitions enriched and at peace and complete — more full of love and forgiveness for themselves and everyone else for having had Louise in their lives — and with a quiet respect for having created that precise learning experience.

I have been gifted in my life with many great teachers, some of them saints, I'm sure, and even avatars, perhaps. Yet Louise is a great teacher one can speak with and be with because of her enormous capacity to listen and to be in unconditional love while sharing doing the dishes. (In the same way another teacher I hold as great makes terrific potato salad.) Louise teaches by example and lives what she teaches.

I am deeply honored to invite you to make this book part of your life. You — and it — are worth it!

DAVE BRAUN

VENTURES IN SELF-FULFILLMENT
DANA POINT, CALIFORNIA

Part I
INTRODUCTION

Suggestions to My Readers

I have written this book to share with you, my readers, that which I know and teach. It incorporates portions of my little blue book, *Heal Your Body*, which has become widely accepted as an authoritative work on the mental patterns that create dis-eases in the body.

I have had hundreds of letters from readers asking me to share more of my information. Many persons who have worked with me as private clients, and those who have taken my workshops here and abroad, have requested I take the time to write this book.

I have set up this book to take you through a session, just as I would if you came to me as a private client and attended one of my workshops.

If you will do the exercises progressively as they appear in the book, by the time you have finished, you will have begun to change your life.

I suggest you read through the book once. Then slowly read it again, only this time do each exercise in depth. Give yourself time to work with each one.

If you can, work through the exercises with a friend or with a member of your family.

Each chapter opens with an affirmation. Each of these is good to use when you are working on that area of your life. Take two or three days to study and work with each chapter. Keep saying and writing the affirmation that opens the chapter.

The chapters close with a treatment. This is a flow of positive ideas designed to change consciousness. Read over this treatment several times a day.

I close this book by sharing with you my own story. I know it will show you that no matter where we have come from or how lowly it was, we can totally change our lives for the better.

Know that when you work with these ideas, my loving support is with you.

Some Points
of My Philosophy

We are each responsible for all of our experiences.

Every thought we think is creating our future.

The point of power is always in the present moment.

Everyone suffers from self-hatred and guilt.

The bottom line for everyone is,
"I'm not good enough."

It's only a thought, and a thought can be changed.

We create every so-called illness in our body.

Resentment, criticism, and guilt
are the most damaging patterns.

Releasing resentment will dissolve even cancer.

We must release the past and forgive everyone.

We must be willing to begin to learn to love ourselves.

Self-approval and self-acceptance in the now
are the keys to positive changes.

When we really love ourselves, everything in our life works.

In the infinity of life where I am, all is perfect,
whole, and complete, and yet life is ever changing.
There is no beginning and no end,
only a constant cycling and recycling
of substance and experiences.
Life is never stuck or static or stale,
for each moment is ever new and fresh.
I am one with the very Power that created me, and this Power
has given me the power to create my own circumstances.
I rejoice in the knowledge that I have the power
of my own mind to use in any way I choose.
Every moment of life is a new beginning point
as we move from the old. This moment is a new point
of beginning for me right here and right now.
All is well in my world.

 *Chapter One*

WHAT I BELIEVE

"The gateways to wisdom and knowledge
are always open."

Life Is Really Very Simple. What We Give Out, We Get Back

What we think about ourselves becomes the truth for us. I believe that everyone, myself included, is responsible for everything in our lives, the best and the worst. Every thought we think is creating our future. Each one of us creates our experiences by our thoughts and our feelings. The thoughts we think and the words we speak create our experiences.

We create the situations, and then we give our power away by blaming the other person for our frustration. No person, no place, and no thing has any power over us, for "we" are the only thinkers in our mind. When we create peace and harmony and balance in our minds, we will find it in our lives.

Which of these statements sounds like you?

"People are out to get me."
"Everyone is always helpful."

Each one of these beliefs will create quite different experiences. What we believe about ourselves and about life becomes true for us.

The Universe Totally Supports Us in Every Thought We Choose to Think and Believe

Put another way, our subconscious mind accepts whatever we choose to believe. They both mean that what I believe about myself and about life becomes true for me. What you choose to think about yourself and about life becomes true for you. And we have unlimited choices about what we can think.

When we know this, then it makes sense to choose "Everyone is always helpful," rather than "People are out to get me."

The Universal Power Never Judges or Criticizes Us

It only accepts us at our own value. Then it reflects our beliefs in our lives. If I want to believe that life is lonely and that nobody loves me, then that is what I will find in my world.

However, if I am willing to release that belief and to affirm for myself that "Love is everywhere, and I am loving and lovable," and to hold on to that new affirmation and to repeat it often, then it will become true for me. Now, loving people will come into my life, the people already in my life will become more loving to me, and I will find myself easily expressing love to others.

Most of Us Have Foolish Ideas about Who We Are and Many, Many Rigid Rules about How Life Ought to Be Lived

This is not to condemn us, for each of us is doing the very best we can at this very moment. If we knew better, if we had more understanding and awareness, then we would do it differently. Please don't put yourself down for being where you are. The very fact that you have found this book and have discovered me means that you are ready to make a new, positive change in your life. Acknowledge yourself for this. "Men don't cry!" "Women can't handle money!" What limiting ideas to live with.

When We Are Very Little, We Learn How to Feel about Ourselves and about Life by the Reactions of the Adults Around Us

It is the way we learn what to think about ourselves and about our world. Now, if you lived with people who were very unhappy, frightened, guilty, or angry, then you learned a lot of negative things about yourself and about your world.

"I never do anything right." "It's my fault." "If I get angry, I'm a bad person."

Beliefs like this create a frustrating life.

When We Grow Up, We Have a Tendency to Re-create the Emotional Environment of Our Early Home Life

This is not good or bad, right or wrong; it is just what we know inside as "home." We also tend to recreate in our personal relationships the relationships we had with our mothers or with our fathers, or what they had between them. Think how often you have had a lover or a boss who was "just like" your mother or father.

We also treat ourselves the way our parents treated us. We scold and punish ourselves in the same way. You can almost hear the words when you listen. We also love and encourage ourselves in the same way, if we were loved and encouraged as children.

"You never do anything right." "It's all your fault." How often have you said this to yourself?

"You are wonderful." "I love you." How often do you tell yourself this?

However, I Would Not Blame Our Parents for This

We are all victims of victims, and they could not possibly have taught us anything they did not know. If your mother did not know how to love herself, or your father did not know how to love himself, then it would be impossible for them to teach you to love yourself.

They were doing the best they could with what they had been taught as children. If you want to understand your parents more, get them to talk about their own childhood; and if you listen with compassion, you will learn where their fears and rigid patterns come from. Those people who "did all that stuff to you" were just as frightened and scared as you are.

I Believe That We Choose Our Parents

Each one of us decides to incarnate upon this planet at a particular point in time and space. We have chosen to come here to learn a particular lesson that will advance us upon our spiritual, evolutionary pathway. We choose our sex, our color, our country, and then we look around for the particular set of parents who will mirror the pattern we are bringing in to work on in this lifetime. Then, when we grow up, we usually point our fingers accusingly at our parents and whimper, "You did it to me." But really, we chose them because they were perfect for what we wanted to work on overcoming.

We learn our belief systems as very little children, and then we move through life creating experiences to match our beliefs. Look back in your own life and notice how often you have gone through the same experience. Well, I believe you created those experiences over and over because they mirrored something you believed about yourself. It doesn't really matter how long we have had a problem, or how big it is, or how life-threatening it is.

The Point of Power Is Always in the Present Moment

All the events you have experienced in your lifetime up to this moment have been created by your thoughts and beliefs you have held in the past. They were created by the thoughts and words you used yesterday, last week, last month, last year, 10, 20, 30, 40, or more years ago, depending on how old you are.

However, that is your past. It is over and done with. What is important in this moment is what you are choosing to think and believe and say right now. For these thoughts and words will create your future. Your point of power is in the present moment and is forming the experience of tomorrow, next week, next month, next year, and so on.

You might notice what thought you are thinking at this moment. Is it negative or positive? Do you want this thought to be creating your future? Just notice and be aware.

The Only Thing We Are Ever Dealing with Is a Thought, and a Thought Can Be Changed

No matter what the problem is, our experiences are just outer effects of inner thoughts. Even self-hatred is only hating a thought you have about yourself. You have a thought that says, "I'm a bad person." This thought produces a feeling, and you buy into the feeling. However, if you don't have the thought, you won't have the feeling. And thoughts can be changed. Change the thought, and the feeling must go.

This is only to show us where we get many of our beliefs. But let's not use this information as an excuse to stay stuck in our pain. The past has no power over us. It doesn't matter how long we have had a negative pattern. The point of power is in the present moment. What a wonderful thing to realize! We can begin to be free in this moment!

Believe It or Not, We Do Choose Our Thoughts

We may habitually think the same thought over and over so that it does not seem we are choosing the thought. But we did make the original choice. We can refuse to think certain thoughts. Look how often you have refused to think a positive thought about yourself. Well, you can also refuse to think a negative thought about yourself.

It seems to me that everyone on this planet whom I know or have worked with is suffering from self-hatred and guilt to one degree or another. The more self-hatred and guilt we have, the less our lives work. The less self-hatred and guilt we have, the better our lives work, on all levels.

The Innermost Belief for Everyone I Have Worked with Is Always, "I'm Not Good Enough!"

We often add to that, "And I don't do enough," or "I don't deserve." Does this sound like you? Often saying or implying or feeling that you "are not good enough"? But for whom? And according to whose standards?

If this belief is very strong in you, then how can you possibly have created a loving, joyous, prosperous, healthy life? Somehow your main subconscious belief would always be contradicting it. Somehow you would never quite get it together, for something would always be going wrong somewhere.

I Find That Resentment, Criticism, Guilt, and Fear Cause More Problems Than Anything Else

These four things cause the major problems in our bodies and in our lives. These feelings come from blaming others and not taking responsibility for our own experiences. You see, if we are all responsible for everything in our lives, then there is no one to blame. Whatever is happening "out there" is only a mirror of our own inner thinking. I am not condoning other people's poor behavior, but it is OUR beliefs that attract people who will treat us that way.

If you find yourself saying, "Everyone always does such and such to me, criticizes me, is never there for me, uses me like a doormat, abuses me," then this is YOUR PATTERN. There is some thought in you that attracts people who exhibit this behavior. When you no longer think that way, they will go elsewhere and do that to somebody else. You will no longer attract them.

Following are some results of patterns that manifest on the physical level: Resentment that is long held can eat away at the body and become the dis-ease we call cancer. Criticism as a permanent habit can often lead to arthritis in the body. Guilt always looks for punishment, and punishment creates pain. (When a client comes to me with a lot of pain, I know they are holding a lot of guilt.) Fear, and the tension it produces, can create things like baldness, ulcers, and even sore feet.

I have found that forgiving and releasing resentment will dissolve even cancer. While this may sound simplistic, I have seen and experienced it working.

We Can Change Our Attitude Toward the Past

The past is over and done. We cannot change that now. Yet we can change our thoughts about the past. How foolish for us to PUNISH OURSELVES in the present moment because someone hurt us in the long ago past.

I often say to people who have deep resentment patterns, "Please begin to dissolve the resentment now, when it is relatively easy. Don't wait until you are under the threat of a surgeon's knife or on your death bed, when you may have to deal with panic, too."

When we are in a state of panic, it is very difficult to focus our minds on the healing work. We have to take time out to dissolve the fears first.

If we choose to believe we are helpless victims and that it's all hopeless, then the Universe will support us in that belief, and we will just go down the drain. It is vital that we release these foolish, outmoded, negative ideas and beliefs that do not support us and nourish us. Even our concept of God needs to be one that is *for* us, not against us.

To Release the Past, We Must Be Willing to Forgive

We need to choose to release the past and forgive everyone, ourselves included. We may not know how to forgive, and we may not want to forgive, but the very fact that we say we are willing to forgive begins the healing process. It is imperative for our own healing that "we" release the past and forgive everyone.

"I forgive you for not being the way I wanted you to be. I forgive you and I set you free."

This affirmation sets *us* free.

All Dis-ease Comes from a State of Unforgiveness

Whenever we are ill, we need to search our hearts to see who it is we need to forgive.

The *Course in Miracles* says that "all dis-ease comes from a state of unforgiveness," and that "whenever we are ill, we need to look around to see who it is that we need to forgive."

I would add to that concept that the very person you find it hardest to forgive is the one YOU NEED TO LET GO OF THE MOST. Forgiveness means giving up, letting go. It has nothing to do with condoning behavior. It's just letting the whole thing go. We do not have to know HOW to forgive. All we need to do is to be WILLING to forgive. The Universe will take care of the *hows*.

We understand our own pain so well. How hard it is for most of us to understand that THEY, whoever they are we need most to forgive, were also in pain. We need to understand that they were doing the best they could with the understanding, awareness, and knowledge they had at that time.

When people come to me with a problem, I don't care what it is — poor health, lack of money, unfulfilling relationships, or stifled creativity — there is only one thing I ever work on, and that is LOVING THE SELF.

I find that when we really love and accept and APPROVE OF OURSELVES EXACTLY AS WE ARE, then everything in life works. It's as if little miracles are everywhere. Our health improves, we attract more money, our relationships become much more fulfilling, and we begin to express ourselves in creatively fulfilling ways. All this seems to happen without our even trying.

Loving and approving of yourself, creating a space of safety, trusting and deserving and accepting, will create organization in your mind, create more loving relationships in your life, attract a new job and a new and better place to live, and even enable your body weight to normalize. People who love themselves and their bodies neither abuse themselves nor others.

Self-approval and self-acceptance in the now are the main keys to positive changes in every area of our lives.

Loving the self, to me, begins with never ever criticizing ourselves for anything. Criticism locks us into the very pattern we are trying to change. Understanding and being gentle with ourselves helps us to move out of it. Remember, you have been criticizing yourself for years, and it hasn't worked. Try approving of yourself and see what happens.

In the infinity of life where I am,
all is perfect, whole, and complete.
I believe in a power far greater than I am
that flows through me every moment of every day.
I open myself to the wisdom within,
knowing that there is only One Intelligence in this Universe.
Out of this One Intelligence comes all the answers,
all the solutions, all the healings, all the new creations.
I trust this Power and Intelligence,
knowing that whatever I need to know is revealed to me,
and that whatever I need comes to me
in the right time, space, and sequence.
All is well in my world.

Part II

A SESSION WITH LOUISE

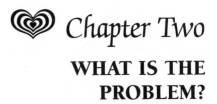 *Chapter Two*

WHAT IS THE
PROBLEM?

"It is safe to look within."

My Body Doesn't Work

It hurts, bleeds, aches, oozes, twists, blows up, limps, burns, ages, can't see, can't hear, is rotting away, and so on. Plus whatever else you may have created. I think I have heard them all.

My Relationships Don't Work

They are smothering, absent, demanding, don't support me, always criticizing me, unloving, never leave me alone, pick on me all the time, don't want to be bothered with me, walk all over me, never listen to me, and so on. Plus whatever else you may have created. Yes, I have heard them all, too.

My Finances Don't Work

They are nonexistent, seldom there, never enough, just out of reach, go out faster than they come in, won't cover the bills, slip through my fingers, and so on. Plus whatever else you may have created. Of course, I have heard them all.

My Life Doesn't Work

I never get to do what I want to do. I can't please anyone. I don't know what I want to do. There is never any time for me. My needs and desires are always left out. I'm only doing this to please them. I am just a doormat. Nobody cares what I want to do. I have no talent. I can't do anything right. All I do is procrastinate. Nothing ever works for me, and so on. Plus whatever else you have created for yourself. All these I have heard and more.

Whenever I ask a new client what is going on in his or her life, I usually get one of the above answers. Or maybe several of these answers. They really think they know the problem. But I know these complaints are only outer effects of inner thought patterns. Beneath the inner thought patterns is another deeper, more fundamental pattern that is the basis of all the outer effects.

I listen to the words they use as I ask some basic questions:

> What is happening in your life?
> How is your health?
> What do you do for a living?
> Do you like your work?
> How are your finances?
> How is your love life?
> How did the last relationship end?
> And the relationship before that, how did it end?
> Tell me about your childhood, briefly.

I watch the body postures and the facial movements. But mostly I really listen to the words they say. Thoughts and words create our future experiences. As I listen to them talk, I can readily understand why they have these particular problems. The words we speak are indicative of our inner thoughts. Sometimes, the words they use do not match the experiences they describe. Then I know that they are either not in touch with what is really going on or they are lying to me. Either one is a starting point and gives us a basis from which to begin.

Exercise: I Should

The next thing I do is to give them a pad and pen and ask them to write on the top of a piece of paper:

I SHOULD

_____

_____

_____

_____

_____

They are to make a list of five or six ways to finish that sentence. Some people find it difficult to begin, and some have so many things to write that it's hard for them to stop.

I then ask them to read the list to me one at a time, beginning each sentence with "I Should..." As they read each one, I ask, "Why?"

The answers that come out are interesting and revealing, such as:

My mother said I should.

Because I am afraid not to.

Because I have to be perfect.

Well, everybody has to do that.

Because I am too lazy, too short, too tall, too fat, too thin, too dumb, too ugly, too worthless.

These answers show me where they are stuck in their beliefs and what they think their limitations are.

I make no comments on their answers. When they are through with their list, I talk about the word SHOULD.

You see, I believe that _should_ is one of the most damaging words in our language. Every time we use _should_, we are, in effect, saying "wrong." Either we _are_ wrong or we _were_ wrong or we are _going to be_ wrong. I don't think we need more wrongs in our life. We need to have more freedom of choice. I would like to take the word _should_ and remove it from the vocabulary forever. I'd replace it with the word _could_. _Could_ gives us choice, and we are never wrong.

I then ask them to reread the list one item at a time, except this time to begin each sentence by saying, "If I really wanted to, I could _____." This puts a whole new light on the subject.

As they do this, I ask them gently, "Why haven't you?" Now we hear different answers:

> I don't want to.
> I am afraid.
> I don't know how.
> Because I am not good enough.
> And so on.

We often find they have been berating themselves for years for something they never wanted to do in the first place. Or they have been criticizing themselves for not doing something when it was never their idea to begin with. Often it was just something that someone else said they "should" do. When they can see that, they can just drop it from the "should list." What a relief that is.

Look at all the people who try to force themselves for years into a career they don't even like only because their parents said they "should" become a dentist or a teacher. How often have we felt inferior because we were told we "should" be smarter or richer or more creative like some relative.

What is there on your "should list" that could be dropped with a sense of relief?

By the time we have gone through this short list, they are beginning to look at their life in a new and different way. They notice that many of the things they thought they "should" do are things they never wanted to do, and they were only trying to please other people. So many times it is because they are afraid or feel they are not good enough.

The problem has now begun to shift. I have started the process of releasing the feeling of "being wrong" because they are not fitting someone else's standards.

Next I begin to explain to them *my philosophy of life* as I did in Chapter One. I believe life is really very simple. What we give out, we get back. The Universe totally supports every thought we choose to think and to believe. When we are little, we learn how to feel about ourselves and about life by the reactions of the adults around us. Whatever these beliefs are, they will be recreated as experiences as we grow up. However, we are only dealing with thought patterns, and *the point of power is always in the present moment.* Changes can begin in this moment.

Loving the Self

I continue to explain that no matter what their problem seems to be, there is only one thing I ever work on with anyone, and this is *Loving the Self.* Love is the miracle cure. Loving ourselves works miracles in our lives.

I am not talking about vanity or arrogance or being stuck-up, for that is not love. It is only fear. I am talking about having a great respect for ourselves and a gratitude for the miracle of our bodies and our minds.

"Love" to me is appreciation to such a degree that it fills my heart to bursting and overflows. Love can go in any direction. I can feel love for:

The very process of life itself.
The joy of being alive.
The beauty I see.
Another person.
Knowledge.
The process of the mind.
Our bodies and the way they work.
Animals, birds, fish.
Vegetation in all its forms.
The Universe and the way it works.

What can you add to this list?

Let's look at some of the ways we don't love ourselves:

31

We scold and criticize ourselves endlessly.
We mistreat our bodies with food, alcohol, and drugs.
We choose to believe we are unlovable.
We are afraid to charge a decent price for our services.
We create illnesses and pain in our bodies.
We procrastinate on things that would benefit us.
We live in chaos and disorder.
We create debt and burdens.
We attract lovers and mates who belittle us.

What are some of *your* ways?

If we *deny our good* in any way, it is an act of not loving ourselves. I remember a client I worked with who wore glasses. One day we released an old fear from childhood. The next day she awakened to find her contact lenses were bothering her too much to wear. She looked around and found her eyesight was perfectly clear.

Yet she spent the whole day saying, "I don't believe it, I don't believe it." The next day she was back to wearing contacts. Our subconscious mind has no sense of humor. She couldn't believe she had created perfect eyesight.

Lack of self-worth is another expression of not loving ourselves.

Tom was a very good artist, and he had some wealthy clients who asked him to decorate a wall or two in their homes. Yet somehow he was always behind in his own bill paying. His original quote was never enough to cover the time involved to complete the work. Anyone who gives a service or creates a one-of-a-kind product can charge any price. People with wealth love to pay a lot for what they get; it gives the item more value. More examples:

Our partner is tired and grouchy. We wonder what *we* have done wrong to cause it.
He takes us out once or twice and never calls again. We think something must be wrong with *us*.
Our marriage ends, and we are sure *we* are a failure.
We are afraid to ask for a raise.
Our bodies do not match those in *Gentleman's Quarterly* or

Vogue magazine, and we feel inferior.

We don't "make the sale," or "get the part," and we are sure we are "not good enough."

We are afraid of intimacy and allowing anyone to get too close, so we have anonymous sex.

We can't make decisions because we are sure they will be wrong.

How do you express *your* lack of self-worth?

The Perfection of Babies

How perfect you were when you were a tiny baby. Babies do not have to do anything to become perfect; they already are perfect, and they act as if they know it. They know they are the center of the Universe. They are not afraid to ask for what they want. They freely express their emotions. You know when a baby is angry— in fact, the whole neighborhood knows. You also know when babies are happy, for their smiles light up a room. They are full of love.

Tiny babies will die if they do not get love. Once we are older, we learn to live without love, but babies will not stand for it. Babies also love every part of their bodies, even their own feces. They have incredible courage.

You were like that. We were all like that. Then we began to listen to adults around us who had learned to be fearful, and we began to deny our own magnificence.

I never believe it when clients try to convince me how terrible they are, or how unlovable they are. My work is to bring them back to the time when they knew how to really love themselves.

Exercise: Mirror

Next, I ask clients to pick up a small mirror, look into their own eyes, and say their names and, "I love and accept you exactly as you are."

This is *so* difficult for many people. Seldom do I get a calm reaction, let alone enjoyment from this exercise. Some cry or are close to tears, some get angry, some belittle their features or qualities, some insist they CAN'T do it. I even had one man throw the mirror across the room and want to run away. It took him several months before he could begin to relate to himself in the mirror.

For years I looked into the mirror only to criticize what I saw there. Recalling the endless hours I spent plucking my eyebrows trying to make myself barely acceptable amuses me now. I remember it used to frighten me to look into my own eyes.

This simple exercise shows me so much. In less than an hour, I am able to get to some of the core issues that are beneath the outer problem. If we work only on the level of the problem, we can spend endless time working out each and every detail; and the minute we think we have it all "fixed up," it will crop up somewhere else.

"The Problem" Is Rarely the Real Problem

She was so concerned with her looks, and especially with her teeth. She went from dentist to dentist feeling each one had only made her look worse. She went to have her nose fixed, and they did a poor job. Each professional was mirroring her belief that she was ugly. Her problem was not her looks, but that she was convinced something was wrong with her.

There was another woman who had terrible breath. It was uncomfortable to be around her. She was studying to be a minister, and her outer demeanor was pious and spiritual. Beneath this was a raging current of anger and jealousy that exploded now and then when she thought someone might be threatening her position. Her inner thoughts were expressed through her breath, and she was offensive even when she pretended to be loving. No one threatened her but herself.

He was only 15 when his mother brought him to me with Hodgkin's dis-ease and three months to live. His mother was understandably hysterical and difficult to deal with, but the boy was bright and clever and wanted to live. He was willing to do anything I told him to, including changing the way he thought and spoke. His separated parents were always arguing, and he really did not have a settled home life.

He wanted desperately to be an actor. The pursuit of fame and fortune far outweighed his ability to experience joy. He thought he could be acceptable and worthwhile only if he had fame. I taught him to love and accept himself, and he got well. He is now grown up and appears on Broadway with regularity. As he learned to experience the joy of being himself, the parts in plays opened up for him.

Overweight is another good example of how we can waste a lot of energy trying to correct a problem that is not the real problem. People often spend years and years fighting fat and are still overweight. They blame all their problems on being overweight. The excess weight is only an outer effect of a deep inner problem. To me, it is always fear and a need for protection. When we feel frightened or insecure or "not good enough," many of us will put on extra weight for protection.

To spend our time berating ourselves for being too heavy, to feel guilty about every bite of food we eat, to do all the numbers we do on ourselves when we gain weight, is just a waste of time. Twenty years later we can still be in the same situation because we have not even begun to deal with the real problem. All that we have done is to make ourselves more frightened and insecure, and then we need more weight for protection.

So I refuse to focus on excess weight or on diets. For diets do not work. The only diet that does work is a mental diet — dieting from negative thoughts. I say to clients, "Let us just put that issue to one side for the time being while we work on a few other things first."

They will often tell me they can't love themselves because they are so fat, or as one girl put it, "too round at the edges." I explain that they are fat because they don't love themselves. When we begin to love and approve of ourselves, it's amazing how weight just disappears from our bodies.

Sometimes clients even get angry with me as I explain how simple it is to change their lives. They may feel I do not understand their problems. One woman became very upset and said, "I came here to get help with my dissertation, not to learn to love myself." To me it was so obvious that her main problem was a lot of self-hatred, and this permeated every part of her life, including the writing of her dissertation. She could not succeed at anything as long as she felt so worthless.

She couldn't hear me and left in tears, coming back one year later with the same problem plus a lot of other problems. Some people are not ready, and there is no judgment. We all begin to make our changes in the right time, space, and sequence for *us*. I did not even begin to make my changes until I was in my forties.

The Real Problem

So here is a client who has just looked into the harmless little mirror, and he or she is all upset. I smile with delight and say, "Good, now we are looking at the 'real problem'; now we can begin to clear out what is really standing in your way." I talk more about loving the self, about how, for me, loving the self begins with never, ever criticizing ourselves for anything.

I watch their faces as I ask them if they criticize themselves. Their reactions tell me so much:

> Well, of course I do.
> All the time.
> Not as much as I used to.
> Well, how am I going to change if I don't criticize myself?
> Doesn't everyone?

To the latter, I answer, "We are not talking about everyone; we are talking about you. Why do you criticize yourself? What is wrong with you?"

As they talk, I make a list. What they say often coincides with their "should list." They feel they are too tall, too short, too fat, too thin, too dumb, too old, too young, too ugly. (The most beautiful or handsome will often say this.) Or they're too late, too early, too lazy, and on and on. Notice how it is almost always "too" something.

Finally, we get down to the bottom line, and they say, "I am not good enough."

Hurrah, hurrah! We have finally found the central issue. They criticize themselves because they have learned to believe they "are not good enough." Clients are always amazed at how fast we have gotten to this point. Now we do not have to bother with any of the side effects like body problems, relationship problems, money problems, or lack of creative expressions. We can put all our energy into dissolving the cause of the whole thing: "NOT LOVING THE SELF!"

In the infinity of life where I am,
all is perfect, whole, and complete.
I am always Divinely protected and guided.
It is safe for me to look within myself.
It is safe for me to look into the past.
It is safe for me to enlarge my viewpoint of life.
I am far more than my personality — past, present, or future.
I now choose to rise above my personality problems
to recognize the magnificence of my being.
I am totally willing to learn to love myself.
All is well in my world.

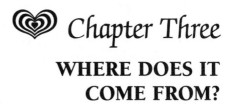 Chapter Three

WHERE DOES IT
COME FROM?

"The past has no power over me."

All right, we have gone through a lot of stuff, and we have sifted through what we *thought* the problem was. Now we have come up with what I believe is the real problem. We feel we are *not good enough*, and there is a *lack of self-love*. From the way I look at life, if there is any problem, then this has to be true. So let us look at where this belief came from.

How did we go from being a tiny baby who knows the perfection of itself and of life to being a person who has problems and feels unworthy and unlovable to one degree or another? People who already love themselves can love themselves even more.

Think of a rose from the time it is a tiny bud. As it opens to full flower, till the last petal falls, it is always beautiful, always perfect, always changing. So it is with us. We are always perfect, always beautiful, and ever changing. We are doing the best we can with the understanding, awareness and knowledge we have. As we gain more understanding, awareness and knowledge, then we will do things differently.

Mental Housecleaning

Now is the time to examine our past a bit more, to take a look at some of the beliefs that have been running us.

Some people find this part of the cleansing process very painful, but it need not be. We must look at what is there before we can clean it out.

If you want to clean a room thoroughly, you will pick up and examine everything in it. Some things you will look at with love, and you will dust them or polish them to give them new beauty. Some things you will see that need refinishing or repair, and you will make a note to do that. Some things will never serve you again, and it becomes time to let those things go. Old magazines and newspapers and dirty paper plates can be dropped into the wastebasket very calmly. There is no need to get angry in order to clean a room.

It is the same thing when we are cleaning our mental house. There is no need to get angry just because some of the beliefs in it are ready to be tossed out. Let them go as easily as you would scrape bits of food into the trash after a meal. Would you really dig into yesterday's garbage to make tonight's meal? Do you dig into old *mental* garbage to create tomorrow's experiences?

If a thought or belief does not serve you, let it go! There is no written law that says that because you once believed something, you have to continue to believe it forever.

Let's look at some limiting beliefs and where they came from:

LIMITING BELIEF: "I'm not good enough."

WHERE IT CAME FROM: A father who repeatedly told him he was stupid.

He said he wanted to be a success so his daddy would be proud of him. But he was riddled with guilt, which created resentment, and all he could produce was one failure after another. Daddy kept financing businesses for him, and one after another, they failed. He used failure to get even. He made his daddy pay and pay and pay. Of course, *he* was the biggest loser.

LIMITING BELIEF: Lack of self-love.

WHERE IT CAME FROM: Trying to win daddy's approval.

The last thing she wanted was to be like her father. They couldn't agree on anything and were always arguing. She only wanted his approval, but instead all she got was criticism. Her body was full of pains. Her father had exactly the same kind of pains. She did not realize her anger was creating her pains just as her father's anger was creating pain for him.

LIMITING BELIEF: Life is dangerous.

WHERE IT CAME FROM: A frightened father.

Another client saw life as grim and harsh. It was difficult for her to laugh, and when she did, she would become frightened that something "bad" would happen. She has been reared with the admonition, "Don't laugh or '*they*' might get you."

LIMITING BELIEF: I'm not good enough.

WHERE IT CAME FROM: Being abandoned and ignored.

It was difficult for him to talk. Silence had become a way of life for him. He had just come off drugs and alcohol and was convinced that he was terrible. I discovered his mother had died when he was very young, and he had been reared by an aunt. The aunt seldom spoke except to give an order, and he was brought up in silence. He even ate alone in silence and stayed quietly in his room day after day. He had a lover who was also a silent man, and they spent most of their time alone in silence. The lover died, and once again he was alone.

Exercise: Negative Messages

The next exercise we do is to get a large sheet of paper and make a list of all the things your parents said were wrong with you. What were the negative messages you heard? Give yourself enough time to remember as many as you can. A half hour usually works well.

What did they say about money? What did they say about your body? What did they say about love and relationships? What did they say about your creative talents? What were the limiting or negative things they said to you?

If you can, just look objectively at these items and say to yourself, "So that's where that belief came from."

Now, let's take a new sheet of paper and dig a little deeper. What other negative messages did you hear as a child?

From relatives _____

From teachers _____

From friends _____

From authority figures _____

From your church _____

Write them all down. Take your time. Be aware of what feelings are going on in your body.

What you have on these two pieces of paper are the thoughts that need to be removed from your consciousness. These are the very beliefs you have that are making you feel "not good enough."

Seeing Yourself as a Child

If we were to take a three-year-old child and put him in the middle of the room, and you and I were to start yelling at the child, telling him how stupid he was, how he could never do anything right, how he should do this, and shouldn't do that, and look at the mess he made; and maybe hit him a few times, we would end up with a frightened little child who sits docilely in the corner, or who tears up the place. The child will go one of these two ways, but we will never know the potential of that child.

If we take the same little child and tell him how much we love him, how much we care, that we love the way he looks and love how bright and clever he is, that we love the way he does things, and that it's okay for him to make mistakes as he learns — and that we will always be there for him no matter what — then the potential that comes out of that child will blow your mind!

Each one of us has a three-year-old child within us, and we often spend most of our time yelling at that kid in ourselves. Then we wonder why our lives don't work.

If you had a friend who was always criticizing you, would you want to be around that person? Perhaps you were treated this way as a child, and that is sad. However, that was a long time ago, and if you are now choosing to treat yourself in the same way, then it is sadder still.

So now, here in front of us, we have a list of the negative messages we heard as a child. How does this list correspond with what *you* believe to be wrong with you? Are they almost the same? Probably yes.

We base our life script on our early messages. We are all good little children and obediently accept what "they" tell us as truth. It would be very easy just to blame our parents and be victims for the rest of our lives. But that wouldn't be much fun, and it certainly wouldn't get us out of our stuck position.

Blaming Your Family

Blame is one of the surest ways to stay *in* a problem. In blaming another, we give away our power. Understanding enables us to rise above the issue and take control of our future.

The past cannot be changed. The future is shaped by our current thinking. It is imperative for our freedom to understand that our parents were doing the best they could with the understanding, awareness, and knowledge they had. Whenever we blame someone else, we are not taking responsibility for ourselves.

Those people who did all those terrible things to us were just as frightened and scared as you are. They felt just the same helplessness as you do. The only things they could possibly teach you are what they had been taught.

How much do you know about your parents' childhoods, especially before the age of ten? If it's still possible for you to find out, ask them. If you're able to find out about your parents' childhoods, you will more easily understand why they did what they did. Understanding will bring you compassion.

If you don't know and can't find out, try to imagine what it must have been like for them. What kind of childhood would create an adult like that?

You need this knowledge for your own freedom. You can't free yourself until you free them. You can't forgive yourself until you forgive them. If you demand perfection from them, you will demand perfection from yourself, and you will be miserable all your life.

Choosing Our Parents

I agree with the theory that we choose our parents. The lessons that we learn seem perfectly matched to the "weaknesses" of the parents we have.

I believe we are all on an endless journey through eternity. We come to this planet to learn particular lessons that are necessary for our spiritual evolution. We choose our sex, our color, our country; and then we look around for the perfect set of parents who will "mirror" our patterns.

Our visits to this planet are like going to school. If you want to become a beautician, you go to beauty school. If you want to become a mechanic, you go to mechanics school. If you want to become a lawyer, you to go law school. The parents you picked this time around are the perfect couple who are "experts" in what you have chosen to learn.

When we grow up, we have a tendency to point our fingers accusingly at our parents and say, "You did it to me!" But I believe we chose them.

Listening to Others

Our older brothers and sisters are gods to us when we are little. If they were unhappy, they probably took it out on us physically or verbally. They might have said things like:

> "I'll tell on you for..." (instilling guilt)
> "You're just a baby, you can't do that."
> "You're too stupid to play with us."

Teachers at school often influence us greatly. In the fifth grade, a teacher told me emphatically I was too tall to be a dancer. I believed her and put away my dancing ambitions until I was too old to make dancing a career.

Did you understand that tests and grades were only to see how much knowledge you had at a given time, or were you a child who allowed tests and grades to measure self-worth?

Our early friends share their own misinformation about life with us. The other kids at school can tease us and leave lasting hurts. When I was a child, my last name was Lunney and the kids used to call me "lunatic."

Neighbors also have an influence, not only because of their remarks but also because we're asked, "What will the neighbors think?"

Think back to the other authority figures who were influential in your childhood.

And, of course, there are the strong and very persuasive statements made by advertisements in periodicals and on television. All too many products are sold by making us feel we are unworthy or wrong if we don't use them.

* * *

We are all here to transcend our early limitations, whatever they were. We're here to recognize our own magnificence and divinity no matter what *they* told us. You have *your* negative beliefs to overcome, and I have *my* negative beliefs to overcome.

In the infinity of life where I am,
all is perfect, whole, and complete.
The past has no power over me
because I am willing to learn and to change.
I see the past as necessary to bring me to where I am today.
I am willing to begin where I am right now
to clean the rooms of my mental house.
I know it does not matter where I start,
so I now begin with the smallest and the easiest rooms,
and in that way I will see results quickly.
I am thrilled to be in the middle of this adventure,
for I know I will never go through
this particular experience again.
I am willing to set myself free.
All is well in my world.

Chapter Four

IS IT TRUE?

"Truth is the unchangeable part of me."

The question, "Is it true or real?" has two answers: "Yes" and "No." It is true if you *believe* it to be true. It is not true if you *believe* it isn't true. The glass is both half full and half empty, depending on how you look at it. There are literally billions of thoughts we can choose to think.

Most of us choose to think the same kinds of thoughts our parents used to think, but we don't have to continue to do this. There is no law written that says we can only think in one way.

Whatever I choose to believe becomes true for me. Whatever you choose to believe becomes true for you. Our thoughts can be totally different. Our lives and experiences are totally different.

Examine Your Thoughts

Whatever we believe becomes true for us. If you have a sudden financial disaster, then on some level you may believe you are unworthy of being comfortable with money, or you believe in burdens and debt. Or if you believe that nothing good ever lasts, maybe you believe that life is out to get you, or, as I hear so often, "I just can't win."

If you seem unable to attract a relationship, you may believe "Nobody loves me," or "I am unlovable." Perhaps you fear being dominated as your mother was, or maybe you think, "People just hurt me."

If you have poor health, you may believe, "Illness runs in our family." Or that you are a victim of the weather. Or perhaps it's: "I was born to suffer," or "It's just one thing after another."

Or you may have a different belief. Perhaps you're not even aware of your belief. Most people really aren't. They just see the outer circumstances as being the way the cookie crumbles. Until someone can show you the connection between the outer experiences and the inner thoughts, you remain a victim in life.

PROBLEM	BELIEF
Financial disaster	I am not worthy of having money.
No friends	Nobody loves me.
Problems with work	I'm not good enough.
Always pleasing others	I never get my way.

Whatever the problem is, it comes from a thought pattern, and *thought patterns can be changed!*

It may feel true, it may *seem* true — all these problems we're wrestling with and juggling in our lives. However, no matter how difficult an issue we are dealing with, it is only an outer result or the effect of an inner thought pattern.

If you don't know what thoughts are creating your problems, you're in the right place now, because this book is designed to help you find out. Look at the problems in your life. *Ask yourself, "What kinds of thoughts am I having that create this?"*

If you allow yourself to sit quietly and ask this question, your inner intelligence will show you the answer.

It's Only a Belief You Learned as a Child

Some of the things we believe *are* positive and nourishing. These thoughts serve us well all of our lives, such as: "Look both ways before you cross the street."

Other thoughts are very useful at the beginning, but as we grow older they are no longer appropriate. "Don't trust strangers" may be good advice for a small child, but for an adult, to continue this belief will only create isolation and loneliness.

Why do we so seldom sit down and ask ourselves, "Is that really true?" For instance, why do I believe things like, "It's difficult for me to learn"?

Better questions to ask are: "Is it true for me now?" "Where did that belief come from?" "Do I still believe it because a first grade teacher told me that over and over?" "Would I be better off if I dropped that belief?"

Beliefs that "Boys don't cry," and "Girls don't climb trees," create men who hide their feelings and women who are afraid to be physical.

If we were taught as a child that the world is a frightening place, then everything we hear that fits that belief we will accept as true for us. The same is true for "Don't trust strangers," "Don't go out at night," or "People cheat you."

On the other hand, if we were taught early in life that the world is a safe place, then we would hold other beliefs. We could easily accept that love is everywhere, and people are so friendly, and I always have whatever I need.

If you were taught as a child that, "It's all my fault," then you will walk around always feeling guilt no matter what happens. Your belief will turn you into someone who's always saying, "I'm sorry."

If you learned to believe as a child, "I don't count," then this belief will always keep you at the end of the line wherever you are. Like my childhood experience about not getting any cake (see *My Story*, Chapter 16). Sometimes you will feel you're invisible when others fail to notice you.

Did your childhood circumstances teach you to believe, "Nobody loves me"? Then you are sure to be lonely. Even when you bring a friend or relationship into your life, it will be short-lived.

Did your family teach you, "There is not enough"? Then I am sure you often feel as though the cupboard is bare, or you find you just get by or are always in debt.

I had a client who had been brought up in a household where they believed everything was wrong and could only get worse. His main joy in life was playing tennis, and then he hurt his knee. He went to every doctor he could find, and it only got worse. Finally, he could not play at all.

Another person had been brought up as a preacher's son, and as a child he was taught that everybody else came first. The preacher's family always came last. Today he is wonderful at helping his clients get the best deal, yet he's usually in debt, with little pocket money. His belief still makes him last in line.

If You Believe It, It Seems True

How often have we said, "That's the way I am," or "That's the way it is"? Those specific words are really saying that that's what we *believe* to be true for us. Usually, what we believe is only someone else's opinion we have incorporated into our belief systems. No doubt it fits right in with all the other things we believe.

Are you one of the many people who will get up in the morning, see that it's raining, and say, "Oh, what a lousy day!"?

It is *not* a lousy day. It is only a wet day. If we wear the appropriate clothing and change our attitude, we can have a lot of rainy day fun. If it is really our belief that rainy days are lousy days, then we will always greet rain with a sinking heart. We will fight the day rather than flow with what is happening in the moment.

If we want a joyous life, we must think joyous thoughts. If we want a prosperous life, we must think prosperous thoughts. If we want a loving life, we must think loving thoughts. *Whatever we send out mentally or verbally will come back to us in like form.*

Each Moment Is a New Beginning

I repeat, *The Point of Power is always in the present moment.* You are *never* stuck. This is where the changes take place, right here and right now *in our own minds!* It doesn't matter how long we've had a negative pattern or an illness or a poor relationship or lack of finances or self-hatred. We can begin to make a shift today!

Your problem no longer needs to be the truth for you. It can now fade back to the nothingness from whence it came. You can do it.

Remember: *you are the only person who thinks in your mind!* You are the power and authority in your world!

Your thoughts and beliefs of the past have created this moment, and all the moments up to this moment. What you are now choosing to believe and think and say will create the next moment and the next day and the next month and the next year.

Yes, you, darling! I can give you the most marvelous advice, coming from my years of experience, yet you can continue to choose to think the same old thoughts, you can refuse to change and keep all your problems.

You are the power in your world! You get to have whatever you choose to think!

This moment begins the new process. Each moment is a new beginning, and this moment is a new beginning for you right here and right now! Isn't that great to know! This moment is the *Point of Power!* This moment is where the change begins!

Is It True?

Stop for a moment and catch your thought. What are you thinking right now? If it is true that your thoughts shape your life, would you want what you were just thinking right now to become true for you? If it's a thought of worry or anger or hurt or revenge or fear, how do you think this thought will come back to you?

It is not always easy to catch our thoughts because they move so swiftly. However, we can begin right now to watch and listen to what we say. If you hear yourself expressing negative words of any sort, stop in mid-sentence. Either rephrase the sentence or just drop it. You could even say to it, "Out!"

Imagine yourself in line at a cafeteria, or perhaps at a buffet in a luxurious hotel, where instead of dishes of food, there are dishes of thoughts. You get to choose any and all the thoughts you wish. These thoughts will create your future experiences.

Now, if you choose thoughts that will create problems and pain, that's rather foolish. It's like choosing food that always makes you ill. We may do this once or twice, but as soon as we learn which foods upset our bodies, we stay away from them. It's the same with thoughts. *Let us stay away from thoughts that create problems and pain.*

One of my early teachers, Dr. Raymond Charles Barker, would repeatedly say, "When there is a problem, there is not something to do, there is something to know."

Our minds create our future. When we have something in our present that is undesirable, then we must use our minds to change the situation. And we can begin to change it this very second.

It is my deep desire that the topic "How Your Thoughts Work" would be the very first subject taught in school. I have never understood the importance of having children memorize battle dates. It seems like such a waste of mental energy. Instead, we could teach them important subjects such as How the Mind Works, How to Handle Finances, How to Invest Money for Financial Security, How to Be a Parent, How to Create Good Relationships, and How to Create and Maintain Self-Esteem and Self-Worth.

Can you imagine what a whole generation of adults would be like if they had been taught these subjects in school along with their regular curriculum? Think how these truths would manifest. We would have happy people who feel good about themselves. We would have people who are comfortable financially and who enrich the economy by investing their money wisely. They would have good relationships with everyone and would be comfortable with the role of parenthood and then go on to create another generation of children who feel good about themselves. Yet within all this, each person would remain an individual expressing his or her own creativity.

There is no time to waste. Let's continue with our work.

In the infinity of life where I am,
all is perfect, whole, and complete.
I no longer choose to believe in old limitations and lack.
I now choose to begin to see myself
as the Universe sees me — perfect, whole, and complete.
The truth of my Being is that I was created
perfect, whole, and complete.
I will always be perfect, whole, and complete.
I now choose to live my life from this understanding.
I am in the right place at the right time, doing the right thing.
All is well in my world.

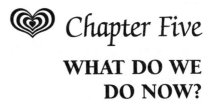 *Chapter Five*

WHAT DO WE DO NOW?

"I see my patterns, and I choose to make changes."

Decide to Change

Throwing up our hands in horror at what we may call the mess of our lives and just giving up are the ways many people react at this point. Others get angry at themselves or at life and also give up.

By giving up, I mean deciding, "It's all hopeless and impossible to make any changes, so why try?" The rest of it goes, "Just stay the way you are. At least you know how to handle that pain. You don't like it, but it is familiar, and you hope it won't get any worse."

To me, habitual anger is like sitting in a corner with a dunce cap on. Does this sound familiar? Something happens, and you get angry. Something else happens, and you get angry again. Something else happens, and you get angry again. Something else happens, and once again you get angry. But you never go beyond getting angry.

What good does that do? It's a foolish reaction to waste your time only getting angry. It's also a refusal to perceive life in a new and different way.

It would be much more helpful to ask yourself how you are creating so many situations to get angry at.

What are you believing that causes all these frustrations? What are you giving out that attracts in others the need to irritate you? Why do you believe that to get your way you need to get angry?

Whatever you give out comes back to you. The more you give out anger, the more you are creating situations for you to get angry at, like sitting in a corner with a dunce cap on, getting nowhere.

Does this paragraph bring up feelings of anger? Good! It must be hitting home. This is something you could be willing to change.

Make a Decision to Be "Willing to Change"!

If you really want to know how stubborn you are, just approach the idea of being *willing to change*. We all want to have our lives change, to have situations become better and easier, but *we* don't want to have to change. We would prefer that *they* change. In order to have this happen, *we must change inside*. We must change our way of thinking, change our way of speaking, change our way of expressing ourselves. Only then will the outer changes occur.

This is the next step. We are now fairly clear on what the problems are, and where they came from. Now it is time to be *willing to change*.

I have always had a streak of stubbornness within me. Even now sometimes when I decide to make a change in my life, this stubbornness can come to the surface, and my resistance to changing *my* thinking is strong. I can temporarily become self-righteous, angry, and withdrawn.

Yes, this still goes on within me after all these years of work. It's one of my lessons. However, when this happens now, I know I'm hitting an important point of change. Every time I decide to make a change in my life, to release something else, I'm going ever deeper into myself to do this.

Each old layer must give way in order to be replaced with new thinking. Some of it is easy, and some of it is like trying to lift a boulder with a feather.

The more tenaciously I hold on to an old belief when I say I want to make a change, the more I know this is an important one for me to release. It is only by learning these things that I can teach others.

It is my opinion that many really good teachers do not come from joyful households where all was easy. They come from a place of much pain and suffering, and they've worked through the layers to reach the place where they can now help others to become free. Most good teachers are continually working to release even more, to remove ever-deeper layers of limitation. This becomes a lifetime occupation.

The main difference between the way I used to work at releasing beliefs, and the way I do it today, is that now I don't have to be angry at myself in order to do so. I no longer choose to believe that I'm a bad person just because I find something else to change within me.

Housecleaning

The mental work I do now is like cleaning a house. I go through my mental rooms and examine the thoughts and beliefs in them. Some I love, so I polish and shine them and make them even more useful. Some I notice need replacement or repair, and I get around to them as I can. Some are like yesterday's newspapers and old magazines or clothing that's no longer suitable. These I either give away or toss into the trash, and I let them be gone forever.

It's not necessary for me to be angry or to feel I'm a bad person in order to do this.

Exercise: I Am Willing to Change

Let's use the affirmation, "I am willing to change." Repeat this often. "I am willing to change. I am willing to change." You can touch your throat as you say this. The throat is the energy center in the body where change takes place. By touching your throat, you are acknowledging you are in the process of changing.

Be willing to allow the changes to happen when they come up in your life. Be aware that where you DO NOT WANT TO CHANGE is exactly the area where you NEED to change the most. "I am willing to change."

The Universal Intelligence is always responding to your thoughts and words. Things will definitely begin to change as you make these statements.

Many Ways to Change

Working with my ideas is not the only way to change. There are many other methods that work quite well. In the back of the book, I have included a list of many of the ways you could approach your own growth process.

Just think of a few now. There is the spiritual approach, there is the mental approach, and the physical approach. Holistic healing includes body, mind, and spirit. You can begin in any one of these areas as long as you eventually include all the areas. Some begin with the mental approach and do workshops or therapy. Some begin in the spiritual area with meditation or prayer.

When you begin to *clean your house*, it really doesn't matter which room you start in. Just begin in the area that appeals to you most. The others will happen almost by themselves.

Junk food eaters who begin on the spiritual level often find that they are drawn to nutrition. They meet a friend or find a book or go to a class that brings them to an understanding that what they put into their bodies will have a lot to do with how they feel and look. One level will always lead to another as long as there is the willingness to grow and change.

I give very little nutritional advice because I have discovered that all systems work for some people. I do have a local network of good practitioners in the holistic field, and I refer clients to them when I see the necessity for nutritional knowledge. This is an area where you must find your own way or go to a specialist who can test you.

Many of the books on nutrition have been written by persons who were very ill and worked out a system for their own healing. Then they wrote a book to tell everyone else the methods they used. However, everyone is not alike.

For instance, the macrobiotic and the natural raw food diets are two totally different approaches. The raw food people never cook anything, seldom eat bread or grains, and are very careful not to eat fruits and vegetables at the same meal. And they never use salt. The macrobiotic people cook almost all of their food, have a different system of food combining, and use a lot of salt. Both systems work.

Both systems have healed bodies. But neither system is good for everybody's body.

My personal nutritional approach is simple. If it grows, eat it. If it doesn't grow, don't eat it.

Be conscious of your eating. It's like paying attention to our thoughts. We also can learn to pay attention to our bodies and the signals we get when we eat in different ways.

Cleaning the mental house after a lifetime of indulging in negative mental thoughts is a bit like going on a good nutritional program after a lifetime of indulging in junk foods. They both can often create healing crises. As you begin to change your physical diet, the body begins to throw off the accumulation of toxic residue, and as this happens, you can feel rather rotten for a day or two. So it is when you make a decision to change the mental thought patterns — your circumstances can begin to seem worse for a while.

Recall for a moment the end of a Thanksgiving dinner. The food is eaten, and it's time to clean the turkey pan. The pan is all burnt and crusty, so you put in hot water and soap and let it soak for a while. Then you begin to scrape the pan. Now you *really* have a mess; it looks worse than ever. But, if you just keep scrubbing away, soon you will have a pan as good as new.

It's the same thing with cleaning up a dried-on crusty mental pattern. When we soak it with new ideas, all the gook comes to the surface to look at. Just keep doing the new affirmations, and soon you will have totally cleared an old limitation.

Exercise: Willing to Change

So we have decided we are willing to change, and we will use any and all methods that work for us. Let me describe one of the methods I use with myself and with others.

First: go look in a mirror and say to yourself, "I am willing to change."

Notice how you feel. If you are hesitant or resistant or just don't want to change, ask yourself why. What old belief are you holding on to? Please don't scold yourself, just notice what it is. I'll bet that belief has been causing you a lot of trouble. I wonder where it came from. Do you know?

Whether we know where it came from or not, let's do something to dissolve it, now. Again, go to the mirror, and look deep into your own eyes, touch your throat, and say out loud ten times, "I am willing to release all resistance."

Mirror work is very powerful. As children we received most of our negative messages from others looking us straight in the eye and perhaps shaking a finger at us. Whenever we look into the mirror today, most of us will say something negative to ourselves. We either criticize our looks or berate ourselves for something. To look yourself straight in the eye and make a positive declaration about yourself is, in my opinion, the quickest way to get results with affirmations.

In the infinity of life where I am,
all is perfect, whole, and complete.
I now choose calmly and objectively to see my old patterns,
and I am willing to make changes.
I am teachable. I can learn. I am willing to change.
I choose to have fun doing this.
I choose to react as though I have found a treasure
when I discover something else to release.
I see and feel myself changing moment by moment.
Thoughts no longer have any power over me.
I am the power in the world. I choose to be free.
All is well in my world.

⟠ Chapter Six
RESISTANCE TO CHANGE

"I am in the rhythm and flow of ever-changing life."

Awareness Is the First Step in Healing or Changing

When we have some pattern buried deeply within us, we must become aware of it in order to heal the condition. Perhaps we begin to mention the condition, to complain about it or to see it in other people. It rises to the surface of our attention in some way, and we begin to relate to it. We often attract a teacher, a friend, a class or workshop, or a book to ourselves that begins to awaken new ways to approach the dissolving of the problem.

My awakening began with a chance remark of a friend who had been told about a meeting. My friend did not go, but something within me responded, and I went. That little meeting was the first step on my pathway of unfoldment. I didn't recognize the significance of it until sometime later.

Often, our reaction to this first stage is to think the approach is silly, or that it doesn't make sense. Perhaps it seems too easy, or unacceptable to our thinking. We don't want to do it. Our resistance comes up very strong. We may even feel angry about the thought of doing it.

Such a reaction is very good, if we can understand that it is the first step in our healing process.

I tell people that any reaction they may feel is there to show them they are already in the process of healing even though the total healing is not yet completed. The truth is that the process begins the moment we begin to think about making a change.

Impatience is only another form of resistance. It is resistance to learning and to changing. When we demand that it be done right now, completed at once, then we don't give ourselves time to learn the lesson involved with the problem we have created.

If you want to move to another room, you have to get up and move step by step in that direction. Just sitting in your chair and demanding that you be in the other room will not work. It's the same thing. We all want our problem to be over with, but we don't want to do the small things that will add up to the solution.

Now is the time to acknowledge our responsibility in having created the situation or condition. I'm not talking about having guilt, nor about being a "bad person" for being where you are. I am saying to acknowledge the "power within you" that transforms our every thought into experience. In the past we unknowingly used this power to create things we did not want to experience. We were not aware of what we were doing. Now, by acknowledging our responsibility, we *become* aware and learn to use this power consciously in positive ways for our benefit.

Often when I suggest a solution to the client — a new way to approach a matter or forgiving the person involved — I will see the jaw begin to clench and jut out, and arms cross tightly over the chest. Maybe even fists will form. Resistance is coming to the fore, and I know we have hit upon exactly what needs to be done.

We all have lessons to learn. The things that are so difficult for us are only the lessons we have chosen for ourselves. If things are easy for us, then they are not lessons, but are things we already know.

Lessons Can Be Learned Through Awareness

If you think of the hardest thing for you to do and how much you resist it, then you're looking at your greatest lesson at the moment. Surrendering, giving up the resistance, and allowing yourself to learn what you need to learn, will make the next step even easier. Don't let your resistance stop you from making the changes. We can work on two levels: 1) Looking at the resistance, and 2) Still making the mental changes. Observe yourself, watch how you resist, and then go ahead anyway.

Nonverbal Clues

Our actions often show our resistance. For instance:

Changing the subject
Leaving the room
Going to the bathroom
Being late
Getting sick
Procrastinating by:
    doing something else
    doing busy work
    wasting time
Looking away, or out the window
Flipping through a magazine
Refusing to pay attention
Eating, drinking, or smoking
Creating or ending a relationship
Creating breakdowns; cars, appliances, plumbing, etc.

Assumptions

We often assume things about others to justify our resistance. We make statements such as:

It wouldn't do any good anyway.
My husband/wife won't understand.
I would have to change my whole personality.
Only crazy people go to therapists.
They couldn't help me with my problem.
They couldn't handle my anger.

My case is different.
I don't want to bother them.
It will work itself out.
Nobody else does it.

Beliefs

We grow up with beliefs that become our resistance to changing. Some of our limiting ideas are:

It's not done.
It's just not right.
It's not right for me to do that.
That wouldn't be spiritual.
Spiritual people don't get angry.
Men/women just don't do that.
My family never did that.
Love is not for me.
It's too far to drive.
It's too much work.
It's too expensive.
It will take too long.
I don't believe in it.
I'm not that kind of person.

Them

We give our power to others and use that excuse as our resistance to changing. We have ideas like:

God doesn't approve.
I'm waiting for the stars to say it's okay.
This isn't the right environment.
They won't let me change.
I don't have the right teacher/book/class/tools.

My doctor doesn't want me to.
I can't get time off work.
I don't want to be under their spell.
It's all their fault.
They have to change first.
As soon as I get _____ , I'll do it.
You/they don't understand.
I don't want to hurt them.
It's against my upbringing, religion, philosophy.

Self Concepts

We have ideas about ourselves that we use as limitations or resistance to changing. We are:

Too old.
Too young.
Too fat.
Too thin.
Too short.
Too tall.
Too lazy.
Too strong.
Too weak.
Too dumb.
Too smart.
Too poor.
Too worthless.
Too frivolous.
Too serious.
Too stuck.
Maybe it's just all too much.

Delaying Tactics

Our resistance often expresses itself as delaying tactics. We use excuses like:

I'll do it later.
I can't think right now.
I don't have the time right now.
It would take too much time away from my work.
Yes, that's a good idea; I'll do it some other time.
I have too many other things to do.
I'll think about it tomorrow.
As soon as I get through with _____ .
As soon as I get back from this trip.
The time isn't right.
It's too late, or too soon.

Denial

This form of resistance shows up in denial of the need to do any changing. Things like:

There is nothing wrong with me.
I can't do anything about this problem.
I was all right last time.
What good would it do to change?
If I ignore it, maybe the problem will go away.

Fear

By far the biggest category of resistance is fear — fear of the unknown. Listen to these:

I'm not ready yet.
I might fail.
They might reject me.
What would the neighbors think?

I'm afraid to tell my husband/wife.
I might get hurt.
I may have to change.
It might cost me money.
I would rather die first, or get a divorce first.
I don't want anyone to know I have a problem.
I'm afraid to express my feelings.
I don't want to talk about it.
I don't have the energy.
Who knows where I might end up?
I may lose my freedom.
It's too hard to do.
I don't have enough money now.
I might hurt my back.
I wouldn't be perfect.
I might lose my friends.
I don't trust anyone.
It might hurt my image.
I'm not good enough.

And on and on the list goes. Do you recognize some of these as the ways *you* resist? Look for the resistance in these examples:

A client came to me because she was in a lot of pain. She had broken her back, her neck, and her knee in three separate auto accidents. Yet she was late, got lost, and then was stuck in traffic.

It was easy for her to tell me all her problems, but the minute I said, "Let me talk for a moment," all sorts of turmoil began. Her contact lenses began to bother her. She wanted to sit in another chair. She had to go to the bathroom. Then her lenses had to come out. I could not keep her attention for the rest of the session.

It was all resistance. She wasn't ready to let go and be healed. I discovered her sister also had broken her back twice, and so had her mother.

Another client was an actor, a mime, a street performer, and quite good at it. He bragged about how clever he was at cheating others, especially institutions. He knew how to get away with almost anything, and yet he got away with nothing. He was always broke, at least a month behind in the rent, often without a telephone. His clothes were tacky, work was very sporadic, he had a lot of pains in his body, and his love life was zilch.

His theory was that he couldn't stop cheating until some good came into his life. Of course, with what he was giving out, no good could come into his life. He had to stop cheating first.

His resistance was that he was not ready to let go of the old ways.

Leave Your Friends Alone

Too often instead of working on our own changes, we decide which of our friends needs to change. This, too, is resistance.

In the early days of my work, I had a client who would send me to all her friends in the hospital. Instead of sending them flowers, she would have me go to fix up their problems. I would arrive with my tape recorder in hand, usually finding someone in bed who didn't know why I was there or understand what I was doing. This was before I learned never to work with anyone unless he or she requested it.

Sometimes clients come to me because a friend has given them a session as a present. This usually doesn't work too well, and they seldom come back for further work.

When something works well for us, we often want to share it with others. But they may not be ready to make a change at that point in time and space. It's hard enough to make changes when we want to, but to try to make someone else change when he or she doesn't want to is impossible, and it can ruin a good friendship. I push my clients because they come to me. I leave my friends alone.

Mirror Work

Mirrors reflect back to us our feelings about ourselves. They show us clearly the areas to be changed if we want to have a joyous, fulfilling life.

I ask people to look in their eyes and say something positive about themselves every time they pass a mirror. The most powerful way to do affirmations is to look in a mirror and say them out loud. You are immediately aware of the resistance and can move through it quicker. It's good to have a mirror with you as you read this book. Use it often for affirmations and to check where you are resisting and where you are open and flowing.

Now, look in a mirror and say to yourself, "I am willing to change."

Notice how you feel. If you are hesitant, resistant, or just don't want to change, ask yourself why. What old belief are you holding on to? This is not a time to scold yourself. Just notice what is going on and what belief rises to the surface. That is the one that has been causing you a lot of trouble. Can you recognize where it came from?

When we do our affirmations and they don't feel right or nothing seems to happen, it's so easy to say, "Oh, affirmations don't work." It's not that the affirmations don't work, it's that we need to do another step before we begin affirmations.

Repeated Patterns Show Us Our Needs

For every habit we have, for every experience we go through over and over, for every pattern we repeat, there is a NEED WITHIN US for it. The need corresponds to some belief we have. If there were not a need, we wouldn't have it, do it, or be it. There is something within us that needs the fat, the poor relationships, the failures, the cigarettes, the anger, the poverty, the abuse, or whatever there is that's a problem for us.

How many times have we said, "I won't ever do that again!"? Then, before the day is up, we have the piece of cake, smoke the cigarettes, say hateful things to the ones we love, and so on. Then we compound the whole problem by angrily saying to ourselves, "Oh, you have no willpower, no discipline. You're just weak." This only adds to the load of guilt we already carry.

It Has Nothing to Do with Willpower or Discipline

Whatever we are trying to release in our lives is just a symptom, an outer effect. Trying to eliminate the symptom without working on dissolving the cause is useless. The moment we release our willpower or discipline, the symptom crops up again.

Willingness to Release the Need

I say to clients, "There must be a need in you for this condition, or you wouldn't have it. Let's go back a step and work on the WILLINGNESS TO RELEASE THE NEED. When the need is gone, you will have no desire for the cigarette or the overeating or the negative pattern."

One of the first affirmations to use is: "I am willing to release the NEED for the resistance, or the headache, or the constipation, or the excess weight, or the lack of money or whatever." Say: "I am willing to release the need for..." If you are resisting at this point, then your other affirmations cannot work.

The webs we create around ourselves need to be unwound. If you have ever untangled a ball of string, you know that yanking and pulling only makes it worse. You need to very gently and patiently unravel the knots. Be gentle and patient with *yourself* as you untangle your own mental knots. Get help if you need it. Above all, love yourself in the process. The *willingness* to let go of the old is the key. That is the secret.

When I say "needing the problem," I mean that according to our particular set of thought patterns, we "need" to have certain outer effects or experiences. Every outer effect is the natural expression of an inner thought pattern. To battle only the outer effect or symptom is wasted energy and often increases the problem.

"I Am Unworthy" Creates Procrastination

If one of my inner belief systems or thought patterns is, "I am unworthy," then one of my outer effects will probably be procrastination. After all, procrastination is one way to keep us from getting where we say we want to go. Most people who procrastinate will spend a lot of time and energy berating themselves for procrastinating. They will call themselves lazy and generally will make themselves out to feel they are "bad persons."

Resentment of Another's Good

I had a client who loved attention and usually came to class late so he could create a stir. He had been the baby of 18 children, and he came last on the list of getting. As a child he watched everyone else "have" while he just longed for his own. Even now when someone had good fortune, he would not rejoice with them. Instead he would say, "Oh, I wish I had that," or "Oh, why don't I ever get that?"

His resentment of their good was a barrier to his own growth and change.

Self-Worth Opens Many Doors

A client who was 79 came to me. She taught singing, and several of her students were making television commercials. She wanted to do this, too, but was afraid. I supported her totally and explained, "There is nobody like you. Just be yourself." I said, "Do it for the fun of it. There are people out there looking for exactly what you have to offer. Let them know you exist."

She called several agents and casting directors, and said, "I am a senior, senior citizen, and I want to do commercials." In a short time, she had a commercial, and since then she's never stopped working. I often see her on TV and in magazines. New careers can start at any age, especially when you do it for the fun of it.

Self-Criticizing Is Totally Missing the Mark

It will only intensify the procrastination and laziness. The place to put the mental energy is into releasing the old and creating a new thought pattern. Say: *"I am willing to release the need to be unworthy. I am worthy of the very best in life, and I now lovingly allow myself to accept it.*

"As I spend a few days doing this affirmation over and over, my outer effect pattern of procrastination will automatically begin to fade.

"As I internally create a pattern of self-worth, then I no longer have the need to delay my good."

Do you see how this could apply to some of the negative patterns or outer effects in your life? Let's stop wasting time and energy putting ourselves down for something we can't help doing if we have certain inner beliefs. *Change the beliefs.*

No matter how you approach it, or what subject matter we are talking about, we are only dealing with thoughts, and thoughts can be changed.

When we want to change a condition, we need to say so.

"I am willing to release the pattern within me that is creating this condition."

You can say this to yourself over and over every time you think of your illness or problem. The minute you say it, you are stepping out of the victim class. You are no longer helpless; you are acknowledging your own power. You are saying, "I am beginning to understand that I created this. I now take my own power back. I am going to release this old idea and let it go."

Self-Criticism

I have a client who will eat a pound of butter and everything else she can get ahold of when she cannot bear to be with her own negative thoughts. The next day she will be angry at her body for being heavy. When she was a little girl, she would walk around the family dinner table finishing off everyone's leftovers and eating a whole stick of butter. The family would laugh and think it was cute. It was almost the only approval she got from her family.

When you scold yourself, when you berate yourself, when you "beat yourself up," who do you think you're treating this way?

Almost all of our programming, both negative and positive, was accepted by us by the time we were three years old. Our experiences since then are based upon what we accepted and believed about ourselves and about life at that time. The way we were treated when we were very little is usually the way we treat ourselves now. The person you are scolding is a three-year-old child within you.

If you are a person who gets angry at yourself for being afraid and fearful, think of yourself as being three years old. If you had a little three-year-old child in front of you who was afraid, what would you do? Would you be angry at him, or would you reach out your arms and comfort the child until he felt safe and at ease? The adults around you when you were a child may not have known how to comfort you at that time. Now *you* are the adult in your life, and if you're not comforting the child within you, then that is very sad indeed.

What was done in the past is done, and it is over now. But this is present time, and you now have the opportunity to treat yourself the way you wish to be treated. A frightened child needs comforting, not scolding. Scolding yourself only makes you more frightened, and there is nowhere to turn. When the child within feels unsafe, it creates a lot of trouble. Remember how it felt to be belittled when you were young? It feels the same way now to that child within.

Be kind to yourself. Begin to love and approve of yourself. That's what that little child needs in order to express itself at its highest potential.

In the infinity of life where I am,
all is perfect, whole, and complete.
I see any resistance patterns within me
only as something else to release.
They have no power over me. I am the power in my world.
I flow with the changes taking place in my life as best I can.
I approve of myself and the way I am changing.
I am doing the best I can. Each day gets easier.
I rejoice that I am in the rhythm and flow
of my ever-changing life.
Today is a wonderful day.
I choose to make it so.
All is well in my world.

❤️ Chapter Seven

HOW TO CHANGE

"I cross bridges with joy and with ease."

I love "how to's." All the theory in the world is useless unless we know how to apply it and make a change. I have always been a very pragmatic, practical person with a great need to know how to do things.

The principles we will be working with at this time are:

Nurturing the willingness to let go,
Controlling the mind, and
Learning how forgiveness of self and others releases us.

Releasing the Need

Sometimes when we try to release a pattern, the whole situation seems to get worse for a while. This is not a bad thing. It is a sign that the situation is beginning to move. Our affirmations are working, and we need to keep going.

Examples

We are working on increasing prosperity, and we lose our wallet.

We are working on improving our relationships, and we have a fight.

We are working on becoming healthy, and we catch a cold.

We are working on expressing our creative talents and abilities, and we get fired.

Sometimes the problem moves in a different direction, and we begin to see and understand more. For example, let's assume you are trying to give up smoking and you are saying, "I am willing to release the 'need' for cigarettes." As you continue to do this, you notice your relationships becoming more uncomfortable.

Don't despair, this is a sign of the process working.

You might ask yourself a series of questions like: "Am I willing to give up uncomfortable relationships? Were my cigarettes creating a smoke screen so I wouldn't see how uncomfortable these relationships are? Why am I creating these relationships?"

You notice the cigarettes are only a symptom and not a cause. Now you are developing insight and understanding that will set you free.

You begin to say, "I am willing to release the 'need' for uncomfortable relationships."

Then you notice the reason you're so uncomfortable is that other people always seem to be criticizing you.

Being aware that we always create all of our experiences, you now begin to say, "I am willing to release the need to be criticized."

You then think about criticism, and you realize that as a child you received a lot of criticism. That little kid inside of you only feels "at home" when it is being criticized. Your way of hiding from this had been to create a "smoke screen."

Perhaps you see the next step as affirming, "I am willing to forgive..."

As you continue to do your affirmations, you may find that cigarettes no longer attract you, and the people in your life no longer criticize you. Then you *know* you have released your need.

This usually takes a little while to work out. If you are gently persistent and are willing to give yourself a few quiet moments each day to reflect on your process of change, you will get the answers. The Intelligence within you is the same Intelligence that created this entire planet. Trust your Inner Guidance to reveal to you whatever it is you need to know.

Exercise: Releasing the Need

In a workshop situation, I would have you do this exercise with a partner. However, you can do it equally as well using a mirror — a big one, if possible.

Think for a moment about something in your life you want to change. Go to the mirror and look into your eyes and say out loud, "I now realize that I have created this condition, and I am now willing to release the pattern in my consciousness that is responsible for this condition." Say it several times, with feeling.

If you were with a partner, I would have your partner tell you if he really thought you meant it. I would want you to convince your partner.

Ask yourself if you really mean it. Convince yourself in the mirror that this time you are ready to step out of the bondage of the past.

At this point many people get scared because they don't know HOW to do this releasing. They are afraid to commit themselves until they know all the answers. It's only more resistance. Just pass through it.

One of the great things is that we do not have to know how. All we need is to be willing. The Universal Intelligence or your subconscious mind will figure out the hows. Every thought you think and every word you speak is being responded to, and the point of power is in the moment. The thoughts you are thinking and the words you are declaring at this moment are creating your future.

Your Mind Is a Tool

You are much more than your mind. You may think your mind is running the show. But that is only because you have trained your mind to think in this way. You can also untrain and retrain this tool of yours.

79

Your mind is a tool for you to use in any way you wish. The way you now use your mind is only a habit, and habits, any habits, can be changed if we want to do so, or even if we only know it is possible to do so.

Quiet the chatter of your mind for a moment, and really think about this concept: YOUR MIND IS A TOOL YOU CAN CHOOSE TO USE ANY WAY YOU WISH.

The thoughts you "choose" to think create the experiences you have. If you believe that it is hard or difficult to change a habit or a thought, then your choice of this thought will make it true for you. If you would choose to think, "It is becoming easier for me to make changes," then your choice of this thought will make that true for you.

Controlling the Mind

There is an incredible power and intelligence within you constantly responding to your thoughts and words. As you learn to control your mind by the conscious choice of thoughts, you align yourself with this power.

Do not think your mind is in control. *You* are in control of your mind. *You* use your mind. You *can* stop thinking those old thoughts.

When your old thinking tries to come back and say, "It's so hard to change," take mental control. Say to your mind, "I now choose to believe it is becoming easier for me to make changes." You may have to have this conversation with your mind several times for it to acknowledge that you are in control and that what you say goes.

The Only Thing You Ever Have Any Control of Is Your Current Thought

Your old thoughts are gone; there is nothing you can do about them except live out the experiences they caused. Your current thought, the one you are thinking right now, is totally under your control.

Example

If you have a little child who has been allowed to stay up as late as he wishes for a long time, and then you make a decision that you now want this child to go to bed at 8:00 every night, what do you think the first night will be like?

The child will rebel against this new rule and may kick and scream and do his best to stay out of bed. If you relent at *this* time, the child wins and will try to control you forever.

However, if you calmly stick to your decision and firmly insist that this is the new bedtime, the rebellion will lessen. In two or three nights, the new routine will be established.

It is the same thing with your mind. Of course it will rebel at first. It does not want to be retrained. But you are in control, and if you stay focused and firm, in a very short time the new way of thinking will be established. And you will feel so good to realize that *you are not a helpless victim of your own thoughts, but rather a master of your own mind.*

Exercise: Letting Go

As you read this, take a deep breath and, as you exhale, allow all the tension to leave your body. Let your scalp and your forehead and your face relax. Your head does not need to be tense in order for you to read. Let your tongue and your throat and your shoulders relax. You can hold a book with relaxed arms and hands. Do that now. Let your back and your abdomen and your pelvis relax. Let your breathing be at peace as you relax your legs and feet.

Is there a big change in your body since you began the previous paragraph? Notice how much you hold on. If you are doing it with your body, you are doing it with your mind.

In this relaxed, comfortable position, say to yourself, "I am willing to let go. I release. I let go. I release all tension. I release all fear. I release all anger. I release all guilt. I release all sadness. I let go of all old limitations. I let go, and I am at peace. I am at peace with myself. I am at peace with the process of life. I am safe."

Go over this exercise two or three times. Feel the ease of letting go. Repeat it whenever you feel thoughts of difficulty coming up. It takes a little practice for the routine to become a part of you. When you put yourself into this peaceful state first, it becomes easy for your affirmations to take hold. You become open and receptive to them. There is no need to struggle or stress or strain. Just relax and think the appropriate thoughts. Yes, it is this easy.

Physical Releasing

Sometimes we need to experience a physical letting go. Experiences and emotions can get locked in the body. Screaming in the car with all the windows rolled up can be very releasing if we have been stifling our verbal expression. Beating the bed or kicking pillows is a harmless way to release pent-up anger, as is playing tennis or running.

Awhile ago, I had a pain in my shoulder for a day or two. I tried to ignore it, but it wouldn't go away. Finally, I sat down and asked myself, "What is happening here? What am I feeling?"

I realized, "It feels like burning. Burning...burning...that means anger. What are you angry about?"

I couldn't think of what I was angry about, so I said, "Well, let's see if we can find out." I put two large pillows on the bed and began to hit them with a lot of energy.

After about twelve hits, I realized exactly what I was angry about. It was so clear. So I beat the pillows even harder and made some noise and released the emotions from my body. When I got through, I felt much better, and the next day my shoulder was fine.

Letting the Past Hold You Back

Many people come to me and say *they cannot enjoy today because of something that happened in the past.* Because they did not do something or do it in a certain way in the past, they cannot live a full life today. Because they no longer have something they had in the past, they cannot enjoy today. Because they were hurt in the past, they will not accept love now. Because something unpleasant happened when they did something once, they are sure it will happen again today. Because they once did something that they are sorry for, they are sure they are bad people forever. Because once someone did something to them, it is now all the other person's fault that their life is not where they want it to be. Because they became angry over a situation in the past, they will hold on to that self-righteousness. Because of some very old experience where they were treated badly, they will never forgive and forget.

Because I did not get invited to the high school prom, I cannot enjoy life today.

Because I did poorly at my first audition, I will be terrified of auditions forever.

Because I am no longer married, I cannot live a full life today.

Because I was hurt by a remark once, I will never trust anyone again.

Because I stole something once, I must punish myself forever.

Because I was poor as a child, I will never get anywhere.

What we often refuse to realize is that holding on to the past — no matter what it was or how awful it was — is ONLY HURTING US. "They" really don't care. Usually, "they" are not even aware. We are only hurting ourselves by refusing to live in this moment to the fullest.

The past is over and done and cannot be changed. This is the only moment we can experience. Even when we lament about the past, we are experiencing our memory of it in this moment, and losing the real experience of this moment in the process.

Exercise: Releasing

Let us now clean up the past in our minds. Release the emotional attachment to it. Allow the memories to be just memories.

If you think back to what you used to wear in the third grade, usually there is no emotional attachment. It's just a memory.

It can be the same for all of the past events in our lives. As we let go, we become free to use all of our mental power to enjoy this moment and to create a great future.

List all the things you are willing to let go of. How willing are you to do this? Notice your reactions. What will you have to do to let these things go? How willing are you to do so? What is your resistance level?

Forgiveness

Next step, *forgiveness*. Forgiveness of ourselves and of others releases us from the past. The *Course in Miracles* says over and over that forgiveness is the answer to almost everything. I know that when we are stuck, it usually means there is some more forgiving to be done. When we do not flow freely with life in the present moment, it usually means we are holding on to a past moment. It can be regret, sadness, hurt, fear, or guilt, blame, anger, resentment, and sometimes even the desire for revenge. *Each one of these states comes from a space of unforgiveness, a refusal to let go and come into the present moment.*

Love is always the answer to healing of any sort. And the pathway to love is forgiveness. Forgiveness dissolves resentment. There are several ways in which I approach this.

Exercise: Dissolving Resentment

There is an old Emmet Fox exercise for dissolving resentment that always works. He recommends that you sit quietly, close your eyes, and allow your mind and body to relax. Then, imagine yourself sitting in a darkened theater, and in front of you is a small stage. On that stage, place the person you resent the most. It could be someone in the past or present, living or dead. When you see this person clearly, visualize good things happening to this person — things that would be meaningful to him. See him smiling and happy.

Hold this image for a few minutes, then let it fade away. I like to add another step. As this person leaves the stage, put yourself up there. See good things happening to you. See yourself smiling and happy. Be aware that the abundance of the Universe is available to all of us.

The above exercise dissolves the dark clouds of resentment most of us carry. For some, it will be very difficult to do. Each time you do it, you may get a different person. Do it once a day for a month, and notice how much lighter you feel.

Exercise: Revenge

Those on the spiritual pathway know the importance of forgiveness. For some of us, there is a step that is necessary before we can totally forgive. Sometimes the little kid in us needs to have revenge before it is free to forgive. For that, this exercise is very helpful.

Close your eyes, sit quietly and peacefully. Think of the people who are hardest to forgive. What would you really like to do to them? What do they need to do to get your forgiveness? Imagine that happening now. Get into the details. How long do you want them to suffer or do penance?

When you feel complete, condense time and let it be over forever. Usually at this point you feel lighter, and it is easier to think about forgiveness. To indulge in this every day would not be good for you. To do it once as a closing exercise can be freeing.

Exercise: Forgiveness

Now we are ready to forgive. Do this exercise with a partner if you can, or do it out loud if you are alone.

Again, sit quietly with your eyes closed and say, "The person I need to forgive is _____ and I forgive you for _____."

Do this over and over. You will have many things to forgive some for and only one or two to forgive others for. If you have a partner, let him say to you, "Thank you, I set you free now." If you do not, then imagine the person you are forgiving saying it to you. Do this for at least five or ten minutes. Search your heart for the injustices you still carry. Then let them go.

When you have cleared as much as you can for now, turn your attention to yourself. Say out loud to yourself, "I forgive myself for _____." Do this for another five minutes or so. These are powerful exercises and good to do at least once a week to clear out any remaining rubbish. Some experiences are easy to let go and some we have to chip away at, until suddenly one day they let go and dissolve.

Exercise: Visualization

Another good exercise. Have someone read this one to you if you can, or put it on tape and listen to it.

Begin to visualize yourself as a little child of five or six. Look deeply into this little child's eyes. See the longing that is there and realize that there is only one thing this little child wants from you, and that is love. So reach out your arms and embrace this child. Hold it with love and tenderness. Tell it how much you love it, how much you care. Admire everything about this child and say that it's okay to make mistakes while learning. Promise that you will always be there no matter what. Now let this little child get very small, until it is just the size to fit into your heart. Put it there so whenever you look down, you can see this little face looking up at you, and you can give it lots of love.

Now visualize your mother as a little girl of four or five, frightened and looking for love and not knowing where to find it. Reach out your arms and hold this little girl and let her know how much you love her, how much you care. Let her know she can rely on you to always be there, no matter what. When she quiets down and begins to feel safe, let her get very small, just the size to fit into your heart. Put her there with your own little child. Let them give each other lots of love.

Now imagine your father as a little boy of three or four — frightened, crying, and looking for love. See the tears rolling down his little face when he doesn't know where to turn. You have become good at comforting frightened little children, so reach out your arms and hold his trembling little body. Comfort him. Croon to him. Let him feel how much you love him. Let him feel that you will always be there for him.

When his tears are dry, and you feel the love and peace in his little body, let him get very small, just the size to fit into your heart. Put him there so those three little children can give each other lots of love and you can love them all.

* * *

There is so much love in your heart that you could heal the entire planet. But just for now let us use this love to heal *you*. Feel a warmth beginning to glow in your heart center, a softness, a gentleness. Let this feeling begin to change the way you think and talk about yourself.

In the infinity of life where I am,
all is perfect, whole, and complete.
Change is the natural law of my life. I welcome change.
I am willing to change. I choose to change my thinking.
I choose to change the words I use.
I move from the old to the new with ease and with joy.
It is easier for me to forgive than I thought.
Forgiving makes me feel free and light.
It is with joy that I learn to love myself more and more.
The more resentment I release, the more love I have to express.
Changing my thoughts makes me feel good.
I am learning to choose to make today a pleasure to experience.
All is well in my world.

❤ Chapter Eight

BUILDING THE NEW

*"The answers within me come to my
awareness with ease."*

I don't want to be fat.
I don't want to be broke.
I don't want to be old.
I don't want to live here.
I don't want to have this relationship.
I don't want to be like my mother/father.
I don't want to be stuck in this job.
I don't want to have this hair/nose/body.
I don't want to be lonely.
I don't want to be unhappy.
I don't want to be sick.

What You Put Your Attention on Grows

The above shows how we are culturally taught to fight the negative mentally — thinking that if we do so, the positive will automatically come to us. It doesn't work that way.

How often have you lamented about what you didn't want? Did it ever bring you what you really wanted? Fighting the negative is a total waste of time if you really want to make changes in your life. *The more you dwell on what you don't want, the more of it you create.*

The things about yourself or your life that you have always disliked are probably still with you.

What you put your attention on grows and becomes permanent in your life. Move away from the negative, and put your attention on what it is that you really *do* want to be or have. Let's turn the above negative affirmations into positive affirmations.

I am slender.
I am prosperous.
I am eternally young.
I now move to a better place.
I have a wonderful new relationship.
I am my own person.
I love my hair/nose/body.
I am filled with love and affection.
I am joyous and happy and free.
I am totally healthy.

Affirmations

Learn to think in positive affirmations. Affirmations can be any statement you make. Too often we think in negative affirmations. Negative affirmations only create more of what you say you don't want. Saying, "I hate my job," will get you nowhere. Declaring, "I now accept a wonderful new job," will open the channels in your consciousness to create that.

Continually make positive statements about how you want your life to be. However, there is one point that is very important in this: *Always make your statement in the PRESENT TENSE,* such as "I am" or "I have." Your subconscious mind is such an obedient servant that if you declare in the future tense, "I want," or "I will have," then that is where that idea will always stay — just out of your reach in the future!

The Process of Loving the Self

As I have said before, no matter what the problem, the main issue to work on is LOVING THE SELF. This is the "magic wand" that dissolves problems. Remember the times when you have felt good about yourself and how well your life was going? Remember the times when you were in love and for those periods you seemed to have no problems? Well, loving yourself is going to bring such a surge of good feelings and good fortune to you that you will be dancing on air. LOVING YOURSELF MAKES YOU FEEL GOOD.

It is impossible to really love yourself unless you have self-approval and self-acceptance. This means no criticism whatsoever. I can hear all the objections right now.

"But I have always criticized myself."
"How can I possibly like that about myself?"
"My parents/teachers/lovers always criticized me."
"How will I be motivated?"
"But it is wrong for me to do those things."
"How am I going to change if I don't criticize myself?"

Training the Mind

Self-criticism such as that illustrated above is just the mind going on with old chatter. See how you have trained your mind to berate you and be resistant to change? Ignore those thoughts and get on with the important work at hand!

Let's go back to an exercise we did earlier. Look into the mirror again, and say, "I love and approve of myself exactly as I am."

How does that feel now? Is it a little easier after the forgiveness work we have done? This is still the main issue. Self-approval and self-acceptance are the keys to positive changes.

In the days when my own self-denial was so prevalent, I would occasionally slap my own face. I didn't know the meaning of self-acceptance. My belief in my own lacks and limitations was stronger than anything anyone else could say to the contrary. If someone told me I was loved, my immediate reaction was, "Why? What could anyone possibly see in me?" Or the classic thought, "If they only knew what I was *really* like inside, they wouldn't love me."

I was not aware that all good begins with accepting that which is within one's self, and loving that self which is you. It took quite a while to develop a peaceful, loving relationship with *myself*.

First, I used to hunt for the little things about myself that I thought were "good qualities." Even this helped, and my own health began to improve. Good health begins with loving the self. So do prosperity and love and creative self-expression. Later I learned to love and approve of all of me, even those qualities I thought were "not good enough." That was when I really began to make progress.

Exercise: I Approve of Myself

I have given this exercise to hundreds of people, and the results are phenomenal. For the next month, say over and over to yourself, "I APPROVE OF MYSELF."

Do this three or four hundred times a day, at least. No, it's not too many times. When you are worrying, you go over your problem at least that many times. Let "I approve of myself" become a walking mantra, something you just say over and over and over to yourself, almost nonstop.

Saying "I approve of myself" is a guaranteed way to bring up everything buried in your consciousness that is in opposition.

When negative thoughts come up, such as, "How can I approve of myself when I am fat?" or "It's silly to think this can do any good," or "I am no good," or whatever your negative babble will be, this is the time to take mental control. Give these thoughts no importance. Just see them for what they are — another way to keep you stuck in the past. Gently say to these thoughts, "I let you go; I approve of myself."

Even considering doing this exercise can bring up a lot of stuff, like "It feels silly," "It doesn't feel true," "It's a lie," "It sounds stuck up," or "How can I approve of myself when I do that?"

Let all these thoughts just pass through. These are only resistance thoughts. They have no power over you unless you choose to believe them.

"I approve of myself, I approve of myself, I approve of myself." No matter what happens, no matter who says what to you, no matter who does what to you, just keep it going. In fact, when you can say that to yourself when someone is doing something you don't approve of, you will know you are growing and changing.

Thoughts have no power over us unless we give in to them. Thoughts are only words strung together. They have NO MEANING WHATSOEVER. Only *we* give meaning to them. Let us choose to think thoughts that nourish and support us.

Part of self-acceptance is releasing other people's opinions. If I were with you and kept telling you, "You are a purple pig, you are a purple pig." You would either laugh at me, or get annoyed with me and think I was crazy. It would be most unlikely that you would think it was true. Yet many of the things we have chosen to believe about ourselves are just as far out and untrue. To believe that your self-worth is dependent on the shape of your body is your version of believing that "You are a purple pig."

Often what we think of as the things "wrong" with us are only our expressions of our own individuality. This is our uniqueness and what is special about us. Nature never repeats itself. Since time began on this planet, there have never been two snowflakes alike or two raindrops the same. And every daisy is different from every other daisy. Our fingerprints are different, and we are different. *We are meant to be different. When we can accept this, then there is no competition and no comparison.* To try to be like another is to shrivel our soul. We have come to this planet to express who *we are*.

I didn't even know who I was until I began to learn to love myself as I am in this moment.

Put Your Awareness into Practice

Think thoughts that make you happy. Do things that make you feel good. Be with people who make you feel good. Eat things that make your body feel good. Go at a pace that makes you feel good.

Planting Seeds

Think for a moment of a tomato plant. A healthy plant can have over a hundred tomatoes on it. In order to get this tomato plant with all these tomatoes on it, we need to start with a small dried seed. That seed doesn't look like a tomato plant. It sure doesn't taste like a tomato plant. If you didn't know for sure, you would not even believe it could be a tomato plant. However, let's say you plant this seed in fertile soil, and you water it and let the sun shine on it.

When the first little tiny shoot comes up, you don't stomp on it and say, "That's not a tomato plant." Rather, you look at it and say, "Oh boy! Here it comes," and you watch it grow with delight. In time, if you continue to water it and give it lots of sunshine and pull away any weeds, you might have a tomato plant with more than a hundred luscious tomatoes. It all began with that one tiny seed.

It is the same with creating a new experience for yourself. The soil you plant in is your subconscious mind. The seed is the new affirmation. *The whole new experience is in this tiny seed.* You water it with affirmations. You let the sunshine of positive thoughts beam on it. You weed the garden by pulling out the negative thoughts that come up. And when you first see the tiniest little evidence, you don't stomp on it and say, "That's not enough!" Instead, you look at this first breakthrough and exclaim with glee, "Oh boy! Here it comes! It's working!"

Then you watch it grow and become your desire in manifestation.

Exercise: Create New Changes

Now is the time to take your list of things that are wrong with you and turn them into positive affirmations. Or you can list all the changes you want to make and have and do. Then select three from this list and turn them into positive affirmations.

Just suppose your negative list was something like this:

> My life is a mess.
> I should lose weight.
> Nobody loves me.
> I want to move.
> I hate my job.
> I should get organized.
> I don't do enough.
> I'm not good enough.

You can then turn them around to something like this:

> I am willing to release the pattern in me that
>   created these conditions.
> I am in the process of positive changes.
> I have a happy, slender body.
> I experience love wherever I go.
> I have the perfect living space.
> I now create a wonderful new job.
> I am now very well organized.
> I appreciate all that I do.
> I love and approve of myself.
> I trust the process of life to bring me my highest good.
> I deserve the best, and I accept it now.

Out of this group of affirmations will come all the things you want to change on your list. Loving and approving of yourself, creating a space of safety, trusting and deserving and accepting, will enable your body weight to normalize. They will create organization in your mind, create loving relationships in your life, attract a new job and a new place to live. It is miraculous the way a tomato plant grows. It is miraculous the way we can demonstrate our desires.

Deserving Your Good

Do you believe that you deserve to have your desire? If you don't, you won't allow yourself to have it. Circumstances beyond your control will crop up to frustrate you.

Exercise: I Deserve

Look in your mirror again, and say, "I deserve to have or be _____, and I accept it now." Say it two or three times.

How do you feel? Always pay attention to your feelings, to what is going on in your body. Does it feel true, or do you still feel unworthy?

If you have any negative feelings in your body, then go back to affirming, "I release the pattern in my consciousness that is creating resistance to my good." "I deserve _____."

Repeat this until you get the acceptance feelings, even if you have to do it several days in a row.

Holistic Philosophy

In our approach to Building the New, we want to use a holistic approach. The holistic philosophy is to nurture and nourish the entire being — the Body, the Mind, and the Spirit. If we ignore any of these areas, we are incomplete; we lack wholeness. It doesn't matter where we start as long as we also include the other areas.

If we begin with the body, we would want to work with nutrition, to learn the relationship between our choice of food and beverages, and how they affect the way we feel. We want to make the best choices for our body. There are herbs and vitamins, homeopathy and Bach Flower Remedies. We might explore colonics.

We would want to find a form of exercise that appeals to us. Exercise is something that strengthens our bones and keeps our bodies young. In addition to sports and swimming, consider dancing, Tai-Chi, martial arts, and yoga. I love my trampoline and use it daily. My slant board enhances my periods of relaxation.

We might want to explore some form of body work such as Rolfing, Heller Work or Trager. Massage, foot reflexology, acupuncture, or chiropractic work are all beneficial, as well. There is also the Alexander Method, Bioenergetics, Feldenkrais, Touch for Health, and Reiki forms of body work.

With the mind, we could explore visualization techniques, guided imagery, and affirmations. There are lots of psychological techniques: Gestalt, hypnosis, rebirthing, psychodrama, past-life regressions, art therapy, and even dream work.

Meditation in any of its forms is a wonderful way to quiet the mind and allow your own "knowingness" to come to the surface. I usually just sit with my eyes closed and say, "What is it I need to know?" and then I wait quietly for an answer. If the answer comes, fine; if it doesn't, fine. It will come another day.

There are *groups* that do workshops for all different tastes such as Insight, Loving Relationships Training, Advocate Experience, the Ken Keyes group, Actualizations, and many more. Many of these groups do weekend workshops. These weekends give you a chance to see a whole new viewpoint about life. No one workshop will totally clear up ALL your problems forever. However, they can assist you in changing your life in the here and now.

In the Spiritual Realm, there is prayer, there is meditation, and becoming connected with your Higher Source. For me, practicing forgiveness and unconditional love are spiritual practices.

There are many spiritual groups. In addition to the Christian churches, there are metaphysical churches, such as Religious Science and Unity. There is the Self-Realization Fellowship, M.S.I.A., Transcendental Meditation, the Siddha Foundation, and so on.

I want you to know that there are many, many avenues you can explore. If one way doesn't work for you, try another. All these suggestions have proved to be beneficial. I cannot say which one is right for you. That is something you will have to discover for yourself. No one method or one person or one group has all the answers for everyone. I don't have all the answers for everyone. I am just one more stepping stone on the pathway to holistic health.

In the infinity of life where I am,
all is perfect, whole, and complete. My life is ever new.
Each moment of my life is new and fresh and vital.
I use my affirmative thinking to create exactly what I want.
This is a new day. I am a new me.
I think differently. I speak differently. I act differently.
Others treat me differently.
My new world is a reflection of my new thinking.
It is a joy and a delight to plant new seeds,
for I know these seeds will become my new experiences.
All is well in my world.

 # Chapter Nine

DAILY WORK

"I enjoy practicing my new mental skills."

If Children Gave Up When They Fell for the First Time, They Would Never Learn to Walk

Like any other new thing you are learning, it takes practice to make it part of your life. First there is a lot of concentration, and some of us choose to make this "hard work." I don't like to think of it as hard work, but rather as something new to learn.

The process of learning is always the same no matter what the subject — whether you're learning to drive a car, or type, or play tennis, or think in a positive manner. First, we fumble and bumble as our subconscious mind learns by trial, and yet, every time we come back to our practicing, it gets easier, and we do it a little better. Of course, you won't be "perfect" the first day. You will be doing whatever you can do. That's good enough for a start.

Say to yourself often, "I'm doing the best I can."

Always Support Yourself

I well remember my first lecture. When I came down from the podium, I immediately said to myself, "Louise, you were wonderful. You were absolutely fantastic for the first time. When you have done five or six of these, you will be a pro."

A couple of hours later, I said to myself, "I think we could change a few things. Let's adjust this, and let's adjust that." I refused to criticize myself in any way.

If I had come off the podium and begun berating myself with, "Oh, you were so awful. You made this mistake, and you made that mistake," then I would have dreaded my second lecture. As it was, the second one was better than the first, and by the sixth one, I was feeling like a pro.

Seeing "The Law" Working All Around Us

Just before I began writing this book, I bought myself a word processor/computer. I called her my "Magic Lady." It was something new I chose to learn. I discovered that learning the computer was very much like learning the Spiritual Laws. When I learned the computer's laws, then she did indeed perform "magic" for me. When I did not follow her laws to the letter, then either nothing would happen or it would not work the way I wanted it to work. She would not give an inch. I could get as frustrated as I wanted while she patiently waited for me to learn her laws, and then she gave me magic. It took practice.

It's the same with the work you're learning to do now. You must learn the Spiritual Laws and follow them to the letter. You cannot bend them to your old way of thinking. You must learn and follow the new language, and when you do, *then* "magic" will be demonstrated in your life.

Reinforce Your Learning

The more ways you can reinforce your new learning, the better. I suggest:

Expressing Gratitude
Writing Affirmations
Sitting in Meditation

Enjoying Exercise
Practicing Good Nutrition
Doing Affirmations Aloud
Singing Affirmations
Taking Time for Relaxation Exercises
Using Visualization, Mental Imagery
Reading and Study

My Daily Work

My own daily work goes something like this.

My first thoughts on awakening before I open my eyes are to be thankful for everything I can think of.

After a shower, I take half an hour or so to meditate and do my affirmations and prayers.

Then after about 15 minutes of exercise, usually on the trampoline, I will sometimes work out with the 6:00 a.m. aerobic program on television.

Now I'm ready for breakfast consisting of fruit and fruit juices and herbal tea. I thank the Earth Mother for providing this food for me, and I thank the food for giving its life to nourish me.

Before lunch I like to go to a mirror and do some affirmations out loud; I may even sing them — something like:

Louise, you are wonderful, and I love you.
This is one of the best days of your life.
Everything is working out for your highest good.
Whatever you need to know is revealed to you.
Whatever you need comes to you.
All is well.

Lunch is often a large salad. Again, the food is blessed and thanked.

In the late afternoon, I spend a few minutes on my slant board, allowing my body to experience some deep relaxation. I may listen to a tape at this time.

Dinner will be steamed vegetables and a grain. Sometimes I'll eat fish or chicken. My body works best on simple food. I like to share dinner with others, and we bless each other in addition to the food.

Sometimes in the evening, I take a few moments to read and study. There is always more to learn. At this time I may also write out my current affirmation 10 or 20 times.

As I go to bed, I collect my thoughts. I go over the events of the day and bless each activity. I affirm that I will sleep deeply and soundly, awakening in the morning bright and refreshed and looking forward to the new day.

Sounds overwhelming, doesn't it? To begin with, it seems like a lot to cope with, but after a short period of time, your new way of thinking will become as much a part of your life as bathing or brushing your teeth. You will do it automatically and easily.

It would be wonderful for a family in the morning to do some of these things together. Meditating together in the morning to start the day or just before dinner brings peace and harmony to all. If you think you don't have the time, you might get up half an hour earlier. The benefits would be well worth the effort.

How Do You Begin Your Day?

What is the first thing you say in the morning when you wake up? We all have something we say almost every day. Is it positive or negative? I can remember when I used to awaken in the morning and say with a groan, "OH GOD, ANOTHER DAY." And that is exactly the sort of day I would have, one thing after another going wrong. Now when I awaken and before I even open my eyes, I thank the bed for a good night's sleep. After all, we have spent the whole night together in comfort. Then with my eyes still closed, I spend about ten minutes just being thankful for all the good in my life. I program my day a bit, affirming that everything will go well and that I will enjoy it all. This is before I get up and do my morning meditation or prayers.

Meditation

Give yourself a few minutes every day to sit in quiet *meditation*. If you are new at meditation, begin with five minutes. Sit quietly, observe your breathing, and allow the thoughts to pass gently through your mind. Give them no importance, and they will pass on. It is the nature of the mind to think, so don't try to get rid of thoughts.

There are many classes and books you can explore to find ways to meditate. No matter how or where you begin, you will eventually create the method best for you. I usually just sit quietly and ask, "What is it that I need to know?" I allow the answer to come if it wants to; if not, I know it will come later. There is no right or wrong way to meditate.

Another form of meditation is to sit quietly and observe the breath as it goes in and out of your body. As you inhale, count one, and as you exhale, count two. Continue counting until you get to 10, then begin again at one. If you notice your counting takes you to 25 or so, just go back to one.

There was one client who seemed to me to be so bright and intelligent. Her mind was unusually clever and quick, and she had a great sense of humor. Yet she could not get her act together. She was overweight, broke, frustrated in her career, and without a romance for many years. She could accept all the metaphysical concepts quickly; they made a lot of sense to her. Yet she was too clever, too quick. She found it difficult to slow herself down enough to practice over a meaningful period of time the ideas she could grasp so quickly on a moment-by-moment basis.

Daily meditation helped her enormously. We began with only 5 minutes a day and very gradually worked up to 15 or 20 minutes.

Exercise: Daily Affirmations

Take one or two affirmations and write them 10 or 20 times a day. Read them aloud with enthusiasm. Make a song out of your affirmations and sing them with joy. Let your mind go over these affirmations all day long.

Affirmations that are used consistently become beliefs and will always produce results, sometimes in ways that we cannot even imagine.

One of my beliefs is that I always have good relationships with my landlord. My last landlord in New York City was a man known to be extremely difficult, and all the tenants complained. In the five years I lived there, I saw him only three times. When I decided to move to California, I wanted to sell all my possessions and start fresh and unencumbered by the past. I began to do affirmations such as:

"All my possessions are sold easily and quickly."
"The move is very simple to do."
"Everything is working in Divine Right Order."
"All is well."

I did not think about how difficult it would be to sell things or where I would sleep the last few nights or any other negative ideas. I just kept doing my affirmations. Well, my clients and students quickly bought all the little stuff and most of the books. I informed my landlord in a letter that I would not be renewing my lease, and to my surprise, I received a phone call from him expressing his dismay at my leaving. He offered to write a letter of recommendation to my new landlord in California and asked if he could please buy the furniture, as he had decided to rent that apartment furnished.

My Higher Consciousness had put the two beliefs together in a way I could not have conceived of: "I always have good relationships with my landlord," and "Everything will sell easily and quickly." To the other tenants' amazement, I was able to sleep in my own bed in a comfortable furnished apartment until the last moment, AND BE PAID FOR IT! I walked out with a few clothes, my juicer, my blender, my hair dryer, and my typewriter, plus a large check, and I leisurely took the train to Los Angeles.

Do Not Believe in Limitations

Upon arriving in California, it was necessary for me to buy a car. Not having owned a car before nor having made a major purchase before, I did not have any established credit. The banks would not give me credit. Being a woman and self-employed did not help my case any. I did not want to spend all my savings to buy a new car. Establishing credit became a Catch-22.

I refused to have any negative thoughts about the situation or about the banks. I rented a car and kept affirming that, "I have a beautiful new car, and it comes to me easily."

I also told everybody I met that I wanted to buy a new car and had not been able to establish credit so far. In about three months' time, I met a businesswoman who instantly liked me. When I told her my story about the car, she said, "Oh, well, I will take care of that."

She called a friend at the bank who owed her a favor, and told her that I was an "old" friend, and gave me the highest references. Within three days, I drove off a car dealer's lot with a beautiful new car.

I was not excited so much as I was "in awe of the process." I believe the reason it took me three months to manifest the car was that I had never committed myself to monthly payments before, and the little kid in me was scared and needed time to get up the courage to make the step.

Exercise: I Love Myself

I assume you are already saying, "I approve of myself" almost nonstop. This is a powerful foundation. Keep it up for at least a month.

Now take a pad of paper and at the top write, "I LOVE MYSELF; THEREFORE..."

Finish this sentence in as many ways as you can. Read it over daily, and add to it as you think of new things.

If you can work with a partner, do so. Hold hands and alternate saying, "I love myself; therefore..." The biggest benefit of doing this exercise is that you learn it is almost impossible to belittle yourself when you say you love yourself.

Exercise: Claim the New

Visualize or imagine yourself having or doing or being what you are working toward. Fill in all the details. Feel, see, taste, touch, hear. Notice other people's reactions to your new state. Make it all okay with you no matter what their reactions are.

Exercise: Expand Your Knowledge

Read everything you can to expand your awareness and understanding of how the mind works. There is so much knowledge out there for you. This book is only ONE STEP on your pathway! Get other viewpoints. Hear other people say it in a different way. Study with a group for a while until you go beyond them.

This is a life work. The more you learn, the more you know, the more you practice and apply, the better you get to feel, and the more wonderful your life will be. Doing this work makes YOU FEEL GOOD!

Begin to Demonstrate Results

By practicing as many of these methods as you can, you will begin to demonstrate your results of this work. You will see the little miracles occur in your life. The things you are ready to eliminate will go of their own accord. The things and events you want will pop up in your life seemingly out of the blue. You will get bonuses you never imagined!

I was so surprised and delighted when after a few months of doing mental work, I began to look younger. Today I look ten years younger than I did ten years ago!

Love who and what you are and what you do. Laugh at yourself and at life, and nothing can touch you. It's all temporary anyway. Next lifetime you will do it differently anyway, so why not do it differently right now?

You could read one of Norman Cousins' books. He cured himself of a fatal dis-ease with laughter. Unfortunately, he didn't change the mental patterns that created that dis-ease, and so just created another one. However, he also laughed himself to health on that one, too!

There are so many ways you can approach your healing. Try them all, and then use the ones that appeal to you the most.

When you go to bed at night, close your eyes and again be thankful for all the good in your life. It will bring more good in.

Please do not listen to the news or watch it on TV the last thing at night. The news is only a list of disasters, and you don't want to take that into your dream state. Much clearing work is done in the dream state, and you can ask your dreams for help with anything you are working on. You will often find an answer by morning.

Go to sleep peacefully. Trust the process of life to be on your side and take care of everything for your highest good and greatest joy.

There is no need to make drudgery out of what you are doing. It can be fun. It can be a game. It can be a joy. It's up to you! Even practicing forgiveness and releasing resentment can be fun, if you want to make it so. Again, make up a little song about that person or situation that is so hard to release. When you sing a ditty, it lightens up the whole procedure. When I work with clients privately, I bring laughter into the procedure as soon as I can. The quicker we can laugh about the whole thing, the easier it is to let it go.

If you saw your problems on a stage in a play by Neil Simon, you would laugh yourself right out of the chair. Tragedy and comedy are the same thing. It just depends on your viewpoint! "Oh, what fools we mortals be."

Do whatever you can to make your transformational change a joy and a pleasure. Have fun!

In the infinity of life where I am,
all is perfect, whole, and complete.
I support myself, and life supports me.
I see evidence of The Law working all around me
and in every area of my life.
I reinforce that which I learn in joyous ways.
My day begins with gratitude and joy.
I look forward with enthusiasm to the adventures of the day,
knowing that in my life, "All is good."
I love who I am and all that I do.
I am the living, loving, joyous expression of life.
All is well in my world.

Part III

PUTTING THESE IDEAS TO WORK

💗 Chapter Ten

RELATIONSHIPS

"All my relationships are harmonious."

It seems all of life is relationships. We have relationships with everything. You are even having a relationship now with the book you are reading and with me and my concepts.

The relationships you have with objects and foods and weather and transportation and with people all reflect the relationship you have with yourself. The relationship you have with yourself is highly influenced by the relationships you had with the adults around you as a child. The way the adults reacted to us then is often the way we react toward ourselves now, both positively and negatively.

Think for a moment of the words you use when you are scolding yourself. Aren't they the same words your parents used when they were scolding you? What words did they use when they praised you? I'm sure you use the same words to praise yourself.

Perhaps they never praised you, so then you have no idea how to praise yourself and probably think you have nothing to praise. I am not blaming our parents, because we are all victims of victims. They could not possibly teach you anything they did not know.

Sondra Ray, the great rebirther who has done so much work with relationships, claims that every major relationship we have is a reflection of the relationship we had with one of our parents. She also claims that until we clean up that first one, we will never be free to create exactly what we want in relationships.

Relationships are mirrors of ourselves. What we attract always mirrors either qualities we have or beliefs we have about relationships. This is true whether it is a boss, a co-worker, an employee, a friend, a lover, a spouse, or child. The things you don't like about these people are either what you yourself do or would not do, or what you believe. You could not attract them or have them in your life if the way they are didn't somehow complement your own life.

Exercise: Us Versus Them

Look for a moment at someone in your life who bothers you. Describe three things about this person that you don't like, things that you want him or her to change.

Now, look deeply inside of you and ask yourself, "Where am I like that, and when do I do the same things?"

Close your eyes and give yourself the time to do this.

Then ask yourself if you ARE WILLING TO CHANGE. When you remove these patterns, habits, and beliefs from your thinking and behavior, either the other person will change or he or she will leave your life.

If you have a boss who is critical and impossible to please, look within. Either you do that on some level or you have a belief that "bosses are always critical and impossible to please."

If you have an employee who won't obey or doesn't follow through, look to see where you do that and clean it up. Firing someone is too easy; it doesn't clear your pattern.

If there is a co-worker who won't cooperate and be part of the team, look to see how you could have attracted this. Where are you noncooperative?

If you have a friend who is undependable and lets you down, turn within. Where in your life are you undependable, and when do you let others down? Is that your belief?

If you have a lover who is cold and seems unloving, look to see if there is a belief within you that came from watching your parents in your childhood that says, "Love is cold and undemonstrative."

If you have a spouse who is nagging and nonsupportive, again look to your childhood beliefs. Did you have a parent who was nagging and nonsupportive? Are you that way?

If you have a child who has habits that irritate you, I will guarantee that they are your habits. Children learn only by imitating the adults around them. Clear it within you, and you'll find that they change automatically.

This is the *only* way to change others — change ourselves first. Change your patterns, and you will find that "they" are different, too.

Blame is useless. Blaming only gives away our power. Keep your power. Without power, we cannot make changes. The helpless victim cannot see a way out.

Attracting Love

Love comes when we least expect it, when we are not looking for it. Hunting for love never brings the right partner. It only creates longing and unhappiness. Love is never outside ourselves; love is within us.

Don't insist that love come immediately. Perhaps you are not ready for it, or you are not developed enough to attract the love you want.

Don't settle for anybody just to have someone. Set your standards. What kind of love do you want to attract? List the qualities in yourself, and you will attract a person who has them.

You might examine what may be keeping love away. Could it be criticism? Feelings of unworthiness? Unreasonable standards? Movie star images? Fear of intimacy? A belief that you are unlovable?

Be ready for love when it does come. Prepare the field and be ready to nourish love. Be loving, and you will be lovable. Be open and receptive to love.

In the infinity of life where I am,
all is perfect, whole, and complete.
I live in harmony and balance with everyone I know.
Deep at the center of my being, there is an infinite well of love.
I now allow this love to flow to the surface.
It fills my heart, my body, my mind, my consciousness,
my very being, and radiates out from me in all directions
and returns to me multiplied.
The more love I use and give, the more I have to give.
The supply is endless.
The use of love makes me feel good;
it is an expression of my inner joy. I love myself;
therefore, I take loving care of my body.
I lovingly feed it nourishing foods and beverages,
I lovingly groom it and dress it, and my body lovingly
responds to me with vibrant health and energy.
I love myself; therefore, I provide for myself a comfortable home,
one that fills all my needs and is a pleasure to be in.
I fill the rooms with the vibration of love
so that all who enter, myself included, will feel this love
and be nourished by it.

I love myself; therefore, I work at a job I truly enjoy doing,
one that uses my creative talents and abilities,
working with and for people I love and who love me,
and earning a good income.
I love myself; therefore, I behave and think in a loving way
to all people for I know that which I give out
returns to me multiplied.
I only attract loving people in my world,
for they are a mirror of what I am.
I love myself; therefore, I forgive and totally release the past
and all past experiences, and I am free.
I love myself; therefore, I live totally in the now,
experiencing each moment as good and knowing that my future
is bright and joyous and secure,
for I am a beloved child of the Universe,
and the Universe lovingly takes care of me
now and forever more. All is well in my world.

💝 Chapter Eleven

WORK

"I am deeply fulfilled by all that I do."

Wouldn't you love to have the above affirmation be true for you? Perhaps you have been limiting yourself by thinking some of these thoughts:

> I can't stand this job.
> I hate my boss.
> I don't earn enough money.
> They don't appreciate me at work.
> I can't get along with the people at work.
> I don't know what I want to do.

This is negative, defensive thinking. What kind of good position do you think this will get you? It is approaching the subject from the wrong end.

If you are in a job you don't care for, if you want to change your position, if you are having problems at work, or if you are out of work, the best way to handle it is this:

Begin by blessing your current position with love. Realize that this is only a stepping stone on your pathway. You are where you are because of your own thinking patterns. If "they" are not treating you the way you would like to be treated, then there is a pattern in your consciousness that is attracting such behavior. So, in your mind, look around your current job or the job you had last, and begin to bless everything with love — the building, the elevators or stairs, the rooms, the furniture and equipment, the people you work for and the people you work with — and each and every customer.

Begin to affirm for yourself that, "I always work for the most wonderful bosses." "My boss always treats me with respect and courtesy," and, "My boss is generous and easy to work for." This will carry forward with you all your life, and if you become a boss, then you will be like that, too.

A young man was about to start a new job and was nervous. I remember saying, "Why wouldn't you do well? *Of course* you will be successful. Open your heart and let your talents flow out of you. Bless the establishment, all of the people you work with, and the people you work for, and each and every customer with love, and all will go well."

He did just that and was a great success.

If you want to leave your job, then begin to affirm that you release your current job with love to the next person who will be delighted to have it. Know that there are people out there looking for exactly what you have to offer, and that you are being brought together on the checkerboard of life even now.

Affirmation for Work

"I am totally open and receptive to a wonderful new position, one that uses all my talents and abilities, and allows me to express creatively in ways that are fulfilling to me. I work with and for people whom I love, and who love and respect me, in a wonderful location and earning good money."

If there is someone at work who bothers you, again bless them with love every time you think of them. In each and every one of us is every single quality. *While we may not choose to do so, we are all capable of being a Hitler or a Mother Teresa.* If this person is critical, begin to affirm that he or she is loving and full of praise. If he or she is grouchy, affirm that this person is cheerful and fun to be around. If he or she is cruel, affirm that this person is gentle and compassionate. If you see only the good qualities in this person, then that is what he or she has to show to you, no matter what behavior is displayed toward others.

Example

This man's new job was to play the piano in a club where the boss was known for being unkind and mean. The employees used to call the boss "Mr. Death" behind his back. I was asked how to handle this situation.

I replied, "Inside each and every person are all the good qualities. No matter how other people react to him, it has nothing to do with you. Every time you think of this man, bless him with love. Keep affirming for yourself, *I always work for wonderful bosses*. Keep doing this over and over."

He took my advice and did exactly that. My client began to receive warm greetings, and the boss soon began to slip him bonuses and hired him to play in several other clubs. The other employees who were sending out negative thoughts to the boss were still being mistreated.

If you like your job but feel you are not getting paid enough, then begin to bless your current salary with love. Expressing gratitude for what we already have enables it to grow. Affirm that you are now opening your consciousness to a greater prosperity and that PART of that prosperity is an increased salary. Affirm that you deserve a raise, not for negative reasons, but because you are a great asset to the company and the owners want to share their profits with you. Always do the best you can on the job, for then, the Universe will know that you are ready to be lifted out of where you are to the next and even better place.

Your consciousness put you where you are now. Your consciousness will either keep you there or lift you to a better position. It's up to you.

In the infinity of life where I am,
all is perfect, whole, and complete.
My unique creative talents and abilities flow through me
and are expressed in deeply satisfying ways.
There are people out there who are always
looking for my services. I am always in demand
and can pick and choose what I want to do.
I earn good money doing what satisfies me.
My work is a joy and a pleasure.
All is well in my world.

❤️ Chapter Twelve

SUCCESS

"Every Experience is a Success."

What does "failure" mean anyway? Does it mean that something did not turn out the way you wanted it to, or the way you were hoping? The law of experience is always perfect. We outpicture our inner thoughts and beliefs perfectly. You must have left out a step or had an inner belief that told you that you did not deserve — or you felt unworthy.

It's the same when I work with my computer. If there's a mistake, it is always me. It is something I have not done to comply with the laws of the computer. It only means that there is something else for me to learn.

The old saying, "If at first you don't succeed, try, try again," is so true. It doesn't mean beat yourself up and try the same old way again. It means recognize your error and try another way — until you learn to do it correctly.

I think it is our natural birthright to go from success to success all our life. If we are not doing that, either we are not in tune with our innate capabilities, or we do not believe it can be true for us, or we do not recognize our successes.

When we set standards that are much too high for where we are at this moment, standards we cannot possibly achieve right now, then we will always fail.

When a little child is learning to walk or talk, we encourage him and praise him for every tiny improvement he makes. The child beams and eagerly tries to do better. Is this the way you encourage yourself when you are learning something new? Or do you make it harder to learn because you tell yourself that you are stupid or clumsy or a "failure"?

Many actresses and actors feel they must be performance perfect when they arrive at the first rehearsal. I remind them that the purpose of rehearsal is to learn. Rehearsal is a period of time to make mistakes, to try new ways and to learn. Only by practicing over and over do we learn the new and make it a natural part of us. When you watch an accomplished professional in any field, you are looking at innumerable hours of practice.

Don't do what I used to do — I would refuse to try anything new because I didn't know how to do it, and I didn't want to appear foolish. Learning is making mistakes until our subconscious mind can put together the right pictures.

It doesn't matter how long you have been thinking of yourself as a failure; you can begin to create a "success" pattern now. It doesn't matter what field you want to operate in. The principles are the same. We need to plant the "seeds" of success. These seeds will grow into an abundant harvest.

Here are some "success" affirmations you can use:

> Divine Intelligence gives me all the ideas I can use.
> Everything I touch is a success.
> There is plenty for everyone, including me.
> There are plenty of customers for my services.
> I establish a new awareness of success.
> I move into the Winning Circle.
> I am a magnet for Divine Prosperity.
> I am blessed beyond my fondest dreams.
> Riches of every sort are drawn to me.
> Golden Opportunities are everywhere for me.

Pick one of the above affirmations and repeat it for several days. Then pick another and do the same. Allow these ideas to fill your consciousness. Don't worry about "how" to accomplish this; the opportunities will come your way. Trust the intelligence within you to lead you and guide you. You deserve to be a success in every area of your life.

In the infinity of life where I am,
all is perfect, whole, and complete.
I am one with the Power that created me.
I have within me all the ingredients for success.
I now allow the success formula to flow through me
and manifest in my world.
Whatever I am guided to do will be a success.
I learn from every experience.
I go from success to success and from glory to glory.
My pathway is a series of stepping stones
to ever greater successes.
All is well in my world.

❤️ Chapter Thirteen

PROSPERITY

"I deserve the best, and I accept the best, now."

If you want the above affirmation to be true for you, then you do not want to believe any of the following statements:

Money doesn't grow on trees.

Money is filthy and dirty.

Money is evil.

I am poor, but clean (or good).

Rich people are crooks.

I don't want to have money and be stuck up.

I will never get a good job.

I will never make any money.

Money goes out faster than it comes in.

I am always in debt.

Poor people can never get out from under.

My parents were poor, and I will be poor.

Artists have to struggle.

Only people who cheat have money.

Everyone else comes first.

Oh, I couldn't charge that much.

I don't deserve.

I'm not good enough to make money.

Never tell anyone what I have in the bank.

Never lend money.

A penny saved is a penny earned.
Save for a rainy day.
A Depression could come at any moment.
I resent others having money.
Money only comes from hard work.

How many of these beliefs belong to you? Do you really think that believing any of them will bring you prosperity?

It is old, limited thinking. Perhaps it was what your family believed about money, because family beliefs stay with us unless we consciously release them. Wherever it came from, it must leave your consciousness if you want to prosper.

To me, true prosperity begins with feeling good about yourself. It is also the freedom to do what you want to do, when you want to do it. It is never an amount of money; it is a state of mind. Prosperity or lack of it is an outer expression of the ideas in your head.

Deserving

If we do not accept the idea that we "deserve" to prosper, then even when abundance falls in our laps, we will refuse it somehow. Look at this example:

A student in one of my classes was working to increase his prosperity. He came to class one night *so* excited, for he had just won $500. He kept saying, "I don't believe it! I never win anything." We knew it was a reflection of his changing consciousness. He still felt he did not really deserve it. Next week he could not come to class, as he had broken his leg. The doctor bills came to $500.

He had been frightened to "move forward" in a new "prosperous direction" and felt undeserving, so he punished himself in this way.

Whatever we concentrate on increases, so don't concentrate on your bills. If you concentrate on lack and debt, then you will create more lack and debt.

There is an inexhaustible supply in the Universe. Begin to be aware of it. Take the time to count the stars on a clear evening, or the grains of sand in one handful, the leaves on one branch of a tree, the rain-drops on a windowpane, the seeds in one tomato. Each seed is capable of producing a whole vine with unlimited tomatoes on it. Be grateful for what you do have, and you will find that it increases. I like to bless with love all that is in my life now — my home, the heat, water, light, telephone, furniture, plumbing, appliances, clothing, transportation, jobs — the money I do have, friends, my ability to see and feel and taste and touch and walk and to enjoy this incredible planet.

Our own belief in lack and limitation is the only thing that is limiting us. What belief is limiting you?

Do you want to have money only to help others? Then you are saying you are worthless.

Be sure you are not rejecting prosperity now. If a friend invites you to lunch or dinner, accept with joy and pleasure. Don't feel you are just "trading" with people. If you get a gift, accept it graciously. If you can't use the gift, pass it on to someone else. Keep the flow of things moving through you. Just smile and say "Thank you." In this way you let the Universe know you are ready to receive your good.

Make Room for the New

Make room for the new. Clean out your refrigerator; get rid of all those little bits of stuff wrapped in foil. Clean out your closets; get rid of all the stuff you have not used in the last six months or so. If you haven't used it in a year, definitely get it out of your home. Sell it, trade it, give it away, or burn it.

Cluttered closets mean a cluttered mind. As you clean the closet, say to yourself, "I am cleaning out the closets of my mind." The Universe loves symbolic gestures.

The first time I heard the concept, "The abundance of the Universe is available to everyone," I thought it was ridiculous.

"Look at all the poor people," I said to myself. "Look at my own seemingly hopeless poverty." To hear, "Your poverty is only a belief in your consciousness" only made me angry. It took me many years to realize and accept that I was the only person responsible for my lack of prosperity. It was my belief that I was "unworthy," and "not deserving," that "money is difficult to come by," and that "I do not have talents and abilities," that kept me stuck in a mental system of "not having."

MONEY IS THE EASIEST THING TO DEMONSTRATE! How do you react to this statement? Do you believe it? Are you angry? Are you indifferent? Are you ready to throw this book across the room? If you have any of these reactions, GOOD! I have touched something deep inside you, that very point of resistance to truth. This is the area to work on. It is time to open yourself to the potential of receiving the flow of money and all good.

Love Your Bills

It is essential that we stop worrying about money and stop resenting our bills. Many people treat bills as punishments to be avoided if possible. A bill is an acknowledgment of our ability to pay. The creditor assumes you are affluent enough and gives you the service or the product first. I bless with love each and every bill that comes into my home. I bless with love and stamp a small kiss on each and every check I write. If you pay with resentment, money has a hard time coming back to you. If you pay with love and joy, you open the free-flowing channel of abundance. Treat your money as a friend, not as something you wad up and crush into your pocket.

Your security is not your job, or your bank account, or your investments, or your spouse or parents. Your security is your ability to connect with the cosmic power that creates all things.

I like to think that the power within me that breathes in my body is the same power that provides all that I need, and just as easily and simply. The Universe is lavish and abundant, and it is our birthright to be supplied with everything we need, unless we choose to believe it to the contrary.

I bless my telephone with love each time I use it, and I affirm often that it brings me only prosperity and expressions of love. I do the same with my mail box, and each day it is filled to overflowing with money and love letters of all kinds from friends and clients and far-off readers of my book. The bills that come in I rejoice over, thanking the companies for trusting me to pay. I bless my doorbell and the front door, knowing that only good comes into my home. I expect my life to be good and joyous, and it is.

These Ideas Are for Everyone

The man was a hooker and wanted to increase his business, so he came to me for a prosperity session. He felt he was good at his profession and wanted to make $100,000 a year. I gave him the same ideas I am giving you, and soon he had money to put into Chinese porcelains. He spent so much time at home, he wanted to enjoy the beauty of his ever-increasing investments.

Rejoice in Others' Good Fortune

Don't delay your own prosperity by being resentful or jealous that someone else has more than you. Don't criticize the way they choose to spend their money. It is none of your business.

Each person is under the law of his or her own consciousness. Just take care of your own thoughts. Bless another's good fortune, and know there is plenty for all.

Are you a stingy tipper? Do you stiff washroom attendants with some self-righteous statement? Do you ignore the porters in your office or apartment building at Christmas time? Do you pinch pennies when you don't need to, buying day-old vegetables or bread? Do you do your shopping in a thrift shop, or do you always order the cheapest thing on the menu?

There is a law of "demand and supply." Demand comes first. Money has a way of coming to where it is needed. The poorest family can almost always gather together the money for a funeral.

Visualization — Ocean of Abundance

Your prosperity consciousness is not dependent on money; your flow of money is dependent upon your prosperity consciousness.

As you can conceive of more, more will come into your life.

I love the visualization of standing at the seashore looking out at the vast ocean and knowing that this ocean is the abundance that is available to me. Look down at your hands and see what sort of container you are holding. Is it a teaspoon, a thimble with a hole in it, a paper cup, a glass, a tumbler, a pitcher, a bucket, a wash tub, or perhaps you have a pipeline connected to this ocean of abundance? Look around you and notice that no matter how many people there are and no matter what kind of container they have, there is plenty for everyone. You cannot rob another, and they cannot rob you. And in no way can you drain the ocean dry. Your container is your consciousness, and it can always be exchanged for a larger container. Do this exercise often, to get the feelings of expansion and unlimited supply.

Open Your Arms

I sit at least once a day with my arms stretched out to the side and say, "I am open and receptive to all the good and abundance in the Universe." It gives me a feeling of expansion.

The Universe can only distribute to me what I have in my consciousness, and I can ALWAYS create more in my consciousness. It is like a cosmic bank. I make mental deposits by increasing my awareness of my own abilities to create. Meditation, treatments, and affirmations are mental deposits. Let's make a habit of making daily deposits.

Just having more money is not enough. We want to enjoy the money. Do you allow yourself to have pleasure with money? If not, why not? A portion of everything you take in can go to pure pleasure. Did you have any fun with your money last week? Why not? What old belief is stopping you? Let it go.

Money does not have to be a serious subject in your life. Put it into perspective. Money is a means of exchange. That's all it is. What would you do and what would you have if you didn't need money?

We need to shake up our money concepts. I have found it is easier to teach a seminar on sexuality than it is one on money. People get very angry when their money beliefs are being challenged. Even people who come to a seminar wanting desperately to create more money in their lives will go crazy when I try to change their limiting beliefs.

"I am willing to change." "I am willing to release old negative beliefs." Sometimes we have to work with these two affirmations a lot in order to open the space to begin creating prosperity.

We want to release the "fixed income" mentality. Do not limit the Universe by insisting that you have "ONLY" a certain salary or income. That salary or income is a CHANNEL; IT IS NOT YOUR SOURCE. Your supply comes from one source, the Universe itself.

There are an infinite number of channels. We must open ourselves to them. We must accept in consciousness that supply can come from anywhere and everywhere. Then when we walk down the street and find a penny or a dime, we say "Thank you!" to the source. It may be small, but new channels are beginning to open.

"I am open and receptive to new avenues of income."

"I now receive my good from expected and unexpected sources."

"I am an unlimited being accepting from an unlimited source in an unlimited way."

Rejoice in the Small, New Beginnings

When we work for increasing prosperity, we always gain in accordance with our beliefs about what we deserve. A writer was working to increase her income. One of her affirmations was, "I am making good money being a writer." Three days later, she went to a coffee shop where she often had breakfast. She settled into a booth and spread out some paper she was working on. The manager came over to her and asked, "You are a writer, aren't you? Will you do some writing for me?"

He then brought over several little blank tent signs and asked if she would write, "TURKEY LUNCHEON SPECIAL, $3.95," on each card. He offered her a free breakfast in return.

This small event showed the beginning of her change in consciousness, and she went on to sell her own work.

Recognize Prosperity

Begin to recognize prosperity everywhere, and rejoice in it. Reverend Ike, the well-known evangelist from New York City, remembered that as a poor preacher he used to walk by good restaurants and homes and automobiles and clothing establishments and say out loud, "That's for me, that's for me." Allow fancy homes and banks and fine stores and showrooms of all sorts — and yachts — to give you pleasure. Recognize that all this is part of YOUR abundance, and you are increasing your consciousness to partake of these things if you desire. If you see well-dressed people, think, "Isn't it wonderful that they have so much abundance? There is plenty for all of us."

We don't want someone else's good. We want to have our *own* good.

And yet we do not own anything. We only use possessions for a period of time until they pass on to someone else. Sometimes a possession may stay in a family for a few generations, but eventually it will pass on. There is a natural rhythm and flow of life. Things come, and things go. I believe that when something goes, it is only to make room for something new and better.

Accept Compliments

So many people want to be rich, and yet they won't accept a compliment. I have known many budding actors and actresses who want to be "stars," and yet they cringe when they're paid a compliment.

Compliments are gifts of prosperity. Learn to accept them graciously. My mother taught me early to smile and say, "Thank you" when I received a compliment or a gift. This advice has been an asset all my life.

It is even better to accept the compliment and return it so the giver feels as though he or she has received a gift. It is a way of keeping the flow of good going.

Rejoice in the abundance of being able to awaken each morning and experience a new day. Be glad to be alive, to be healthy, to have friends, to be creative, to be a living example of the joy of living. Live to your highest awareness. Enjoy your transformational process.

In the infinity of life where I am,
all is perfect, whole, and complete.
I am one with the Power that created me.
I am totally open and receptive to the abundant flow of prosperity
that the Universe offers.
All my needs and desires are met before I even ask.
I am Divinely guided and protected,
and I make choices that are beneficial for me.
I rejoice in others' successes, knowing there is plenty for us all.
I am constantly increasing my conscious awareness of abundance,
and this reflects in a constantly increasing income.
My good comes from everywhere and everyone.
All is well in my world.

Chapter Fourteen

THE BODY

"I listen with love to my body's messages."

I believe we create every so-called illness in our body. The body, like everything else in life, is a mirror of our inner thoughts and beliefs. The body is always talking to us, if we will only take the time to listen. Every cell within your body responds to every single thought you think and every word you speak.

Continuous modes of thinking and speaking produce body behaviors and postures and "eases" or dis-eases. The person who has a permanently scowling face did not produce that by having joyous, loving thoughts. Older people's faces and bodies show so clearly a lifetime of thinking patterns. How will you look when you are elderly?

I am including in this section my list of Probable Mental Patterns that create illnesses in the body, as well as the New Thought Patterns or Affirmations to be used to create health. They appear in my book *Heal Your Body*. In addition to those short listings, I will explore a few of the more common conditions to give you an idea of just how we create these problems.

Not every mental equivalent is 100 percent true for everyone. However, it does give us a point of reference to begin our search for the cause of the dis-ease. Many people working in the alternative healing therapies use *Heal Your Body* all the time with their clients and find that the mental causes run 90 to 95 percent true.

*   *   *

THE HEAD represents us. It is what we show the world. It is how we are usually recognized. When something is wrong in the head area, it usually means we feel something is very wrong with "us."

THE HAIR represents strength. When we are tense and afraid, we often create those bands of steel that originate in the shoulder muscles and come up over the top of the head and sometimes even down around the eyes. The hair shaft grows up through the hair follicle. When there is a lot of tension in the scalp, the hair shaft can be squeezed so tightly that the hair can no longer breathe, and it dies and falls out. If this tension is continued, and the scalp is not relaxed, then the follicle remains so tight that the new hair cannot grow through. The result is baldness.

Female baldness has been on the increase ever since women have begun entering the "business world" with all its tensions and frustrations. We are not aware of baldness in women because women's wigs are so natural and attractive. Unfortunately, most men's toupees are still discernible at quite a distance.

Tension is not being strong. Tension is weakness. Being relaxed and centered and peaceful is really being strong and secure. It would be good for us to relax our bodies more, and many of us need to relax our scalps, too.

Try it now. Tell your scalp to relax, and feel if there is a difference. If you notice that your scalp visibly relaxes, then I would suggest you do this little exercise often.

THE EARS represent the capacity to hear. When there are problems with the ears, it usually means something is going on you do not want to hear. An earache would indicate that there is anger about what is heard.

Earaches are common with children. They often have to listen to stuff going on in the household they really don't want to hear. Household rules often forbid a child's expression of anger, and the child's inability to change things creates an earache.

Deafness represents longstanding refusal to listen to someone. Notice that when one partner has a hearing impairment, the other partner often talks and talks and talks.

THE EYES represent the capacity to see. When there are problems with the eyes, it usually means there is something we do not want to see, either about ourselves or about life: past, present, or future.

Whenever I see small children wearing glasses, I know there is stuff going on in their household they do not want to look at. If they can't change the experience, they will diffuse the sight so they don't have to see it so clearly.

Many people have had dramatic healing experiences when they have been willing to go back into the past and clean up what it was they did not want to look at a year or two before they began wearing glasses.

Are you negating what's happening right now? What don't you want to face? Are you afraid to see the present or the future? If you could see clearly, what would you see that you don't see now? Can you see what you are doing to yourself?

Interesting questions to look at.

HEADACHES come from invalidating the self. The next time you get a headache, stop and ask yourself where and how you have just made yourself wrong. Forgive yourself, let it go, and the headache will dissolve back into the nothingness from where it came.

Migraine headaches are created by people who want to be perfect and who create a lot of pressure on themselves. A lot of suppressed anger is involved. Interestingly, migraine headaches can almost always be alleviated by masturbation if you do it as soon as you feel a migraine coming on. The sexual release dissolves the tension and the pain. You may not feel like masturbating then, but it certainly is worth a try. You can't lose.

SINUS problems, felt right in the face and so close to the nose, represent being irritated by someone in your life, someone who is close to you. You might even feel they are bearing down on you.

We forget that we create the situations, then we give our power away by blaming the other person for our frustration. No person, no place, and no thing has any power over us, for "we" are the only thinkers in our mind. We create our experiences, our reality, and everyone in it. When we create peace and harmony and balance in our mind, we will find it in our lives.

THE NECK AND THROAT are fascinating because so much "stuff" goes on there. The neck represents the ability to be flexible in our thinking, to see the other side of a question, and to see another person's viewpoint. When there are problems with the neck, it usually means we are being stubborn about our own concept of a situation.

Whenever I see a person wearing one of those "collars," I know this person is being very self-righteous and stubborn about not seeing the other side of an issue.

Virginia Satir, the brilliant family therapist, said that she did some "silly research" and found that there are more than 250 different ways to wash dishes, depending upon who is washing and the ingredients used. If we are stuck in believing there is only "one way," or "one viewpoint," then we are shutting out most of life.

THE THROAT represents our ability to "speak up" for ourselves, to "ask for what we want," to say "I am," etc. When we have throat problems, it usually means we do not feel we have the right to do these things. We feel inadequate to stand up for ourselves.

Sore throats are always anger. If a cold is involved, then there is mental confusion, too. LARYNGITIS usually means you are so angry you cannot speak.

The throat also represents the creative flow in the body. This is where we express our creativity, and when our creativity is stifled and frustrated, we often have throat problems. We all know many people who live their whole lives for others. They never once get to do what they want to do. They are always pleasing mothers/fathers/spouses/lovers/bosses. TONSILLITIS and THYROID problems are just frustrated creativity, resulting from not being able to do what you want to do.

The energy center in the throat, the fifth chakra, is the place in the body where change takes place. When we are resisting change or are in the middle of change or are trying to change, we often have a lot of activity in our throats. Notice when you cough, or when someone else coughs. What has just been said? What are we reacting to? Is it resistance and stubbornness, or is it the process of change taking place? In a workshop I use coughs as a tool for self-discovery. Every time someone coughs, I have that person touch the throat and say out loud, "I am willing to change," or "I am changing."

THE ARMS represent our ability and capacity to embrace the experiences of life. The upper arms have to do with our capacity, and the lower arms have to do with our abilities. We store old emotions in our joints, and the elbows represent our flexibility in changing directions. Are you flexible about a changing direction in your life, or are old emotions keeping you stuck in one spot?

THE HANDS grasp, hands hold, hands clench. We let things slip through our fingers. Sometimes we hold on too long. We are handy, tightfisted, openhanded, penny pinchers, butterfingers. We give handouts. We can handle ourselves, or we can't seem to handle anything.

We put a handle on something. It's hands down. It's hands off, hanky panky. We give someone a hand, are hand in hand, it's on hand or out of hand, underhanded or overhanded. We have helping hands.

Hands can be gentle or they can be hard, with knotty knuckles from overthinking, or gnarled with arthritic criticism. Grasping hands come from fear — fear of loss, fear of never having enough, fear that it won't stay if you hold lightly.

Tightly grasping a relationship only has the partner run away in desperation. Tightly clenched hands cannot take in anything new. Shaking the hands freely from the wrists gives a feeling of looseness and openness.

That which belongs to you cannot be taken from you, so relax.

THE FINGERS each have meaning. Problems in the fingers show where you need to relax and let go. If you cut your index finger, there is probably anger and fear that has to do with your ego in some current situation. The thumb is mental and represents worry. The index finger is the ego and fear. The middle finger has to do with sex and with anger. When you are angry, hold your middle finger and watch the anger dissolve. Hold the right finger if your anger is at a man and the left if it is at a woman. The ring finger is both unions and grief. The little finger has to do with the family and pretending.

THE BACK represents our support system. Problems with the back usually mean we feel we are not being supported. Too often we think we are only supported by our job or by our family or spouses. In reality, we are totally supported by the Universe, by Life itself.

The upper back has to do with feeling the lack of emotional support. My husband/wife/lover/friend/boss doesn't understand me or support me.

The middle back has to do with guilt. All that stuff that is in back of us. Are you afraid to see what is back there, or are you hiding what is back there? Do you feel stabbed in the back?

Do you feel real "burnt out"? Are your finances in a mess, or do you worry about them excessively? Then your lower back may be bothering you. The lack of money or the fear of money will do it. The amount you have has nothing to do with it.

So many of us feel that money is the most important thing in our lives, and that we could not live without it. This is not true. There is something far more important and precious to us without which we could not live. What is that? It is our breath.

Our breath is the most precious substance in our lives, and yet we totally take for granted when we exhale that our next breath will be there. If we did not take another breath, we would not last three minutes. Now if the Power that created us has given us enough breath to last for as long as we shall live, can we not trust that everything else we need will also be supplied?

THE LUNGS represent our capacity to take in and give out life. Problems with the lungs usually mean we are afraid to take in life, or perhaps we feel we do not have the right to live life fully.

Women have traditionally been very shallow breathers and have often thought of themselves as second-class citizens who did not have the right to take up space and sometimes not even the right to live. Today, this is all changing. Women are taking their place as full members of society and breathing deeply and fully.

It pleases me to see women in sports. Women have always worked in the fields; but this is the first time in history, as far as I know, that women have gone into sports. It is wonderful to see the magnificent bodies that are emerging.

Emphysema and heavy smoking are ways of denying life. They mask a deep feeling of being totally unworthy of existing. Scolding will not change the habit of smoking. It is the basic belief that must change first.

THE BREASTS represent the mothering principle. When there are problems with the breasts, it usually means we are "over-mothering" either a person, a place, a thing, or an experience.

Part of the mothering process is to allow the child to "grow up." We need to know when to take our hands off, when to turn over the reins and let them be. Being overprotective does not prepare the other person to handle his or her own experience. Sometimes our "overbearing" attitudes literally cut off nourishment in a situation.

If cancer is involved, then there is also deep resentment. Release the fear and know the Intelligence of the Universe resides in each one of us.

THE HEART, of course, represents love, while our blood represents joy. Our hearts lovingly pump joy throughout our bodies. When we deny ourselves joy and love, the heart shrivels and becomes cold. As a result, the blood gets sluggish, and we creep our way to ANEMIA, ANGINA, and HEART ATTACKS.

The heart does not "attack" us. We get so caught up in the soap opera and dramas we create that we often forget to notice the little joys that surround us. We spend years squeezing all the joy out of the heart, and it literally falls over in pain. Heart attack people are never joyous people. If they do not take the time to appreciate the joys of life, they will just recreate another heart attack in time.

Heart of gold, cold heart, open heart, black heart, loving heart, warmhearted — where is your heart?

THE STOMACH digests all the new ideas and experiences we have. What or who can't you stomach? What gets you in the gut?

When there are stomach problems, it usually means we don't know how to assimilate the new experience. We are afraid.

Many of us remember when commercial airplanes first became popular. That we could get inside a big metal tube that would carry us safely through the sky was a new idea we found hard to assimilate.

At every seat, there were throw-up bags, and most of us were using them. We would throw up into our barf bags as discreetly as we could, wrap them up and hand them to the stewardess, who spent a lot of her time running up and down the aisle collecting them.

Now it is many years later, and though the bags are still at every seat, they are seldom used. We have assimilated the idea of flying.

ULCERS are no more than fear — tremendous fear of "not being good enough." We fear not being good enough for a parent, we fear not being good enough for a boss. We can't stomach who we are. We rip our guts apart trying to please others. No matter how important our job is, our inner self-esteem is very low. We are afraid they will find out about us.

THE GENITALS represents the most feminine part of a woman, her femininity, or the most masculine part of a man, his masculinity; our masculine principle or our feminine principle.

When we do not feel comfortable with being either a man or a woman, when we reflect our sexuality, when we reject our bodies as dirty or sinful, then we often have problems in the genital area.

I seldom come across a person who was reared in a household where the genitals and their functions were called by their right names. We all grew up with euphemisms of one sort or another. Remember the ones your own family used? It could have been as mild as "down there," to names that made you feel your genitals were dirty and disgusting. Yes, we all grew up believing that something was not quite right between our legs.

I feel the sexual revolution that exploded several years ago was in one way a good thing. We were moving away from Victorian hypocrisy. Suddenly it was okay to have many partners, and women as well as men could have one-night stands. Marital swapping became more open. Many of us began to enjoy the pleasure and freedom of our bodies in a new and open way.

However, few of us thought to deal with what Roza Lamont, founder of the Self-Communication Institute, calls "Mama's God." Whatever your mother taught you about God when you were three years old is still there in your subconscious mind UNLESS you have done some conscious work to release it. Was that God an angry, avenging God? What did that God feel about sex? If we are still carrying those early guilt feelings about our sexuality and our bodies, then we are surely going to create punishment for ourselves.

BLADDER problems, ANAL problems, VAGINITIS, and PRO-STATE and PENIS problems all come under the same area. They stem from distorted beliefs about our bodies and the correctness of their functions.

Every organ in our body is a magnificent expression of life with its own special functions. We do not think of our livers or our eyes as dirty or sinful. Why do we then choose to believe our genitals are?

The anus is as beautiful as the ear. Without our anus we would have no way to release what the body no longer needs, and we would die very quickly. Every part of our body and every function of our body is perfect and normal, natural, and beautiful.

I ask clients with sexual problems to begin to relate to their rectum, penis, or vagina with a sense of love and appreciation for their function and their beauty. If you are beginning to cringe or get irate as you read this, ask yourself why. Who told you to deny any part of your body? Certainly not God. Our sexual organs were created as the most pleasurable part of our body to give us pleasure. To deny this is to create pain and punishment. Sex is not only okay, it is glorious and wonderful. It is as normal for us to have sex as it is for us to breathe or eat.

Just for a moment try to visualize the vastness of the Universe. It is beyond our comprehension. Even our top scientists with their latest equipment cannot measure its size. Within this Universe there are many galaxies.

In one of these smaller galaxies in a far-off corner, there is a minor sun. Around this sun a few pinpoints revolve, one of which is called Planet Earth.

I find it hard to believe that the vast, incredible Intelligence that created this entire Universe is only an old man sitting on a cloud above the Planet Earth...watching my genitals!

Yet so many of us were taught this concept as a child.

It is vital that we release foolish, outmoded ideas that do not support us and nourish us. I feel strongly that even our concept of God needs to be one that is *for us*, not against us. There are so many different religions to choose from. If you have one now that tells you that you are a sinner and a lowly worm, get another one.

I am not advocating that everybody run around having free sex at all times. I am saying that some of our rules do not make sense, and this is why so many people break them and become hypocrites.

When we remove sexual guilt from people and teach them to love and respect themselves, then they will automatically treat themselves and others in ways that are for their highest good and greatest joy. The reason we have so many problems with our sexuality now is because so many of us have self-hatred and self-disgust, and so we treat ourselves and others badly.

It is not enough to teach children in school the mechanics of sexuality. We need on a very deep level to allow children to remember that their bodies, genitals, and sexuality are something to rejoice about. I truly believe that people who love themselves and their bodies will not abuse themselves or others.

I find that most BLADDER problems come from being "pissed off," usually at a partner. Something makes us angry that has to do with our femininity or our masculinity. Women have more bladder problems than men because they are more prone to hide their hurt. VAGINITIS again usually involves feeling romantically hurt by a partner. Men's PROSTATE problems have a lot to do with self-worth and also believing that as he gets older he becomes less of a man. IMPOTENCE adds fear and is sometimes even related to spite against a previous mate. FRIGIDITY comes from fear or a belief that it is wrong to enjoy the body. It also comes from self-disgust, and it can be intensified by an insensitive partner.

PMS, PREMENSTRUAL SYNDROME, which has reached epidemic proportions, is concurrent with the increase of media advertising. These ads continually hammer home the concept that the female body must be sprayed and powdered and douched and over-cleansed in numerous ways to make it even barely acceptable. At the same time that women are coming into their own as equal beings, they are also being bombarded negatively with the idea that the feminine processes are not quite acceptable. This notion, combined with the tremendous amounts of sugar being consumed today, creates a fertile breeding ground for P.M.S.

The feminine processes, all of them, including menstruation and menopause, are normal, natural processes. We must accept them as that. Our bodies are beautiful, magnificent, and wondrous.

It is my belief that VENEREAL DIS-EASE is almost always sexual guilt. It comes from a feeling, often subconscious, that it is not right to express ourselves sexually. A carrier with a venereal dis-ease can have many partners, but only those whose mental and physical immune systems are weak will be susceptible to it. In addition to the old standards, in recent years the heterosexual population has created an increase of HERPES. This is a dis-ease that comes back again and again "to punish us" for our belief that "we are bad." Herpes has a tendency to flare up when we are emotionally upset. That tells us a lot right there.

Now, let's take that same theory over into the gay community, where they have all the same problems everybody else has, plus much of society pointing their fingers at them and saying, "Bad!" Usually, their own mothers and fathers are also saying, "You're bad." This is a heavy load to carry, and it's difficult to love yourself under these circumstances. It is not surprising that gay men were amongst the first to experience the dread dis-ease, aids.

In heterosexual society, many women dread growing old because of the belief systems we have created around the glory of youth. It is not so difficult for the men, for they become distinguished with a bit of gray hair. The older man often gets respect, and people may even look up to him.

Not so for most gay men, for they have created a culture that places tremendous emphasis on youth and beauty. While everyone is young to start with, only a few fit the standard of beauty. So much emphasis has been placed on the physical appearance of the body that the feelings inside have been totally disregarded. If you are not young and beautiful, it's almost as though you don't count. The person does not count; only the body counts.

This way of thinking is a disgrace to the whole culture. It's another way of saying, "Gay is not good enough."

Because of the ways gay people often treat other gays, for many gay men the experience of getting old is something to dread. It is almost better to die than to get old. And aids is a dis-ease that often kills.

Too often gay men feel that when they get older, they will be useless and unwanted. It is almost better to destroy themselves first, and many have created a destructive lifestyle. Some of the concepts and attitudes that are so a part of the gay lifestyle — the meat rack, the constant judging, the refusal to get close to another, and so on — are monstrous. And aids is a monstrous dis-ease.

These sorts of attitudes and behavior patterns can only create guilt on a very deep level, no matter how much we may "camp." Camping, which can be such fun, can also be extremely destructive, both to givers and recipients. It is another way of avoiding closeness and intimacy.

In no way am I trying to create guilt for anyone. However, we need to look at the things that need to be changed in order for all of our lives to function with love and joy and respect. Fifty years ago, almost all gay men were closeted, and now they have been able to create pockets in society where they can at least be relatively open. I feel it is unfortunate that much of what they have created gives so much pain to their gay brothers. While it is often deplorable the way straights treat gays, it is *tragic* the way many gays treat other gays.

Men traditionally have always had more sexual partners than women; and when men get together, of course there will be a great deal more sex. That's all fine and good. The bathhouses fulfill a wonderful need, unless we are using our sexuality for the wrong reasons. Some men like having lots of partners to satisfy their deep need for self-esteem rather than for the joy of it. I do not believe there is anything wrong with having several partners, and the use of alcohol and some recreational drugs on an "occasional basis" is fine. However, if we are getting bombed out of our heads every night, and if we "need" several partners a day just to prove our self-worth, then we are not coming from a nourishing space. We need to make some mental changes.

This is a time for healing, for making whole, not for condemnation. We must rise out of the limitations of the past. We are all Divine, Magnificent expressions of Life. Let's claim that now!

THE COLON represents our ability to let go, to release that which we no longer need. The body, being in the perfect rhythm and flow of life, needs a balance of intake, assimilation, and elimination. It is only our fears that block the releasing of the old.

Even if constipated people are not actually stingy, they usually do not trust that there will ever be enough. They hold on to old relationships that give them pain. They are afraid to throw out clothes that have been in the closet for years because they might need them some day. They stay in stifling jobs, or never give themselves pleasure, because they must save for that rainy day. We do not rummage in last night's garbage to find today's meal. Learn to trust the process of life to always bring you what you need.

Our LEGS carry us forward in life. Leg problems often indicate a fear of moving forward or a reluctance to move forward in a certain direction. We run with our legs, we drag our legs, we pussyfoot, we are knock-kneed, pigeon-toed; and we have big, fat, angry thighs filled with childhood resentments. Not wanting to do things will often produce minor leg problems. VARICOSE VEINS represent standing in a job or place that we hate. The veins lose their ability to carry joy.

Are *you* going in the direction you want to?

KNEES, like the neck, have to do with flexibility; only they express bending and pride, ego and stubbornness. Often when moving forward, we are fearful of bending, and we become inflexible. This stiffens the joints. We want to move forward, but we do not want to change our ways. This is why knees take so long to heal; our ego is involved. The knees take a long time because we get our pride and our self-righteousness involved.

The next time you have a knee problem, ask yourself where you are being self-righteous, where you are refusing to bend. Drop the stubbornness and let go. Life is flow, life is movement; and to be comfortable, we must be flexible and move with it. A willow tree bends and sways and flows with the wind and is always graceful and at ease with life.

Our FEET have to do with our understanding, our understanding of ourselves and of life — past, present, and future.

Many old people have a difficult time walking. Their understanding has been warped, and they often feel there is no place to go. Little children move on happy, dancing feet. Elderly people often shuffle as if they are reluctant to move.

Our SKIN represents our individuality. Skin problems usually mean we feel our individuality is being threatened somehow. We feel that others have power over us. We are thin-skinned. Things tend to get under our skin, we feel skinned alive, our nerves are right under our skin.

One of the quickest ways to heal skin problems is to nurture yourself by saying in your mind, "I approve of myself," several hundred times a day. Take back your own power.

ACCIDENTS are no accident. Like everything else in our lives, we create them. It's not that we necessarily say, "I want to have an accident," but we do have the mental thought patterns that can attract an accident to us. Some people seem to be "accident prone," and others go for a lifetime without ever getting a scratch.

Accidents are expressions of anger. They indicate built-up frustrations resulting from not feeling the freedom to speak up for one's self. Accidents also indicate rebellion against authority. We get so mad we want to hit people, and instead, *we* get hit.

When we are angry at ourselves, when we feel guilty, when we feel the need for punishment, an accident is a marvelous way of taking care of that.

It seems as though any accident is not our fault, that we are helpless victims of a quirk of fate. An accident allows us to turn to others for sympathy and attention. We get our wounds bathed and attended to. We often get bedrest, sometimes for an extended period of time. And we get pain.

Where this pain occurs in the body gives us a clue to which area of life we feel guilty about. The degree of physical damage lets us know how severely we felt we needed to be punished and how long the sentence should be.

ANOREXIA-BULIMIA is denying the self life, an extreme form of self-hatred.

Food is nourishment on the most basic level. Why would you deny yourself nourishment? Why do you want to die? What is going on in your life that is so awful that you want to get out completely?

Self-hatred is only hating a thought you have about yourself. Thoughts can be changed.

What is so terrible about you? Were you reared in a critical family? Did you have critical teachers? Did your early religious training tell you that you were "not good enough" as you are? So often we try to find reasons that "make sense to us" for why we are not loved and accepted just as we are.

Because of the fashion industry's obsession with slenderness, many women who have as their main messages, "I am not good enough; what's the use," will use their bodies as a focal point for self-hatred. On one level they are saying, "If I were only thin enough, then they would love me." But it doesn't work.

Nothing works from the outside. Self-approval and self-acceptance are the key.

ARTHRITIS is a dis-ease that comes from a constant pattern of criticism. First of all, criticism of the self, and then criticism of other people. Arthritic people often attract a lot of criticism because it is their pattern to criticize. They are cursed with "perfectionism," the need to be perfect at all times in every situation.

Do you know of anyone on this planet who is "perfect"? I do not. Why do we set up standards that say we have to be "Super Person," in order to be barely acceptable? It's such a strong expression of "not being good enough," and such a heavy burden to carry.

ASTHMA we call "smother love." There is a feeling that you do not have the right to breathe for yourself. Asthmatic children often have "overdeveloped consciences." They take on guilt feelings for whatever seems wrong in their environment. They feel "unworthy," therefore guilty, and in need of self-punishment.

Geographic cures sometimes work with asthma, especially if the family does *not* go along.

Usually, asthmatic children will "outgrow" their dis-ease. This really means they go away to school, get married, or leave home somehow, and the dis-ease dissolves. Oftentimes, later in life, an experience will happen that pushes an old button within them, and they have another attack. When that happens, they are not really responding to the current circumstances, but rather to what used to go on in their childhood.

BOILS AND BURNS, CUTS, FEVERS, SORES, "ITIS," AND INFLAMMATIONS all are indications of anger expressing in the body. Anger will find its way to express, no matter *how* much we try to suppress it. Steam that is built up must be released. We fear our anger, lest we destroy our world, yet anger can be released as simply as saying, "I am angry about this." True, we can't always say this to our bosses. We can, however, beat the bed or scream in the car or play tennis. These are harmless ways to physically releasing anger.

Spiritual people often believe they "shouldn't" get angry. True, we are all working toward the time when we no longer blame others for our feelings, but until we arrive there, it is healthier to acknowledge what we do feel in the moment.

CANCER is a dis-ease caused by deep resentment held for a long time until it literally eats away at the body. Something happens in childhood that destroys the sense of trust. This experience is never forgotten, and the individual lives with a sense of self-pity, finding it hard to develop and maintain long-term, meaningful relationships. Because of that belief system, life seems to be a series of disappointments. A feeling of hopelessness and helplessness and loss permeates the thinking, and it becomes easy to blame others for all our problems. People with cancer are also very self-critical. To me, learning to love and accept the self is the key to healing cancers.

OVERWEIGHT represents a need for protection. We seek protection from hurts, slights, criticism, abuse, sexuality, and sexual advances; from a fear of life in general and also specifically. Take your choice.

I am not a heavy person, yet I have learned over the years that when I am feeling insecure and not at ease, I will put on a few pounds. When the threat is gone, the excess weight goes away by itself.

Fighting fat is a waste of time and energy. Diets don't work. The minute you stop, the weight goes back up. Loving and approving of yourself, trusting in the process of life and feeling safe because you know the power of your own mind make up the best diet I know of. Go on a diet from negative thoughts, and your weight will take care of itself.

Too many parents stuff food in a baby's mouth no matter what the problem is. These babies grow up to stand in front of an open refrigerator saying, "I don't know what I want," whenever there is a problem.

PAIN of any sort, to me, is an indication of guilt. Guilt always seeks punishment, and punishment creates pain. Chronic pain comes from chronic guilt, often so deeply buried that we are not even aware of it anymore.

Guilt is a totally useless emotion. It never makes anyone feel better, nor does it change a situation.

Your "sentence" is now over, so let yourself out of prison. Forgiving is only giving up, letting go.

STROKES are blood clots; congestion in the bloodstream in the area of the brain cutting off the blood supply to the brain.

The brain is the computer of the body. Blood is joy. The veins and arteries are channels of joy. Everything works under the law and the action of love. There is love in every bit of intelligence in the Universe. It is impossible to work and function well without love and joy being experienced.

Negative thinking clogs up the brain, and there is no room for love and joy to flow in its free and open way.

Laughter cannot flow if it is not allowed to be free and foolish. It is the same with love and joy. Life is not grim unless we make it so, unless we choose to look at it in that way. We can find total disaster in the smallest upset, and we can find some joy in the greatest tragedy. It is up to us.

Sometimes we try to force our life to go in a certain way when it is not for our highest good. Sometimes we create strokes to force us to go in a totally different direction, to reevaluate our lifestyles.

STIFFNESS in the body represents stiffness in the mind. Fear makes us cling to old ways, and we find it difficult to be flexible. If we believe there is "only one way" to do something, we often find ourselves becoming stiff. We can always find another way to do things. Remember Virginia Satir and her more than 250 different ways to do dishes.

Notice where in the body the stiffness occurs, look it up on my list of mental patterns, and it will show you where in your mind you are being stiff and rigid.

SURGERY has its place. It is good for broken bones and accidents and for conditions beyond the abilities of a beginner to dissolve. It may be easier under these conditions to have the operation, and concentrate all the mental healing work on seeing that the condition is not recreated.

More and more each day there are many wonderful people in the medical profession who are truly dedicated to helping humanity. More and more doctors are turning to holistic ways of healing, treating the whole person. Yet most doctors do not work with the *cause* of any illness; they only treat the symptoms, the effects.

They do this in one of two ways: They poison or they mutilate. Surgeons cut, and if you go to surgeons, they will usually recommend cutting. However, if the decision for surgery is made, prepare yourself for the experience so it will go as smoothly as possible, and you will heal as rapidly as possible.

Ask the surgeon and staff to cooperate with you in this. Surgeons and their staffs in the operating rooms are often unaware that even though the patient is unconscious, he or she is still hearing and picking up everything said on a subconscious level.

I heard one New Age leader say she needed some emergency surgery and, before the operation, she had a talk with the surgeon and the anesthesiologist. She asked them please to play soft music during the operation and for them to talk to her and each other continuously in positive affirmations. She had the nurse in the recovery room do the same thing, so the operation went easily, and her recovery was rapid and comfortable.

With my own clients, I always suggest they affirm that, "Every hand that touches me in the hospital is a healing hand and expresses only love," and, "The operation goes quickly and easily and perfectly." Another is, "I am totally comfortable at all times."

After the surgery, have some soft and pleasant music playing as much as possible, and affirm to yourself, "I am healing rapidly, comfortably, and perfectly." Tell yourself, "Every day I feel better and better."

If you can, make yourself a tape of a series of positive affirmations. Take your tape recorder to the hospital, and play your tape over and over while you rest and recuperate. Notice sensations, not pain. Imagine love flowing from your own heart down through your arms and into your hands. Place your hands over the part that is healing, and say to this place, "I love you, and I am helping you to get well."

SWELLING of the body represents clogging and stagnation in the emotional thinking. We create situations where we get "hurt," and we cling to these memories. Swelling often represents bottled-up tears, feeling stuck and trapped, or blaming others for our own limitations.

Release the past, let it wash away. Take back your own power. Stop dwelling on what you don't want. Use your mind to create what you "do want." Let yourself flow with the tide of life.

TUMORS are false growths. An oyster takes a tiny grain of sand and, to protect itself, grows a hard and shiny shell around it. We call it a pearl and think it is beautiful.

We take on old hurt and nurse it and keep pulling the scab off it, and in time we have a tumor.

I call this running the old movie. I believe the reason women have so many tumors in the uterus area is that they take an emotional hurt, a blow to their femininity, and nurse it. I call this the "He done me wrong" syndrome.

Just because a relationship ends does not mean there is something wrong with us, nor does it lessen our self-worth.

It is not *what happens*, it is how we *react* to it. We are each responsible for all our experiences. What beliefs about yourself do you need to change in order to attract more loving kinds of behavior?

In the infinity of life where I am,
all is perfect, whole, and complete.
I recognize my body as a good friend.
Each cell in my body has Divine Intelligence.
I listen to what it tells me, and know that its advice is valid.
I am always safe, and Divinely protected and guided.
I choose to be healthy and free.
All is well in my world.

❤ Chapter Fifteen

THE LIST

"I am healthy, whole, and complete."

As you look through the list (see pages 200–269 in this collection) from my book *Heal Your Body,* see if you can find the correlation between dis-eases you may have had or are having now and the probable causes I have listed.

A good way to use this list when you have a physical problem is:

1. Look up the mental cause. See if this could be true for you. If not, sit quietly and ask yourself, "What could be the thoughts in me that created this?"
2. Repeat to yourself, "I am willing to release the pattern in my consciousness that has created this condition."
3. Repeat the new thought pattern to yourself several times.
4. Assume that you are already in the process of healing.

Whenever you think of the condition, repeat the steps.

Part IV

CONCLUSION

❤ Chapter Sixteen

MY STORY

"We are all one."

"Will you tell me a little about your childhood, briefly." This is a question I have asked so many clients. It's not that I need to hear all the details, but I want to get a general pattern of where they are coming from. If they have problems now, the patterns that created them began a long time ago.

When I was a little girl of 18 months, I experienced my parents divorcing. I don't remember that as being so bad. What I do remember with horror is when my mother went to work as a live-in domestic and boarded me out. The story goes that I cried nonstop for three weeks. The people taking care of me couldn't handle that, and my mother was forced to take me back and make other arrangements. How she managed as a single parent brings my admiration today. Then, however, all I knew and cared about was that I was not getting all the loving attention I once had.

I have never been able to determine if my mother loved my step-father or whether she just married him in order to provide a home for us. But it was not a good move. This man had been brought up in Europe in a heavy Germanic home with much brutality, and he had never learned any other way to manage a family. My mother became pregnant with my sister, and then the 1930s Depression descended upon us, and we found ourselves stuck in a home of violence. I was five years old.

To add to the scenario, it was just about this time that a neighbor, an old wino, as I remember it, raped me. The doctor's examination is still vivid in my mind, as was the court case in which I was the star witness. The man was sentenced to 15 years in prison. I was told repeatedly that, "It was your fault," so I spent many years fearing that when he was released he would come and get me for being so terrible as to put him in jail.

Most of my childhood was spent enduring both physical and sexual abuse, with a lot of hard labor thrown in. My self-image became lower and lower, and few things seemed to go right for me. I began to express this pattern in the outside world.

There was an incident in the fourth grade that was so typical of what my life was like. We were having a party at school one day, and there were several cakes to share. Most of the children in this school except for me were from comfortable middle-class families. I was poorly dressed, with a funny bowl haircut, high-topped black shoes, and I smelled from the raw garlic I had to eat every day to "keep the worms away." We never had cake. We couldn't afford it. There was an old neighbor woman who gave me ten cents every week, and a dollar on my birthday and at Christmas. The ten cents went into the family budget, and the dollar bought my underwear for the year at the dime store.

So, this day we were having the party at school, and there was so much cake that, as they were cutting it, some of the kids who could have cake almost every day were getting two or three pieces. When the teacher finally got around to me (and of course I was last), there was no cake left. Not one piece.

I see clearly now that it was my "already confirmed belief" that I was worthless and did not DESERVE anything that put me at the end of the line with no cake. It was MY pattern. THEY were only being a mirror for my beliefs.

When I was 15, I could not take the sexual abuse any longer, and I ran away from home and from school. The job I found as a waitress in a diner seemed so much easier than the heavy yard work I had to do at home.

Being starved for love and affection and having the lowest of self-esteem, I willingly gave my body to whoever was kind to me; and just after my 16th birthday, I gave birth to a baby girl. I felt it was impossible to keep her; however, I was able to find her a good, loving home. I found a childless couple who longed for a baby. I lived in their home for the last four months, and when I went to the hospital, I had the child in their name.

Under such circumstances, I never experienced the joys of motherhood, only the loss and guilt and shame. Then it was only a shameful time to get over with as soon as possible. I only remember her big toes, which were unusual, like mine. If we ever meet, I will know for sure if I see her toes. I left when the child was five days old.

I immediately went back home and said to my mother who had continued to be a victim, "Come on, you don't have to take this any longer. I'm getting you out of here." She came with me, leaving my ten-year-old sister, who had always been Daddy's darling, to stay with her father.

After helping my mother get a job as a domestic in a small hotel and settling her into an apartment where she was free and comfortable, I felt my obligations were over. I left for Chicago with a girlfriend to stay a month — and did not return for over 30 years.

In those early days, the violence I experienced as a child, combined with the sense of worthlessness I developed along the way, attracted men into my life who mistreated me and often beat me. I could have spent the rest of my life berating men, and I probably would still be having the same experiences. Gradually, however, through positive work experiences, my self-esteem grew, and those kind of men began to leave my life. They no longer fit my old pattern of unconsciously believing I deserved abuse. I do not condone their behavior, but if it were not "my pattern," they would not have been attracted to me. Now, a man who abuses women does not even know I exist. Our patterns no longer attract.

After a few years in Chicago doing rather menial work, I went to New York and was fortunate enough to become a high-fashion model. Yet, even modeling for the big designers did not help my self-esteem very much. It only gave me more ways to find fault with myself. I refused to recognize my own beauty.

I was in the fashion industry for many years. I met and married a wonderful, educated English gentleman. We traveled the world, met royalty, and even had dinner at the White House. Though I was a model and had a wonderful husband, my self-esteem still remained low until years later when I began the inner work.

One day after 14 years of marriage, my husband announced his desire to marry another, just when I was beginning to believe that good things can last. Yes, I was crushed. But time passes, and I lived on. I could feel my life changing, and a numerologist one spring confirmed it by telling me that in the fall a small event would occur that would change my life.

It was so small that I didn't notice it until several months later. Quite by chance, I had gone to a meeting at the Church of Religious Science in New York City. While their message was new to me, something within me said, "Pay attention," and so I did. I not only went to the Sunday services, but I began to take their weekly classes. The beauty and fashion world was losing its interest to me. How many years could I remain concerned with my waist measurement or the shape of my eyebrows? From a high school dropout who never studied anything, I now became a voracious student, devouring everything I could lay my hands on that pertained to metaphysics and healing.

The Church of Religious Science became a new home for me. Even though most of my life was going on as usual, this new course of study began to take up more and more of my time. The next thing I knew, it was three years later, and I was eligible to apply to become one of the Church's licensed practitioners. I passed the test, and that's where I began, as a church counselor, many years ago.

It was a small beginning. During this time I became a Transcendental Meditator. My church was not giving the Ministerial Training Program for another year, so I decided to do something special for myself. I went to college for six months — MIU, Maharishi International University — in Fairfield, Iowa.

It was the perfect place for me at that time. In the freshman year, every Monday morning we began a new subject, things I had only heard of, such as biology, chemistry, and even the theory of relativity. Every Saturday morning there was a test. Sunday was free, and Monday morning we began anew.

There were none of the distractions so typical of my life in New York City. After dinner we all went to our rooms to study. I was the oldest kid on campus and loved every moment of it. No smoking, drinking, or drugs were allowed, and we meditated four times a day. The day I left, I thought I would collapse from the cigarette smoke in the airport.

Back to New York I went to resume my life. Soon I began taking the Ministerial Training Program. I became very active in the church and in its social activities. I began speaking at their noon meetings and seeing clients. This quickly blossomed into a full-time career. Out of the work I was doing, I was inspired to put together the little book *Heal Your Body*, which began as a simple list of metaphysical causations for physical illnesses in the body. I began to lecture and travel and hold small classes.

Then one day I was diagnosed as having cancer.

With my background of being raped at five and having been a battered child, it was no wonder I manifested cancer in the vaginal area.

Like anyone else who has just been told they have cancer, I went into total panic. Yet because of all my work with clients, I knew that mental healing worked, and here I was being given a chance to prove it to myself. After all, I had written the book on mental patterns, and I knew cancer was a dis-ease of deep resentment that has been held for a long time until it literally eats away at the body. I had been refusing to be willing to dissolve all the anger and resentment at "them" over my childhood. There was no time to waste; I had a lot of work to do.

The word *incurable*, which is so frightening to so many people, means to me that this particular condition cannot be cured by any outer means and that we must go within to find the cure. If I had an operation to get rid of the cancer and did not clear the mental pattern that created it, then the doctors would just keep cutting Louise until there was no more Louise to cut. I didn't like that idea.

If I had the operation to remove the cancerous growth and also cleared the mental pattern that was causing the cancer, then it would not return. If cancer or any other illness returns, I do not believe it is because they did not "get it all out," but rather that the patient has made no mental change. He or she just recreates the same illness, perhaps in a different part of the body.

I also believe that if I could clear the mental pattern that created this cancer, then I would not even need the operation. So I bargained for time, and the doctors grudgingly gave me three months when I said I did not have the money.

I immediately took responsibility for my own healing. I read and investigated everything I could find on alternative ways to assist my healing process.

I went to several health food stores and bought every book they had on the subject of cancer. I went to the library and did more reading. I checked out foot reflexology and colon therapy and thought they both would be beneficial to me. I seemed to be led to exactly the right people. After reading about foot reflexology, I wanted to find a practitioner. I attended a lecture, and while I usually sat in the front row, this night I was compelled to sit in the back. Within a minute, a man came and sat beside me and — guess what? He was a foot reflexologist who visited the home. He came to me three times a week for two months and was a great help.

I knew I also had to love myself a great deal more than I was. There was little love expressed in my childhood, and no one had made it okay for me to feel good about myself. I had adopted "their" attitudes of continually picking on and criticizing me, which had become second nature.

I had come to the realization through my work with the Church that it was okay and even essential for me to love and approve of myself. Yet I kept putting it off — rather like the diet you will always start tomorrow. But I could no longer put it off. At first it was very difficult for me to do things like stand in front of the mirror and say things like, "Louise, I love you. I really love you." However, as I persisted, I found that several situations came up in my life where in the past I would have berated myself, and now, because of the mirror exercise and other work, I was not doing so. I was making some progress.

I knew I had to clear the patterns of resentment I had been holding since childhood. It was imperative for me to let go of the blame.

Yes, I had had a very difficult childhood with a lot of abuse — mental, physical, and sexual. But that was many years ago, and it was no excuse for the way I was treating myself now. I was literally eating my body with cancerous growth because I had not forgiven.

It was time for me to go beyond the incidents themselves and to begin to UNDERSTAND what types of experiences could have created people who would treat a child that way.

With the help of a good therapist, I expressed all the old, bottled-up anger by beating pillows and howling with rage. This made me feel cleaner. Then I began to piece together the scraps of stories my parents had told me of their own childhoods. I started to see a larger picture of their lives. With my growing understanding, and from an adult viewpoint, I began to have compassion for their pain; and the blame slowly began to dissolve.

In addition, I hunted for a good nutritionist to help me cleanse and detoxify my body from all the junky foods I had eaten over the years. I learned that junky foods accumulate and create a toxic body. Junky thoughts accumulate and create toxic conditions in the mind. I was given a very strict diet with lots of green vegetables and not much else. I even had colonics three times a week for the first month.

I did not have an operation — however, as a result of all the thorough mental and physical cleansing, six months after my diagnosis I was able to get the medical profession to agree with what I already knew — that I no longer had even a trace of cancer! Now I knew from personal experience that DIS-EASE CAN BE HEALED, IF WE ARE WILLING TO CHANGE THE WAY WE THINK AND BELIEVE AND ACT!

Sometimes what seems to be a big tragedy turns out to become the greatest good in our lives. I learned so much from that experience, and I came to value life in a new way. I began to look at what was really important to me, and I made a decision finally to leave the treeless city of New York and its extreme weather. Some of my clients insisted they would "die" if I left them, and I assured them I would be back twice a year to check on their progress, and telephones can reach everywhere. So I closed my business and took a leisurely train trip to California, deciding to use Los Angeles as a starting point.

Even though I had been born here many years before, I knew almost no one anymore except for my mother and sister, who both now lived on the outskirts about an hour away. We have never been a close family nor an open one, but still I was unpleasantly surprised to learn that my mother had been blind for a few years, and no one had bothered to tell me. My sister was too "busyish" to see me, so I let her be and began to set up my new life.

My little book *Heal Your Body* opened many doors for me. I began to go to every New Age type of meeting I could find. I would introduce myself, and when appropriate, give out a copy of the little book. For the first six months, I went to the beach a lot, knowing that when I became busy, there would be less time for such leisurely pursuits. Slowly, the clients appeared. I was asked to speak here and there, and things began to come together as Los Angeles welcomed me. Within a couple of years, I was able to move into a lovely home.

My new lifestyle in Los Angeles was a large jump in consciousness from my early upbringing. Things were going smoothly, indeed. How swiftly our lives can change completely.

One night I received a phone call from my sister, the first call in two years. She told me that our mother, now 90, blind, and almost deaf, had fallen and broken her back. In one moment my mother went from being a strong, independent woman to being a helpless child in pain.

She broke her back and also broke open the wall of secrecy around my sister. Finally, we were all beginning to communicate. I discovered that my sister also had a severe back problem that impaired her sitting and walking and which was very painful. She suffered in silence, and though she looked anorexic, her husband did not know she was ill.

After spending a month in the hospital, my mother was ready to go home. But in no way could she take care of herself, so she came to live with me.

Though trusting in the process of life, I did not know how I could handle it all, so I said to God, "Okay, I will take care of her, but you have to give me help, and you have to provide the money!"

It was quite an adjustment for both of us. She arrived on a Saturday; and the following Friday, I had to go to San Francisco for four days. I could not leave her alone, and I had to go. I said, "God, you handle this. I have to have the right person to help us before I leave."

On the following Thursday, the perfect person had "appeared," and moved in to organize my home for my mother and me. It was another confirmation of one of my basic beliefs: "Whatever I need to know is revealed to me, and whatever I need comes to me in Divine right order."

I realized it was lesson time for me once again. Here was an opportunity to clean up a lot of that garbage from childhood.

My mother had not been able to protect me when I was a child; however, I could and would take care of her now. Between my mother and my sister, a new whole adventure began.

To give my sister the help she asked for presented another challenge. I learned that when I had rescued my mother so many years ago, my stepfather then turned his rage and pain against my sister, and it was her turn to be brutalized.

I realized that what started out to be a physical problem was then greatly exaggerated by fear and tension, plus the belief that no one could help her. So here was Louise, not wanting to be a rescuer and yet wanting to give her sister an opportunity to choose wellness at this point in her life.

Slowly the unraveling began, and now, today, it's still going on. We progress step by step as I provide an atmosphere of safety while we explore various avenues of healing.

My mother,* on the other hand, responds very well. She exercises as best she can four times a day. Her body gets stronger and more flexible. I took her to get a hearing aid, and she became more interested in life. In spite of her Christian Science beliefs, I persuaded her to have a cataract removed from one eye. What a joy for her to begin to see again and for us to see the world through her eyes. She is so pleased to read again.

My mother and I began to find time to sit and talk to each other in ways we had never done before. A new understanding developed between us. Today, we both become freer as we cry and laugh and hug together. Sometimes she pushes my buttons, which only tells me there is something further for me to clear.

*　　*　　*

*My mother left the planet peacefully several years ago. I miss her and love her. We completed all we could together, and now we are both free.

Afterword

I t's hard to believe that more than 30 years have gone by since I first wrote *You Can Heal Your Life.* During this time, the book has been translated into 42 different languages, has become available in more than 132 different countries, and has now sold over 40 million copies throughout the world.

When I first wrote *You Can Heal Your Life,* my original dream was to go beyond the students in my workshops and reach as many other people as possible in order to help them change their lives for the better. Little did I know how the Universe would fulfill this dream, and how many people would really be helped. From the moment this book was written, it seems that Life has said, "This book must go out; it must be available worldwide." I think the success of this work is due to the fact that I have the ability to help people change, and learn to love themselves, without laying guilt on them. I also think the simplicity of the message helps it to cross over many different cultures with success.

At a trade book fair in Los Angeles (BookExpo America), I met a man who told me that I'm a best-selling author in his bookstore in Kathmandu, Nepal. I keep his business card on my desk as a reminder of the extraordinary connection I have with people everywhere. And today, the Internet brings me masses of mail from all over the globe each month. Many of these letters are from young people who find the message just as relevant and healing as did those who first read it 30 years ago.

So much has happened over the years. For six and a half years three decades ago, I spent time working with people with AIDS. It began with six men in my living room in Los Angeles one evening, and in a couple of years grew to a weekly meeting of more than 800 people. I called it "The Hayride." This was such a growing period for me. My heart was constantly being stretched. I will remember those experiences for the rest of my life. It had a long life, and continued even after I moved out of town, but The Hayride Support Group no longer exists in West Hollywood.

Sometime after I wrote *You Can Heal Your Life,* several of the Hayride people went on the *Oprah* show with me to put out positive messages about AIDS. The same week, I appeared on *Donahue* with Dr. Bernie Siegel. *You Can Heal Your Life* hit the *New York Times* bestseller list and stayed there for 14 weeks. I was in constant awe of how Life was moving me in so many directions. I was working ten-hour days, seven days a week, for a long period of time.

Life goes in cycles. There is a time to do certain things, and then there is a time to move on. For many years, I had the pleasure of spending much of my time in my garden creating compost and feeding the earth. Really healthy soil grows flowers and fruits that are spectacular. I also grew most of the food I ate. Then I tried living in a high-rise condominium in downtown San Diego for a while. I thought having a terrace would be enough for my gardening needs, but it wasn't. Now I've come back to the soil and happily spend every free moment I have digging in the earth, planting and harvesting fruits and vegetables. There is nothing more delicious and healthy than fresh-picked produce.

Painting had been on my wish list for a long time, and I have dabbled a bit over the years and taken a few classes. I've had two wonderful art teachers who really advanced my painting ability: Lynn Hays, who taught me to paint large oil portraits; and Linda Bounds, who besides inspiring *me,* also encourages Alzheimer's patients to participate in group classes where they all work on one large painting. The only time these patients speak normally is when they are in Linda's class. Painting has certainly enlarged *my* creative boundaries, as well as those of others!

Over the last 25 years, I've also rescued several animals. I told each one, "I cannot do anything about your past; however, I promise you that you will live a life of love and joy for the rest of your days." They all lived out their allotted times and have now moved on. My intuition tells me not to have any more animals for the time being, as I need to be free to move around the world. Besides, I have neighbors on both sides who have dogs, so it's easy for me to get my daily animal fix.

In the early days, there were few people doing the kind of work I was, and I felt the need to be everywhere, teaching constantly. Now there are so many good teachers out there that I no longer feel the pressure to personally rescue everyone. I've written more than 30 books and have produced numerous audios and videos, so there's plenty of material for people to study. I've cut down my speaking schedule to almost nothing, and now work behind the scenes supporting new authors and talented teachers.

Another first for me came in 2008, when I made my first movie! Many women in the film industry who are 35 cannot get parts because they're considered too old. At 81, I got my turn to be a star. A number of people over the years have wanted to film the story of my life, but I just never felt as if the right person had come along. Then in late 2007, Life brought to me director Michael Goorjian. I looked into his kind eyes and saw his gentle smile, and my heart said yes, this is the one!

Although Michael and filmmaker Noah Veneklasen were newcomers to my way of thinking, I knew that the filming process and the long editing process would give them time to allow these ideas to sink into their consciousness. Not only is *You Can Heal Your Life, the movie* a success, but everyone involved with the filmmaking process has seen positive changes occur in their lives.

Reading books is good, but there's something about watching a film that brings the message deeper into one's consciousness. I've received innumerable letters telling me about the positive effects this film has had on people. The most dramatic was from a man who had spent five years in a Japanese internment camp, and after watching this film, he was finally able to forgive his captors and free himself from all the bitterness he'd carried with him for so many years.

There has been enormous interest in this film, and I taped two more shows with Oprah, talking about both the book and the movie. As it happens, more than two decades ago, my book *You Can Heal Your Life* was on the *New York Times* bestseller list for 14 weeks. And then it went back on the list—22 years later, which was almost unheard of.

When I first printed *You Can Heal Your Life*, I started a publishing company called Hay House to self-publish my book, since I then believed that no other publisher would have published it back when these thoughts were considered so radical. At that time, there wasn't even a self-help section in the bookstore. Today, more than half of the *New York Times* bestsellers are self-help books. How the consciousness of people has changed! It feels good to know that I was one of the early pioneers of spreading the message that we all do have the ability to improve the quality of our lives.

Based in California, Hay House has since grown to be one of the world's top publishers in the self-help/mind-body-spirit field. We now even have offices in Australia, the U.K., South Africa, India, and New York City. All these changes were beyond my wildest dreams. In the beginning, all I wanted to do was to help people I couldn't see personally.

I truly believe that the growth of Hay House has been supervised by the Universe itself. When we choose a new book to publish, it's always something that helps others improve themselves. I love supporting promising authors who are helping change people's lives.

I'm blessed to have excellent people running Hay House publishing for me. Reid Tracy, president and CEO, is invaluable to me and to the company. His insights have helped take my messages and those of our other splendid authors to the ends of the planet. Shelley Anderson, my personal assistant, is also invaluable. I love all the people who work in the editorial, art, publicity, customer care, marketing, sales, accounting, and radio areas; as well as those who work in the warehouse. They all make up the wonderful mix of Hay House family that makes us all so successful. I believe we shall all continue to bring our high level of information to the world for many years to come—blessing and prospering all those we touch.

An astrologer once told me that when I was born, there was a configuration in my chart that showed that I would be helping many, many people on a one-to-one basis. Of course 86 years ago, tape recorders had not been invented, so it would be hard to interpret that configuration. However, because of the miracle of technology, the sound of my voice on tape (and now on CD and in other audio formats) accompanies thousands of people to bed each night. My voice can put anyone to sleep!

As a result, many people whom I have never met feel that they know me because we spend so many intimate moments together. One of the wonderful things about what I do is that it gives me the opportunity to be greeted with love almost everywhere I go. People feel that I'm an old friend who has helped them through many a sticky moment.

*   *   *

I'd also like to share my thoughts about aging with you. No matter what age we are, we can always let go of our baggage and break through a new barrier. Let me tell you about one of my later breakthroughs.

Ten years ago when I turned 76, I decided to do something I'd never done before because I was always afraid to: I took up ballroom dancing. I had wanted to dance since I was a child, but could never get up the courage. For many years I'd said, "In the next lifetime, I'll be a dancer. It's too late to do it now." Talk about a negative affirmation.

Then one day I passed a dance studio with a sign outside that read: "We teach you to dance one step at a time." And I thought, *One step at a time . . . maybe I could do that.* And the thought that followed was: *I'm going to live quite a few more years. Why am I waiting for the next lifetime?!*

And so a new era began for me.

The first two months were absolute hell for me. I dreaded the lesson on Wednesday afternoon, but I knew I had to go through with it. I think I held my breath the entire first lesson. Every little-kid piece of garbage I had left in me came up: Embarrassment, humiliation, and shame all flooded through my body. I couldn't even *find* an affirmation to fix it.

One of my early teachers said one day, "Louise, I can just *see* the fear in your eyes. Where does it come from?" I couldn't answer right then, but later that night I really thought about it, and the answer was that there was a part of me that was convinced that I would be hit in the face if I did it "wrong." That was a real revelation to me. The little kid inside was terrified of being slapped, and I was 76 years old!

At the next lesson when I told the teacher about my breakthrough, her eyes filled with tears. And that was the turning point for me. All those feelings began to subside, and I could concentrate on my steps. Now, ten years later, I've taken many private and group lessons, and it has become great fun for me. I often go dancing. So, my dears, if I can do it, so can you. It's never too late to learn something new.

The older I get, the more important my health becomes to me. I eat simply: protein, vegetables, and some fruit. I'm not a vegetarian now, although I have been; however, I do eat lots of vegetables. I no longer consume wheat, dairy, sugar, corn, citrus, beans, or caffeine, except on very rare occasions; and I exercise more than I used to. The practice of yoga entered my life when I was 75, and I've been taking classes several times a week. I've actually become more limber than I was as a child. In addition, I take Pilates classes, and I walk for an hour three times a week. All this helps keep my body in good shape.

In October of 2007, I had my 80th birthday party. What a gala occasion it was! The entire Hay House family of employees and authors was there, all of whom I love and adore; and many of my personal friends attended, too. As I looked out over the festive gathering, I announced that the coming decade would be the best of my life so far. The whole group loved hearing that. I even received a special Louise Hay Rose. I loved having a rose named after me! This really touched my heart because long after I'm gone, its pleasure will remain. I also received a beautiful Louise Hay Orchid, a yellow cymbidium. (The cymbidiums are only available to those in Southern California who can grow them outdoors.) That whole evening really began my fabulous ninth decade.

Who knows what the next 20 years hold for me? I have some ideas; however, Life knows so much more than I do. One of the next subjects I would like to teach is how to make dying a joyful experience. We have so many negative beliefs about death, yet it's a normal and natural process. We are all born and we all die. Why are we so frightened to die? We weren't afraid to be born. My feelings at the moment are that if we learn to live a joyous life, then we will automatically have a joyous death. I guess I will have to show people what this type of passing can be like. I shall explore this more, and then I will share my findings with you.

All is well. Life is good.

Louise L. Hay

Spring 2013

In the infinity of life where I am,
all is perfect, whole, and complete.
Each one of us, myself included, experiences the richness
and fullness of life in ways that are meaningful to us.
I now look at the past with love and choose
to learn from my old experiences.
There is no right or wrong, nor good or bad.
The past is over and done.
There is only the experience of the moment.
I love myself for bringing myself
through this past into this present moment.
I share what and who I am,
for I know we are all one in Spirit.
All is well in my world.

Deep at the center of my being there is an infinite well of Love. I now allow this Love to flow to the surface. It fills my heart, my body, my mind, my consciousness, my very being, and radiates out from me in all directions and returns to me multiplied. The more Love I use and give, the more I have to give, the supply is endless. The use of love makes Me feel good, it is an expression of my inner joy. I love myself therefore, I take loving care of my body. I lovingly feed it nourishing foods and beverages, I lovingly groom it and dress it, and my body lovingly responds to me with vibrant health and energy. I love myself therefore I provide for myself a comfortable home, one that fills all my needs and is a pleasure to be in. I fill the rooms with the vibration of love so that all who enter, myself included, will feel this love and be nourished by it. I love myself therefore, I work at a job that I truly enjoy doing, one that uses my creative talents and abilities, working with and for people that I love and that love me, and earning a good income. I love myself therefore, I behave and think in a loving way to all people for I know that that which I give out returns to me multiplied. I only attract loving people in my world for they are a mirror of what I am. I love myself therefore, I forgive and totally release the past and all past experiences and I am free. I love myself therefore, I live totally in the now, experiencing each moment as good and knowing that my future is bright, and joyous, and secure for I am a beloved child of the universe and the universe lovingly takes care of me now and forever more. And so it is.

Reprinted by permission from "Heal Your Body" by Louise L. Hay

181

Holistic Healing Recommendations

BODY

Nutrition

   Diet, Food Combining, Macrobiotic,
   Natural Herbs, Vitamins, Bach Flower Remedies,
   Homeopathy.

Exercise

   Yoga, Trampoline, Walking, Dance, Cycling,
   Tai-Chi, Martial Arts, Swimming, Sports, etc.

Alternative Therapies

   Acupuncture, Acupressure, Colon Therapy,
   Reflexology, Radionics, Chromotherapy,
   Massage & Body Work
      Alexander, Bioenergetics, Touch for Health,
      Feldenkrais, Deep Tissue Work, Rolfing,
      Polarity, Trager, Reiki.

Relaxation Techniques

   Systematic Desensitization, Deep Breathing,
   Biofeedback, Sauna, Water Therapy (Hot Tub),
   Slant Board, Music.

Books

   Food Is Your Best Medicine - Bieler
   Love Your Body - Hay
   Healthy Healing - Linda Page Rector
   Herbally Yours - Royal
   Getting Well Again - Simonton

MIND

   Affirmations, Mental Imagery, Guided Imagery,
   Meditation, Loving the Self.

Psychological Techniques

   Gestalt, Hypnosis, NLP, Focusing, T.A., Rebirthing,
   Dream Work, Psychodrama, Past-Life Regression, Jung
   Humanistic Psychotherapies, Astrology, Art Therapy.

Groups

> Insight, Loving Relationship Training,
> ARAS, Ken Keyes Groups, All 12-Step Programs,
> Aids Project, Rebirthing.

Books

> *Visualization* - Bry
> *The Power of Affirmations* - Fankhauser
> *Creative Visualization* - Gawain
> *Focusing* - Gendlin
> *Heal Your Body* - Hay
> *Love Is Letting Go of Fear* - Jampolsky
> *Teach Only Love* - Jampolsky
> *A Conscious Person's Guide to Relationships* - Keyes
> *The Superbeings* - Price
> *Celebration of Breath* - Ray
> *Loving Relationships* - Ray

SPIRIT

> Asking for What You Want, Forgiveness,
> Receiving (Allowing the Presence of God to Enter),
> Accepting, Surrendering.

Spiritual Group Work

> M.S.I.A., T.M., Siddah Foundation,
> Self-Realization, Religious Science,
> Unity.

Books

> *Your Needs Met* - Addington
> *Ageless Body, Timeless Mind* - Chopra
> *Real Magic* - Dyer
> Any book by Emmet Fox
> *Course in Miracles* - Foundation for Inner Peace
> *The Science of Mind* - Holmes
> *The Mutant Message Down Under* - Morgan
> *The Manifestation Process* - Price
> *The Celestine Prophecy* - Redfield
> *The Nature of Personal Reality* - Roberts
> *Autobiography of a Yogi* - Yogananda
> *Adventures of a Psychic* - Browne

HEAL YOUR BODY

DEDICATION

I have long believed the following: "Everything I need to know is revealed to me." "Everything I need comes to me." "All is well in my life." There is no new knowledge. All is ancient and infinite. It is my joy and pleasure to gather together wisdom and knowledge for the benefit of those on the healing pathway. I dedicate this offering to all of you who have taught me what I know: to my clients, to my friends in the field, to my teachers, and to the Divine Infinite Intelligence for channeling through me that which others need to hear.

ACKNOWLEDGMENTS

I wish to acknowledge Robert Lang, M.D., Associate Professor of Medicine, Yale University; Pete Grim, D.C.; and René Espy, D.C., who all shared their ideas and wisdom with me.

PREFACE

Little did I know when I first wrote the original version of *Heal Your Body* that today I would be writing a Preface for the 67th edition. This little blue book has become an indispensable item to many. I've sold hundreds of thousands of copies, far beyond my vision in the early days. *Heal Your Body* has opened countless doors and created friends for me everywhere. Wherever I travel, I meet people who show me well-worn copies carried constantly in their purses or pockets.

This little book doesn't "heal" anyone, but it does awaken within you the ability to contribute to your own healing process. For us to become whole and healthy, we must balance the body, mind, and spirit. We need to take good care of our bodies. We need to have a positive mental attitude about ourselves and about life. And we need to have a strong spiritual connection. When these three things are balanced, we rejoice in living. No doctor or health practitioner can give us this unless we choose to take part in our healing process.

You will find many new additions in this version, and it is also cross-referenced to provide more input. I suggest that you make a list of every ailment you've ever had and look up the mental causes. You'll discover a pattern that will show you a lot about yourself. Select a few of the affirmations and do them for a month. This will help eliminate old patterns that you've been carrying for a long time.

Louise L. Hay

INTRODUCTION

In this newly revised edition, I want to share with you one of the reasons why *I know* that dis-ease can be reversed by simply reversing mental patterns.

A number of years ago, I was diagnosed with cancer of the vagina. With my background of being raped when I was five years old and being a battered child, it was no wonder that I'd manifested cancer in the vaginal area. Having already been a teacher of healing for several years, I was very aware that I was now being given a chance to practice on myself and prove what I'd been teaching others.

Like anyone who has just been told that they have cancer, I went into a total panic, yet I knew that mental healing worked. Being aware that cancer comes from a pattern of deep resentment that is held for a long time until it literally eats away at the body, I knew that I had a lot of mental work to do.

I realized that if I had the operation to get rid of the cancer but did not clear the mental pattern that created it, then the doctors would just keep cutting Louise until there was no more Louise to cut. If I had the operation and cleared the mental pattern that was causing the cancer, then the cancer wouldn't return.

When cancer or any other illness returns, I don't believe that it's because the doctor didn't "get it all out," but rather, that the patient has made no mental changes and so just re-creates the same illness. I also knew that if I could clear the mental pattern that created the condition called cancer, I wouldn't need the doctor. So I bargained for time. The doctor grudgingly gave me three months, at the same time warning me that my life was endangered by the delay.

I immediately began to work with my own teacher to clear old patterns of resentment. Up till that time, I hadn't acknowledged that I harbored deep resentment. We're often so blind to our own patterns. A lot of forgiveness work was in order. The other thing I did was to go to a good nutritionist and completely detoxify my body. So between the mental and physical cleansing, in six months I was able to get the medical profession to agree with what I already know: that I no longer had any form of cancer. I still keep the original lab report as a reminder of how negatively creative I could be.

Now when I hear about someone's illness, no matter what dire their predicament seems to be, I *know* that if they're *willing* to do the mental work of releasing and forgiving, almost anything can be healed. The word *incurable,* which is so frightening to so many people, really only means that the particular condition cannot be cured by "outer" methods and that we must *go within* to effect the healing. The condition came from nothing and will go back to nothing.

❖❖❖ ❖❖❖

THE POINT OF POWER IS IN
THE PRESENT MOMENT

The point of power is in the present moment . . . right here and right now in our minds. It doesn't matter how long we've had negative patterns, an illness, a rotten relationship, lack of finances, or self-hatred. We can begin to make a change today. The thoughts we've held and the words we've repeatedly used have created our life and experiences up to this point. Yet, that is past thinking; we've already done that. What we're choosing to think and say, today, at this moment, will create tomorrow and the next day and the next week and the next month and the next year, and so on. *The point of power is always in the present moment.* This is where we begin to make changes. What a liberating idea. We can begin to let the old nonsense go. Right now. The smallest beginning will make a difference.

When you were a tiny baby, you were pure joy and love. You knew how important you were; you felt that you were the center of the universe. You had such courage that you asked for what you wanted and you expressed all your feelings openly. You loved yourself totally—every part of your body, including your feces. You knew that you were perfect. And that is the truth of your being. All the rest is learned nonsense and can be unlearned.

How often have we said, "That's the way I am," or "That's the way it is." What we're really saying is that it is what we "believe to be true for us." Usually what we believe is only someone else's opinion that we've accepted and incorporated into our own belief system.

It fits in with other things that we believe. If we were taught as a child that the world is a frightening place, then everything we hear that fits in with that belief we will accept as true for us—for example: "Don't trust strangers," "Don't go out at night," "People cheat you," and so on. On the other hand, if we were taught early in life that the world is a safe and joyous place, then we would believe other things, such as: "Love is everywhere," "People are so friendly," and "Money comes to me easily." Life experiences mirror our beliefs.

We seldom sit down and question our beliefs. For instance, I could ask myself: "Why do I believe that it's difficult for me to learn? Is that really true? Is it true for me now? Where did that belief come from? Do I still believe it simply because a first-grade teacher told me so over and over? Would I be better off if I dropped that belief?"

Stop for a moment and catch your thought. What are you thinking right now? If thoughts shape your life and experiences, would you want this thought to become true for you? If it's a thought of worry, anger, hurt, or revenge, how do you think that this thought will come back for you? If we want a joyous life, we must think joyous thoughts. Whatever we send out mentally or verbally will come back to us in like form.

Take a little time to listen to the words you say. If you hear yourself saying something three times, write it down. It has become a pattern for you. At the end of a week, look at the list you've made and you'll see how your words fit your experiences. Be willing to change your words and thoughts and watch your life change. The way to control your life is to control your choice of words and thoughts. No one thinks in your mind but you.

❖❖❖ ❖❖❖

MENTAL EQUIVALENTS:
The Mental Thought Patterns That Form Our Experience

B oth the good in our lives and the dis-ease are the results of mental thought patterns that form our experiences. We all have many thought patterns that produce good, positive experiences, and these we enjoy. It's the negative thought patterns that produce uncomfortable, unrewarding experiences with which we're concerned. It's our desire to change our dis-ease in life into perfect health.

We've learned that for every effect in our lives, there's a thought pattern that precedes and maintains it. Our consistent thinking patterns create our experiences. Therefore, by changing our thinking patterns, we can change our experiences.

What a joy it was when I first discovered the words *metaphysical causations*. This describes the power in the words and thoughts that create experiences. This new awareness brought me an understanding of the connection between thoughts and the different parts of the body and physical problems. I learned how I had unknowingly created dis-ease in myself, and this made a great difference in my life. Now I could stop blaming life and other people for what was wrong in my life and my body. I could now take full responsibility for my own health. Without either reproaching myself or feeling guilty, I began to see how to avoid creating thought patterns of dis-ease in the future.

For example, I couldn't understand why I repeatedly had problems with a stiff neck. Then I discovered that the neck represented being flexible on issues, being willing to see different sides of a question. I had been a very inflexible person, often refusing to listen to another side of a question out of fear. But, as I became more flexible in my thinking and able, with a loving understanding, to see another person's viewpoint, my neck ceased to bother me. Now, if my neck becomes a bit stiff, I look to see where my thinking is stiff and rigid.

❖❖❖ ❖❖❖

REPLACING OLD PATTERNS

In order to permanently eliminate a condition, we must first work to dissolve the mental cause. But most often, since we don't know what the cause is, we find it difficult to know where to begin. So, if you're saying, "If I only knew what's causing this pain," I hope that this booklet will provide both a clue to find the causes and a helpful guide for building new thought patterns that will produce health in mind and body.

I've learned that for every condition in our lives, there's a *need for it*. Otherwise, we wouldn't have it. The symptom is only an outer effect. We must go within to dissolve the mental cause. This is why willpower and discipline don't work. They're only battling the outer effect. It's like cutting down the weed instead of getting the root out. So before you begin the New Thought Pattern affirmations, work on the *willingness to release the need* for the cigarettes, the headache, the excess weight, or whatever. When the need is gone, the outer effect must die. No plant can live if the root is cut away.

The mental thought patterns that cause the most dis-ease in the body are *criticism, anger, resentment,* and *guilt.* For instance, criticism indulged in long enough will often lead to dis-eases such as arthritis. Anger turns into things that boil, burn, and infect the body. Resentment long held festers and eats away at the self and ultimately can lead to tumors and cancer. Guilt always seeks punishment and leads to pain. It's so much easier to release these negative thinking patterns from our minds when we're healthy than to try to dig them out when we're in a state of panic and under the threat of the surgeon's knife.

The following list of mental equivalents has been compiled from many years of study, my own work with clients, and my lectures and workshops. It's helpful as a quick-reference guide to the probable mental patterns behind the dis-ease in your body. I offer these with love and a desire to share this simple method of helping to *Heal Your Body.*

❖❖❖ ❖❖❖

HEALING AFFIRMATIONS

PROBLEM	PROBABLE CAUSE	NEW THOUGHT PATTERN
Abdominal Cramps	Fear. Stopping the process.	I trust the process of life. I am safe.
Abscess	Fermenting thoughts over hurts, slights, and revenge.	I allow my thoughts to be free. The past is over. I am at peace.
Accidents	Inability to speak up for the self. Rebellion against authority. Belief in violence.	I release the pattern in me that created this. I am at peace. I am worthwhile.
Aches	Longing for love. Longing to be held.	I love and approve of myself. I am loving and lovable.
Acne	Not accepting the self. Dislike of the self.	I am a Divine expression of life. I love and accept myself where I am right now.
Addictions	Running from the self. Fear. Not knowing how to love the self.	I now discover how wonderful I am. I choose to love and enjoy myself.

Addison's Disease See: Adrenal Problems	Severe emotional malnutrition. Anger at the self.	*I lovingly take care of my body, my mind, and my emotions.*
Adenoids	Family friction, arguments. Child feeling unwelcome, in the way.	*This child is wanted and welcomed and deeply loved.*
Adrenal Problems See: Addison's Disease, Cushing's Disease	Defeatism. No longer caring for the self. Anxiety.	*I love and approve of myself. It is safe for me to care for myself.*
Aging Problems	Social beliefs. Old thinking. Fear of being one's self. Rejection of the now.	*I love and accept myself at every age. Each moment in life is perfect.*
AIDS	Feeling defenseless and hopeless. Nobody cares. A strong belief in not being good enough. Denial of the self. Sexual guilt.	*I am part of the Universal design. I am important, and I am loved by Life itself. I am powerful and capable. I love and appreciate all of myself.*
Alcoholism	"What's the use?" Feeling of futility, guilt, inadequacy. Self-rejection.	*I live in the now. Each moment is new. I choose to see my self-worth. I love and approve of myself.*

Allergies See: Hay Fever	Who are you allergic to? Denying your own power.	*The world is safe and friendly. I am safe. I am at peace with life.*
Alzheimer's Disease See: Dementia, Senility	Refusal to deal with the world as it is. Hopelessness and help-lessness. Anger.	*There is always a new and better way for me to experience life. I forgive and release the past. I move into joy.*
Amenorrhea See: Female Problems, Menstrual Problems	Not wanting to be a woman. Dislike of the self.	*I rejoice in who I am. I am a beautiful expression of life, flowing perfectly at all times.*
Amnesia	Fear. Running from life. Inabil-ity to stand up for the self.	*Intelligence, courage, and self-worth are always present. It is safe to be alive.*
Amyotrophic Lateral Sclerosis (Lou Gehrig's Disease)	Unwillingness to accept self-worth. Denial of success.	*I know I am worthwhile. It is safe for me to succeed. Life loves me.*
Anemia	"Yes-but" attitude. Lack of joy. Fear of life. Not feeling good enough.	*It is safe for me to experience joy in every area of my life. I love life.*

Problem	Probable Cause	New Thought Pattern
Ankle(s)	Inflexibility and guilt. Ankles represent the ability to receive pleasure.	I deserve to rejoice in life. I accept all the pleasure life has to offer.
Anorectal Bleeding (Hematochezia)	Anger and frustration.	I trust the process of life. Only right and good action is taking place in my life.
Anorexia See: Appetite, Loss of	Denying the self life. Extreme fear, self-hatred, and rejection.	It is safe to be me. I am wonderful just as I am. I choose to live. I choose joy and self-acceptance.
Anus See: Hemorrhoids	Releasing point. Dumping ground.	I easily and comfortably release that which I no longer need in life.
— Abscess	Anger in relation to what you don't want to release.	It is safe to let go. Only that which I no longer need leaves my body.
— Bleeding See: Anorectal Bleeding		
— Fistula	Incomplete releasing of trash. Holding on to garbage of the past.	It is with love that I totally release the past. I am free.
— Itching (Pruritis Ani)	Guilt over the past. Remorse.	I lovingly forgive myself. I am free.

— Pain	Guilt. Desire for punishment. Not feeling good enough.	*The past is over. I choose to love and approve of myself in the now.*
Anxiety	Not trusting the flow and the process of life.	*I love and approve of myself, and I trust the process of life. I am safe.*
Apathy	Resistance to feeling. Deadening of the self. Fear.	*It is safe to feel. I open myself to life. I am willing to experience life.*
Appendicitis	Fear. Fear of life. Blocking the flow of good.	*I am safe. I relax and let life flow joyously.*
Appetite		
— Excessive	Fear. Needing protection. Judging the emotions.	*I am safe. It is safe to feel. My feelings are normal and acceptable.*
— Loss of See: Anorexia	Fear. Protecting the self. Not trusting life.	*I love and approve of myself. I am safe. Life is safe and joyous.*
Arm(s)	Represents the capacity and ability to hold the experiences of life.	*I lovingly hold and embrace my experiences with ease and with joy.*
Arteries	Carry the joy of life.	*I am filled with joy. It flows through me with every beat of my heart.*

Arteriosclerosis	Resistance, tension. Hardened narrow-mindedness. Refusing to see good.	*I am completely open to life and to joy. I choose to see with love.*
Arthritic Fingers	A desire to punish. Blame. Feeling victimized.	*I see with love and understanding. I hold all my experiences up to the light of love.*
Arthritis See: Joints	Feeling unloved. Criticism, resentment.	*I am love. I now choose to love and approve of myself. I see others with love.*
Asphyxiating Attacks See: Breathing Problems, Hyperventilation	Fear. Not trusting the process of life. Getting stuck in childhood.	*It is safe to grow up. The world is safe. I am safe.*
Asthma	*Smother* love. Inability to breathe for oneself. Feeling stifled. Suppressed crying.	*It is safe now for me to take charge of my own life. I choose to be free.*
— Babies and Children	Fear of life. Not wanting to be here.	*This child is safe and loved. This child is welcomed and cherished.*

205

Athlete's Foot	Frustration at not being accepted. Inability to move forward with ease.	I love and approve of myself. I give myself permission to go ahead. It's safe to move.
Back	Represents the support of life.	I know that Life always supports me.
Back Problems See: Spinal Misalignments: Special Section		
— Lower	Fear of money. Lack of financial support.	I trust the process of life. All I need is always taken care of. I am safe.
— Middle	Guilt. Stuck in all that stuff back there. "Get off my back."	I release the past. I am free to move forward with love in my heart.
— Upper	Lack of emotional support. Feeling unloved. Holding back love.	I love and approve of myself. Life supports and loves me.
Bad Breath See: Halitosis	Anger and revenge thoughts. Experiences backing up.	I release the past with love. I choose to voice only love.
Balance, Loss of	Scattered thinking. Not centered.	I center myself in safety and accept the perfection of my life. All is well.

Problem	Probable Cause	New Thought Pattern
Baldness	Fear. Tension. Trying to control everything. Not trusting the process of life.	*I am safe. I love and approve of myself. I trust life.*
Bedwetting (Enuresis)	Fear of parent, usually the father.	*This child is seen with love, with compassion, and with understanding. All is well.*
Belching	Fear. Gulping life too quickly.	*There is time and space for everything I need to do. I am at peace.*
Bell's Palsy See: Palsy, Paralysis	Extreme control over anger. Unwillingness to express feelings.	*It is safe for me to express my feelings. I forgive myself.*
Birth	Represents the entering of this segment of the movie of life.	*This baby now begins a joyous and wonderful new life. All is well.*
— Defects	Karmic. You selected to come that way. We choose our parents and our children. Unfinished business.	*Every experience is perfect for our growth process. I am at peace with where I am.*
Bites	Fear. Open to every slight.	*I forgive myself, and I love myself now and forevermore.*
— Animal	Anger turned inward. A need for punishment.	*I am free.*

207

— Bug	Guilt over small things.	I am free of all irritations. All is well.
Blackheads	Small outbursts of anger.	I calm my thoughts, and I am serene.
Bladder Problems (Cystitis)	Anxiety. Holding on to old ideas. Fear of letting go. Being pissed off.	I comfortably and easily release the old and welcome the new in my life. I am safe.
Bleeding	Joy running out. Anger. But where?	I am the joy of Life expressing and receiving in perfect rhythm.
Bleeding Gums	Lack of joy in the decision made in life.	I trust that right action is always taking place in my life. I am at peace.
Blisters	Resistance. Lack of emotional protection.	I gently flow with life and each new experience. All is well.
Blood	Represents joy in the body, flowing freely.	I am the joy of Life expressing and receiving.

Blood Pressure

— High Hypertension	Long-standing emotional problem not solved.	*I joyously release the past. I am at peace.*
— Low	Lack of love as a child. Defeatism. "What's the use? It won't work anyway."	*I now choose to live in the ever-joyous NOW. My life is a joy.*
Blood Problems See: Leukemia	Lack of joy. Lack of circulation of ideas.	*Joyous new ideas are circulating freely within me.*
— Anemic See: Anemia		
— Clotting	Closing down the flow of joy.	*I awaken new life within me. I flow.*
Body Odor	Fear. Dislike of the self. Fear of others.	*I love and approve of myself. I am safe.*
Boils (Furuncle) See: Carbuncle	Anger. Boiling over. Seething.	*I express love and joy, and I am at peace.*
Bone(s) See: Skeleton	Represent the structure of the Universe.	*I am well structured and balanced.*

Bone Marrow
Represents deepest beliefs about the self. How you support and care for yourself.
Divine Spirit is the structure of my life. I am safe and loved and totally supported.

Bone Problems

— Breaks/Fractures
Rebelling against authority.
In my world, I am my own authority, for I am the only one who thinks in my mind.

— Deformity
See: Osteomyelitis, Osteoporosis
Mental pressures and tightness. Muscles can't stretch. Loss of mental mobility.
I breathe in life fully. I relax and trust the flow and the process of life.

Bowels
Represent the release of waste.
Letting go is easy.

— Problems
Fear of letting go of the old and no longer needed.
I freely and easily release the old and joyously welcome the new.

Brain
Represents the computer, the switchboard.
I am the loving operator of my mind.

— Tumor
Incorrect computerized beliefs. Stubborn. Refusing to change old patterns.
It is easy for me to reprogram the computer of my mind. All of life is change, and my mind is ever new.

Breast(s)

Represents mothering, nurturing, and nourishment.

I take in and give out nourishment in perfect balance.

Breast Problems

A refusal to nourish the self. Putting everyone else first.

I am important. I count. I now care for and nourish myself with love and with joy. I allow others the freedom to be who they are. We are all safe and free.

— Cysts, Lumps, Soreness (Mastitis)

Overmothering. Overprotection. Overbearing attitudes.

Breath

Represents the ability to take in life.

I love life. It is safe to live.

Breathing Problems
See: Asphyxiating Attacks, Hyperventilation

Fear or refusal to take in life fully. Not feeling the right to take up space or even exist.

It is my birthright to live fully and freely. I am worth loving. I now choose to live life fully.

Bright's Disease
See: Nephritis

Feeling like a kid who can't do it right and is not good enough. A failure. Loss.

I love and approve of myself. I care for me. I am totally adequate at all times.

Bronchitis
See: Respiratory Ailments

Inflamed family environment. Arguments and yelling. Sometimes silent.

I declare peace and harmony within me and around me. All is well.

Bruises (Ecchymoses)

The little bumps in life. Self-punishment.

I love and cherish myself. I am kind and gentle with me. All is well.

Bulimia	Hopeless terror. A frantic stuffing and purging of self-hatred.	*I am loved and nourished and supported by Life itself. It is safe for me to be alive.*
Bunions	Lack of joy in meeting the experiences of life.	*I joyously run forward to greet life's wonderful experiences.*
Burns	Anger. Burning up. Incensed.	*I create only peace and harmony within myself and in my environment. I deserve to feel good.*
Bursitis	Repressed anger. Wanting to hit someone.	*Love relaxes and releases all unlike itself.*
Buttocks	Represent power. Loose buttocks, loss of power.	*I use my power wisely. I am strong. I am safe. All is well.*
Callouses	Hardened concepts and ideas. Fear solidified.	*It is safe to see and experience new ideas and new ways. I am open and receptive to good.*
Cancer	Deep hurt. Long-standing resentment. Deep secret or grief eating away at the self. Carrying hatreds. "What's the use?"	*I lovingly forgive and release all of the past. I choose to fill my world with joy. I love and approve of myself.*

Problem		Affirmation
Candida (Candidiasis) See: Thrush, Yeast Infections	Feeling very scattered. Lots of frustration and anger. Demanding and untrusting in relationships. Great takers.	I give myself permission to be all that I can be, and I deserve the very best in life. I love and appreciate myself and others.
Canker Sores	Festering words held back by the lips. Blame.	I create only joyful experiences in my loving world.
Car Sickness See: Motion Sickness	Fear. Bondage. Feeling of being trapped.	I move with ease through time and space. Only love surrounds me.
Carbuncle See: Boils	Poisonous anger about personal injustices.	I release the past and allow time to heal every area of my life.
Carpal-Tunnel Syndrome See: Wrist	Anger and frustration at life's seeming injustices.	I now choose to create a life that is joyous and abundant. I am at ease.
Cataracts	Inability to see ahead with joy. Dark future.	Life is eternal and filled with joy. I look forward to every moment.
Cellulite	Stored anger and self-punishment.	I forgive others. I forgive myself. I am free to love and enjoy life.
Cerebral Palsy See: Palsy	A need to unite the family in an action of love.	I contribute to a united, loving, and peaceful family life. All is well.

Cerebrovascular Accident
See: Stroke

Childhood Diseases

Belief in calendars and social concepts and false laws. Childish behavior in the adults around them.

This child is Divinely protected and surrounded by love. We claim mental immunity.

Chills

Mental contraction, pulling away and in. Desire to retreat. "Leave me alone."

I am safe and secure at all times. Love surrounds me and protects me. All is well.

Cholelithiasis
See: Gallstones

Cholesterol (Atherosclerosis)

Clogging the channels of joy. Fear of accepting joy.

I choose to love life. My channels of joy are wide open. It is safe to receive.

Chronic Diseases

A refusal to change. Fear of the future. Not feeling safe.

I am willing to change and to grow. I now create a safe, new future.

Circulation

Represents the ability to feel and express the emotions in positive ways.

I am free to circulate love and joy in every part of my world. I love life.

Cold Sores (Fever Blisters) See: Herpes Simplex	Festering angry words and fear of expressing them.	*I only create peaceful experiences because I love myself. All is well.*
Colds (Upper-Respiratory Illness) See: Respiratory Ailments	Too much going on at once. Mental confusion, disorder. Small hurts. "I get three colds every winter," type of belief.	*I allow my mind to relax and be at peace. Clarity and harmony are within me and around me. All is well.*
Colic	Mental irritation, impatience, annoyance in the surroundings.	*This child responds only to love and to loving thoughts. All is peaceful.*
Colitis See: Colon, Intestines, Mucus Colon, Spastic Colitis	Insecurity. Represents the ease of letting go of that which is over.	*I am part of the perfect rhythm and flow of life. All is in Divine right order.*
Colon	Holding on to the past. Fear of letting go.	*I easily release that which I no longer need. The past is over, and I am free.*
Coma	Fear. Escaping something or someone.	*We surround you with safety and love. We create a space for you to heal. You are loved.*
Comedones	Small outbursts of anger.	*I calm my thoughts, and I am serene.*

Congestion
See: Bronchitis, Colds, Influenza

Conjunctivitis
See: Pinkeye

Anger and frustration at what you are looking at in life.

I see with eyes of love. There is a harmonious solution, and I accept it now.

Constipation

Refusing to release old ideas. Stuck in the past. Sometimes stinginess.

As I release the past, the new and fresh and vital enter. I allow life to flow through me.

Corns

Hardened areas of thought—stubbornly holding on to the pain of the past.

I move forward, free from the past. I am safe; I am free.

Coronary Thrombosis
See: Heart Attack

Feeling alone and scared. "I'm not good enough. I don't do enough. I'll never make it."

I am one with all of life. The Universe totally supports me. All is well.

Coughs
See: Respiratory Ailments

A desire to bark at the world. "See me! Listen to me!"

I am noticed and appreciated in the most positive ways. I am loved.

Cramps
Tension. Fear. Gripping, holding on.

I relax and allow my mind to be peaceful.

Croup
See: Bronchitis

Crying
Tears are the river of life, shed in joy as well as in sadness and fear.

I am peaceful with all of my emotions. I love and approve of myself.

Cushing's Disease
See: Adrenal Problems

Mental imbalance. Overproduction of crushing ideas. A feeling of being overpowered.

I lovingly balance my mind and my body. I now choose thoughts that make me feel good.

Cuts
See: Injuries, Wounds

Punishment for not following your own rules.

I create a life filled with rewards.

Cyst(s)
Running the old painful movie. Nursing hurts. A false growth.

The movies of my mind are beautiful because I choose to make them so. I love me.

Cystic Fibrosis
A thick belief that life won't work for you. "Poor me."

Life loves me, and I love life. I now choose to take in life fully and freely.

Cystitis
See: Bladder Problems

Deafness

Rejection, stubbornness, isolation. What don't you want to hear? "Don't bother me."

I listen to the Divine and rejoice at all that I am able to hear. I am one with all.

Death

Represents leaving the movie of life.

I joyfully move on to new levels of experience. All is well.

Dementia
See: Alzheimer's Disease, Senility

A refusal to deal with the world as it is. Hopelessness and anger.

I am in my perfect place, and I am safe at all times.

Depression

Anger you feel you do not have a right to have. Hopelessness.

I now go beyond other people's fears and limitations. I create my life.

Diabetes (Hyperglycemia, Mellitus)

Longing for what might have been. A great need to control. Deep sorrow. No sweetness left.

This moment is filled with joy. I now choose to experience the sweetness of today.

Diarrhea

Fear. Rejection. Running off.

My intake, assimilation, and elimination are in perfect order. I am at peace with life.

Problem	Probable Cause	New Thought Pattern
Dizziness (Vertigo)	Flighty, scattered thinking. A refusal to look.	I am deeply centered and peaceful in life. It is safe for me to be alive and joyous.
Dry Eye	Angry eyes. Refusing to see with love. Would rather die than forgive. Being spiteful.	I willingly forgive. I breathe life into my vision and see with compassion and understanding.
Dysentery	Fear and intense anger.	I create peacefulness in my mind, and my body reflects this.
— Amoebic	Believing *they* are out to get you.	I am the power and authority in my world. I am at peace.
— Bacillary	Oppression and hopelessness.	I am filled with life and energy and the joy of living.
Dysmenorrhea See: Female Problems, Menstrual Problems	Anger at the self. Hatred of the body or of women.	I love my body. I love myself. I love all my cycles. All is well.
Ear(s)	Represents the capacity to hear.	I hear with love.
Earache (Otitis: External/ Ear Canal Media/ Inner Ear)	Anger. Not wanting to hear. Too much turmoil. Parents arguing.	Harmony surrounds me. I listen with love to the pleasant and the good. I am a center for love.

219

Ecchymoses
See: Bruises

Eczema

Breathtaking antagonism. Mental eruptions.

Harmony and peace, love and joy surround me and indwell me. I am safe and secure.

Edema
See: Holding Fluids, Swelling

What or whom won't you let go of?

I willingly release the past. It is safe for me to let go. I am free now.

Elbow
See: Joints

Represents changing directions and accepting new experiences.

I easily flow with new experiences, new directions, and new changes.

Emphysema

Fear of taking in life. Not worthy of living.

It is my birthright to live fully and freely. I love life. I love me.

Endometriosis

Insecurity, disappointment, and frustration. Replacing self-love with sugar. Blamers.

I am both powerful and desirable. It's wonderful to be a woman. I love myself, and I am fulfilled.

Enuresis
See: Bed-wetting

Epilepsy

Sense of persecution. Rejection of life. A feeling of great struggle. Self-violence.

I choose to see life as eternal and joyous. I am eternal and joyous and at peace.

Epstein-Barr Virus	Pushing beyond one's limits. Fear of not being good enough. Draining all inner support. Stress virus.	*I relax and recognize my self-worth. I am good enough. Life is easy and joyful.*
Exotropia See: Eye Problems		
Eye(s)	Represents the capacity to see clearly—past, present, and future.	*I see with love and joy.*
Eye Problems See: Sty	Not liking what you see in your own life.	*I now create a life I love to look at.*
— Astigmatism	"I" trouble. Fear of really seeing the self.	*I am now willing to see my own beauty and magnificence.*
— Cataracts	Inability to see ahead with joy. Dark future.	*Life is eternal and filled with joy.*
— Children	Not wanting to see what is going on in the family.	*Harmony and joy and beauty and safety now surround this child.*
— Crossed See: Keratitis	Not wanting to see what's out there. Crossed purposes.	*It is safe for me to see. I am at peace.*
— Farsighted (Hyperopia)	Fear of the present.	*I am safe in the here and now. I see that clearly.*

— Glaucoma	Stony unforgiveness. Pressure from long-standing hurts. Overwhelmed by it all.	I see with love and tenderness.
— Nearsighted See: Myopia	Fear of the future.	I accept Divine guidance and am always safe.
— Walleyed (Exotropia)	Fear of looking at the present, right here.	I love and approve of myself right now.
Face	Represents what we show the world.	It is safe to be me. I express who I am.
Fainting (Vasovagal Attack)	Fear. Can't cope. Blacking out.	I have the power and strength and knowledge to handle everything in my life.
Fat See: Overweight	Oversensitivity. Often represents fear and shows a need for protection. Fear may be a cover for hidden anger and a resistance to forgive.	I am protected by Divine Love. I am always safe and secure. I am willing to grow up and take responsibility for my life. I forgive others, and I now create my own life the way I want it. I am safe.

— Arms	Anger at being denied love.	It is safe for me to create all the love I want.
— Belly	Anger at being denied nourishment.	I nourish myself with spiritual food, and I am satisfied and free.
— Hips	Lumps of stubborn anger at the parents.	I am willing to forgive the past. It is safe for me to go beyond my parents' limitations.
— Thighs	Packed childhood anger. Often rage at the father.	I see my father as a loveless child, and I forgive easily. We are both free.
Fatigue	Resistance, boredom. Lack of love for what one does.	I am enthusiastic about life and filled with energy and enthusiasm.
Feet	Represents our understanding—of ourselves, of life, of others.	My understanding is clear, and I am willing to change with the times. I am safe.

Female Problems
See: Amenorrhea,
Dysmenorrhea,
Fibroid Tumors,
Leukorrhea,
Menstrual Problems,
Vaginitis

Denial of the self. Rejecting femininity. Rejection of the feminine principle.

I rejoice in my femaleness. I love being a woman. I love my body.

Fever

Anger. Burning up.

I am the cool, calm expression of peace and love.

Fever Blisters
See: Cold Sores,
Herpes Simplex

Fibroid Tumors & Cysts
See: Female Problems

Nursing a hurt from a partner. A blow to the feminine ego.

I release the pattern in me that attracted this experience. I create only good in my life.

Fingers

Represent the details of life.

I am peaceful with the details of life.

— Thumb

Represents intellect and worry.

My mind is at peace.

— Index Finger

Represents ego and fear.

I am secure.

224

— Middle Finger	Represents anger and sexuality.	*I am comfortable with my sexuality.*
— Ring Finger	Represents unions and grief.	*I am peacefully loving.*
— Little Finger	Represents the family and pretending.	*I am myself with the family of Life.*
Fistula	Fear. A blockage in the letting-go process.	*I am safe. I trust fully in the process of life. Life is for me.*
Flatulence See: Gas Pains		
Flu See: Influenza		
Food Poisoning	Allowing others to take control. Feeling defenseless.	*I have the strength, power, and skill to digest whatever comes my way.*
Foot Problems	Fear of the future and of not stepping forward in life.	*I move forward in life, with joy and with ease.*
Fractures See: Bone Problems		

225

Frigidity	Fear. Denial of pleasure. A belief that sex is bad. Insensitive partners. Fear of father.	*It is safe for me to enjoy my own body. I rejoice in being a woman.*
Fungus	Stagnating beliefs. Refusing to release the past. Letting the past rule today.	*I live in the present moment, joyous and free.*
Furuncle See: Boils		
Gallstones (Cholelithiasis)	Bitterness. Hard thoughts. Condemning. Pride.	*There is joyous release of the past. Life is sweet, and so am I.*
Gangrene	Mental morbidity. Drowning of joy with poisonous thoughts.	*I now choose harmonious thoughts and let the joy flow freely through me.*
Gas Pains (Flatulence)	Gripping. Fear. Undigested ideas.	*I relax and let life flow through me with ease.*
Gastritis See: Stomach Problems	Prolonged uncertainty. A feeling of doom.	*I love and approve of myself. I am safe.*
Genitals	Represent the masculine and feminine principles.	*It is safe to be who I am.*

— Problems	Worry about not being good enough.	*I rejoice in my own expression of life. I am perfect just as I am. I love and approve of myself.*
Gland(s)	Represent holding stations. Self-starting activity.	*I am the creative power in my world.*
Glandular Fever See: Mononucleosis		
Glandular Problems	Poor distribution of get-up-and-go ideas. Holding yourself back.	*I have all the Divine ideas and activity I need. I move forward right now.*
Globus Hystericus See: Lump in Throat		
Goiter See: Thyroid	Hatred for being inflicted upon. Victim. Feeling thwarted in life. Unfulfilled.	*I am the power and authority in my life. I am free to be me.*
Gonorrhea See: Venereal Disease	A need for punishment for being a *bad* person.	*I love my body. I love my sexuality. I love me.*
Gout	The need to dominate. Impatience, anger.	*I am safe and secure. I am at peace with myself and with others.*

227

Gray Hair	Stress. A belief in pressure and strain.	*I am at peace and comfortable in every area of my life. I am strong and capable.*
Growths	Nursing those old hurts. Building resentments.	*I easily forgive. I love myself and will reward myself with thoughts of praise.*
Gum Problems	Inability to back up decisions. Wishy-washy about life.	*I am a decisive person. I follow through and support myself with love.*
Halitosis See: Bad Breath	Rotten attitudes, vile gossip, foul thinking.	*I speak with gentleness and love. I exhale only the good.*
Hands	Hold and handle. Clutch and grip. Grasping and letting go. Caressing. Pinching. All ways of dealing with experiences.	*I choose to handle all my experiences with love and with joy and with ease.*
Hay Fever See: Allergies	Emotional congestion. Fear of the calendar. A belief in persecution. Guilt.	*I am one with ALL OF LIFE. I am safe at all times.*

Problem	Probable Cause	New Thought Pattern
Headaches See: Migraine Headaches	Invalidating the self. Self-criticism. Fear.	*I love and approve of myself. I see myself and what I do with eyes of love. I am safe.*
Heart See: Blood	Represents the center of love and security.	*My heart beats to the rhythm of love.*
— Attack (M.I./Myocardial Infarction) See: Coronary Thrombosis	Squeezing all the joy out of the heart in favor of money or position, etc.	*I bring joy back to the center of my heart. I express love to all.*
— Problems	Long-standing emotional problems. Lack of joy. Hardening of the heart. Belief in strain and stress.	*Joy. Joy. Joy. I lovingly allow joy to flow through my mind and body and experience.*
Heartburn See: Peptic Ulcer, Stomach Problems, Ulcers	Fear. Fear. Fear. Clutching fear.	*I breathe freely and fully. I am safe. I trust the process of life.*

Hematochezia
See: Anorectal Bleeding

Hemorrhoids
See: Anus

Fear of deadlines. Anger of the past. Afraid to let go. Feeling burdened.

I release all that is unlike love. There is time and space for everything I want to do.

Hepatitis
See: Liver Problems

Resistance to change. Fear, anger, hatred. Liver is the seat of anger and rage.

My mind is cleansed and free. I leave the past and move into the new. All is well.

Hernia

Ruptured relationships. Strain, burdens, incorrect creative expression.

My mind is gentle and harmonious. I love and approve of myself. I am free to be me.

Herpes (Herpes Genitalis)
See: Venereal Disease

Mass belief in sexual guilt and the need for punishment. Public shame. Belief in a punishing God. Rejection of the genitals.

My concept of God supports me. I am normal and natural. I rejoice in my own sexuality and in my own body. I am wonderful.

Herpes Simplex
(Herpes Labialis)
See: Cold Sores

Burning to bitch. Bitter words left unspoken.

I think and speak only words of love. I am at peace with life.

Hip(s)

Carries the body in perfect balance. Major thrust in moving forward.

Hip Hip Hooray—there is joy in every day. I am balanced and free.

Problem	Probable Cause	New Thought Pattern
Hip Problems	Fear of going forward in major decisions. Nothing to move forward to.	*I am in perfect balance. I move forward in life with ease and with joy at every age.*
Hirsutism	Anger that is covered over. The blanket used is usually fear. A desire to blame. There is often an unwillingness to nurture the self.	*I am a loving parent to myself. I am covered with love and approval. It is safe for me to show who I am.*
Hives (Urticaria) See: Rash	Small, hidden fears. Mountains out of molehills.	*I bring peace to every corner of my life.*
Hodgkin's Disease	Blame and a tremendous fear of not being good enough. A frantic race to prove one's self until the blood has no substance left to support itself. The joy of life is forgotten in the race for acceptance.	*I am perfectly happy to be me. I am good enough just as I am. I love and approve of myself. I am joy expressing and receiving.*
Holding Fluids See: Edema, Swelling	What are you afraid of losing?	*I willingly release with joy.*
Huntington's Disease	Resentment at not being able to change others. Hopelessness.	*I release all control to the Universe. I am at peace with myself and with life.*

231

Hyperactivity	Fear. Feeling pressured and frantic.	*I am safe. All pressure dissolves. I AM good enough.*
Hyperglycemia See: Diabetes		
Hyperopia See: Eye Problems		
Hypertension See: Blood Problems		
Hyperthyroidism See: Thyroid	Rage at being left out.	*I am at the center of life, and I approve of myself and all that I see.*
Hyperventilation See: Asphyxiating Attacks, Breathing Problems	Fear. Resisting change. Not trusting the process.	*I am safe everywhere in the Universe. I love myself and trust the process of life.*
Hypoglycemia	Overwhelmed by the burdens in life. "What's the use?"	*I now choose to make my life light and easy and joyful.*
Hypothyroidism See: Thyroid	Giving up. Feeling hopelessly stifled.	*I create a new life with new rules that totally support me.*

Ileitis (Crohn's Disease, Regional Enteritis)	Fear. Worry. Not feeling good enough.	*I love and approve of myself. I am doing the best I can. I am wonderful. I am at peace.*
Impotence	Sexual pressure, tension, guilt. Social beliefs. Spite against a previous mate. Fear of mother.	*I now allow the full power of my sexual principle to operate with ease and with joy.*
Incontinence	Emotional overflow. Years of controlling the emotions.	*I am willing to feel. It is safe for me to express my emotions. I love myself.*
Incurable	Cannot be cured by outer means at this point. We must go *within* to effect the cure. It came from nowhere and will go back to nowhere.	*Miracles happen every day. I go within to dissolve the pattern that created this, and I now accept a Divine healing. And so it is!*
Indigestion	Gut-level fear, dread, anxiety. Griping and grunting.	*I digest and assimilate all new experiences peacefully and joyously.*
Infection See: Viral Infection	Irritation, anger, annoyance.	*I choose to be peaceful and harmonious.*

233

Inflammation
See: "Itis"

Fear. Seeing red. Inflamed thinking.

My thinking is peaceful, calm, and centered.

Influenza
See: Respiratory Ailments

Response to mass negativity and beliefs. Fear. Belief in statistics.

I am beyond group beliefs or the calendar. I am free from all congestion and influence.

Ingrown Toenail

Worry and guilt about your right to move forward.

It is my Divine right to take my own direction in life. I am safe. I am free.

Injuries
See: Cuts, Wounds

Anger at the self. Feeling guilty.

I now release anger in positive ways. I love and appreciate myself.

Insanity (Psychiatric Illness)

Fleeing from the family. Escapism, withdrawal. Violent separation from life.

This mind knows its true identity and is a creative point of Divine Self-Expression.

Insomnia

Fear. Not trusting the process of life. Guilt.

I lovingly release the day and slip into peaceful sleep, knowing tomorrow will take care of itself.

Intestines
See: Colon

Assimilation. Absorption. Elimination with ease.

I easily assimilate and absorb all that I need to know and release the past with joy.

Itching (Pruritus)	Desires that go against the grain. Unsatisfied. Remorse. Itching to get out or get away.	I am at peace just where I am. I accept my good, knowing all my needs and desires will be fulfilled.
"Itis" See: Inflammation	Anger and frustration about conditions you are looking at in your life.	I am willing to change all patterns of criticism. I love and approve of myself.
Jaundice See: Liver Problems	Internal and external prejudice. Unbalanced reason.	I feel tolerance and compassion and love for all people, myself included.
Jaw Problems (Temporomandibular Joint, TMJ Syndrome)	Anger. Resentment. Desire for revenge.	I am willing to change the patterns in me that created this condition. I love and approve of myself. I am safe.
Joints See: Arthritis, Elbow, Knee, Shoulders	Represent changes in direction in life and the ease of these movements.	I easily flow with change. My life is Divinely guided, and I am always going in the best direction.
Keratitis See: Eye Problems	Extreme anger. A desire to hit those or what you see.	I allow the love from my own heart to heal all that I see. I choose peace. All is well in my world.

Kidney Problems	Criticism, disappointment, failure. Shame. Reacting like a little kid.	*Divine right action is always taking place in my life. Only good comes from each experience. It is safe to grow up.*
Kidney Stones	Lumps of undissolved anger.	*I dissolve all past problems with ease.*
Knee See: Joints	Represents pride and ego.	*I am flexible and flowing.*
Knee Problems	Stubborn ego and pride. Inability to bend. Fear. Inflexibility. Won't give in.	*Forgiveness. Understanding. Compassion. I bend and flow with ease, and all is well.*
Laryngitis	So mad you can't speak. Fear of speaking up. Resentment of authority.	*I am free to ask for what I want. It is safe to express myself. I am at peace.*
Left Side of Body	Represents receptivity, taking in, feminine energy, women, the mother.	*My feminine energy is beautifully balanced.*
Leg(s)	Carry us forward in life.	*Life is for me.*

Leg Problems
— Lower

Fear of the future. Not wanting to move.

I move forward with confidence and joy, knowing that all is well in my future.

Leprosy

Inability to handle life at all. A long-held belief in not being good enough or clean enough.

I rise above all limitations. I am Divinely guided and inspired. Love heals all life.

Leukemia
See: Blood Problems

Brutally killing inspiration. "What's the use?"

I move beyond past limitations into the freedom of the now. It is safe to be me.

Leukorrhea
See: Female Problems, Vaginitis

A belief that women are powerless over the opposite sex. Anger at a mate.

I create all my experiences. I am the power. I rejoice in my femaleness. I am free.

Liver

Seat of anger and primitive emotions.

Love and peace and joy are what I know.

Liver Problems
See: Hepatitis, Jaundice

Chronic complaining. Justifying faultfinding to deceive yourself. Feeling bad.

I choose to live through the open space in my heart. I look for love and find it everywhere.

Lockjaw
See: Tetanus

Anger. A desire to control. A refusal to express feelings.

I trust the process of life. I easily ask for what I want. Life supports me.

Lou Gehrig's Disease See: Amyotrophic Lateral Sclerosis		
Lump in Throat (Globus Hystericus)	Fear. Not trusting the process of life.	*I am safe. I trust that Life is here for me. I express myself freely and joyously.*
Lung	The ability to take in life.	*I take in life in perfect balance.*
— Problems See: Pneumonia	Depression. Grief. Fear of taking in life. Not feeling worthy of living life fully.	*I have the capacity to take in the fullness of life. I lovingly live life to the fullest.*
Lupus (Erythematosus)	A giving up. Better to die than stand up for oneself. Anger and punishment.	*I speak up for myself freely and easily. I claim my own power. I love and approve of myself. I am free and safe.*
Lymph Problems	A warning that the mind needs to be recentered on the essentials of life. Love and joy.	*I am now totally centered in the love and joy of being alive. I flow with life. Peace of mind is mine.*
Malaria	Out of balance with nature and with life.	*I am united and balanced with all of life. I am safe.*

Mastitis
See: Breast Problems

Mastoiditis

Anger and frustration. A desire not to hear what is going on. Usually in children. Fear infecting the understanding.

Divine peace and harmony surround and indwell me. I am an oasis of peace and love and joy. All is well in my world.

Mellitus
See: Diabetes

Menopause Problems

Fear of no longer being wanted. Fear of aging. Self-rejection. Not feeling good enough.

I am balanced and peaceful in all changes of cycles, and I bless my body with love.

Menstrual Problems
See: Amenorrhea, Dysmenorrhea, Female Problems

Rejection of one's femininity. Guilt, fear. Belief that the genitals are sinful or dirty.

I accept my full power as a woman and accept all my bodily processes as normal and natural. I love and approve of myself.

Migraine Headaches
See: Headaches

Dislike of being driven. Resisting the flow of life. Sexual fears. (Can usually be relieved by masturbation.)

I relax into the flow of life and let life provide all that I need easily and comfortably. Life is for me.

Miscarriage (Abortion, Spontaneous)	Fear. Fear of the future. "Not now—later." Inappropriate timing.	Divine right action is always taking place in my life. I love and approve of myself. All is well.
Mono, Mononucleosis (Pfeiffer's Disease, Glandular Fever)	Anger at not receiving love and appreciation. No longer caring for the self.	I love and appreciate and take care of myself. I am enough.
Motion Sickness See: Car Sickness, Seasickness	Fear. Fear of not being in control.	I am always in control of my thoughts. I am safe. I love and approve of myself.
Mouth	Represents taking in of new ideas and nourishment.	I nourish myself with love.
— Problems	Set opinions. Closed mind. Incapacity to take in new ideas.	I welcome new ideas and new concepts and prepare them for digestion and assimilation.
Mucus Colon See: Colitis, Colon, Intestines, Spastic Colitis	Layered deposits of old, confused thoughts clogging the channel of elimination. Wallowing in the gummed mire of the past.	I release and dissolve the past. I am a clear thinker. I live in the now in peace and joy.
Multiple Sclerosis	Mental hardness, hard-heartedness, iron will, inflexibility. Fear.	By choosing loving, joyous thoughts, I create a loving, joyous world. I am safe and free.

Muscles	Resistance to new experiences. Muscles represent our ability to move in life.	*I experience life as a joyous dance.*
Muscular Dystrophy	"It's not worth growing up."	*I go beyond my parents' limitations. I am free to be the best me I can.*
Myalgic Encephalomyelitis See: Epstein-Barr Virus		
Myocardial Infarction See: Heart Attack		
Myopia See: Eye Problems	Fear of the future. Not trusting what is ahead.	*I trust the process of life. I am safe.*
Nail(s)	Represent protection.	*I reach out safely.*
Nail Biting	Frustration. Eating away at the self. Spite of a parent.	*It is safe for me to grow up. I now handle my own life with joy and with ease.*

Narcolepsy	Can't cope. Extreme fear. Wanting to get away from it all. Not wanting to be here.	*I rely on Divine wisdom and guidance to protect me at all times. I am safe.*
Nausea	Fear. Rejecting an idea or experience.	*I am safe. I trust the process of life to bring only good to me.*
Nearsightedness See: Eye Problems, Myopia		
Neck (Cervical Spine)	Represents flexibility. The ability to see what's back there.	*I am peaceful with life.*
Neck Problems See: Spinal Misalignments Special Section Stiff Neck	Refusing to see other sides of a question. Stubbornness, inflexibility.	*It is with flexibility and ease that I see all sides of an issue. There are endless ways to do things and see things. I am safe.*
Nephritis See: Bright's Disease	Overreaction to disappointment and failure.	*Only right action is taking place in my life. I release the old and welcome the new. All is well.*

Nerves	Represent communication. Receptive reporters.	I communicate with ease and with joy.
Nervous Breakdown	Self-centeredness. Jamming the channels of communication.	I open my heart and create only loving communication. I am safe. I am well.
Nervousness	Fear, anxiety, struggle, rushing. Not trusting the process of life.	I am on an endless journey through eternity, and there is plenty of time. I communicate with my heart. All is well.
Neuralgia	Punishment for guilt. Anguish over communication.	I forgive myself. I love and approve of myself. I communicate with love.
Nodules	Resentment and frustration and hurt ego over career.	I release the pattern of delay within me, and I now allow success to be mine.
Nose	Represents self-recognition.	I recognize my own intuitive ability.
— Bleeds	A need for recognition. Feeling unrecognized and unnoticed. Crying for love.	I love and approve of myself. I recognize my own true worth. I am wonderful.
— Runny	Asking for help. Inner crying.	I love and comfort myself in ways that are pleasing to me.

— Stuffy	Not recognizing the self-worth.	*I love and appreciate myself.*
Numbness (Paresthesia)	Withholding love and consideration. Going dead mentally.	*I share my feelings and my love. I respond to love in everyone.*
Osteomyelitis See: Bone Problems	Anger and frustration at the very structure of life. Feeling unsupported.	*I am peaceful with and trust the process of life. I am safe and secure.*
Osteoporosis See: Bone Problems	Feeling there is no support left in life.	*I stand up for myself, and Life supports me in unexpected, loving ways.*
Ovaries	Represent point of creation. Creativity.	*I am balanced in my creative flow.*
Overweight See: Fat	Fear, need for protection. Running away from feelings. Insecurity, self-rejection. Seeking fulfillment.	*I am at peace with my own feelings. I am safe where I am. I create my own security. I love and approve of myself.*
Paget's Disease	Feeling there is no longer any foundation to build on. "Nobody cares."	*I know I am supported by Life in grand and glorious ways. Life loves me and cares for me.*

Pain	Guilt. Guilt always seeks punishment.	*I lovingly release the past. They are free and I am free. All is well in my heart now.*
Palsy See: Bell's Palsy, Parkinson's Disease	Paralyzing thoughts. Getting stuck.	*I am a free thinker, and I have wonderful experiences with ease and with joy.*
Pancreas	Represents the sweetness of life.	*My life is sweet.*
Pancreatitis	Rejection. Anger and frustration because life seems to have lost its sweetness.	*I love and approve of myself, and I alone create sweetness and joy in my life.*
Paralysis See: Palsy	Fear. Terror. Escaping a situation or person. Resistance.	*I am one with all of life. I am totally adequate for all situations.*
Parasites	Giving power to others, letting them take over.	*I lovingly take back my power and eliminate all interference.*
Paresthesia See: Numbness		
Parkinson's Disease See: Palsy	Fear and an intense desire to control everything and everyone.	*I relax knowing that I am safe. Life is for me, and I trust the process of life.*

Problem	Probable Cause	New Thought Pattern
Peptic Ulcer See: Heartburn, Stomach Problems, Ulcers	Fear. A belief that you are not good enough. Anxious to please.	I love and approve of myself. I am at peace with myself. I am wonderful.
Periodontitis See: Pyorrhea		
Petit Mal See: Epilepsy		
Pfeiffer's Disease See: Mononucleosis		
Phlebitis	Anger and frustration. Blaming others for the limitation and lack of joy in life.	Joy now flows freely within me, and I am at peace with life.
Piles See: Hemorrhoids		
Pimples See: Blackheads, Whiteheads	Small outbursts of anger.	I calm my thoughts, and I am serene.

Pinkeye
See: Conjunctivitis

Anger and frustration. Not wanting to see.

I release the need to be right. I am at peace. I love and approve of myself.

Pituitary Gland

Represents the control center.

My mind and body are in perfect balance. I control my thoughts.

Plantar Wart

Anger at the very basis of your understanding. Spreading frustration about the future.

I move forward with confidence and ease. I trust and flow with the process of life.

Pneumonia
See: Lung Problems

Desperate. Tired of life. Emotional wounds that are not allowed to heal.

I freely take in Divine ideas that are filled with the breath and the intelligence of Life. This is a new moment.

Poison Ivy

Feeling defenseless and open to attack.

I am powerful, safe, and secure. All is well.

Poison Oak
See: Poison Ivy

Polio

Paralyzing jealousy. A desire to stop someone.

There is enough for everyone. I create my good and my freedom with loving thoughts.

Postnasal Drip	Inner crying. Childish tears. Victim.	*I acknowledge and accept that I am the creative power in my world. I now choose to enjoy my life.*
Premenstrual Syndrome (PMS)	Allowing confusion to reign. Giving power to outside influences. Rejection of the feminine processes.	*I now take charge of my mind and my life. I am a powerful, dynamic woman! Every part of my body functions perfectly. I love me.*
Prostate	Represents the masculine principle.	*I accept and rejoice in my masculinity.*
Prostate Problems	Mental fears weaken masculinity. Giving up. Sexual pressure and guilt. Belief in aging.	*I love and approve of myself. I accept my own power. I am forever young in spirit.*
Pruritis See: Itching		
Pruritis Ani See: Anus		
Psoriasis See: Skin Problems	Fear of being hurt. Deadening the senses of the self. Refusing to accept responsibility for our own feelings.	*I am alive to the joys of living. I deserve and accept the very best in life. I love and approve of myself.*

Psychiatric Illness
  See: Insanity

Pubic Bone
    Represents genital protection.

    My sexuality is safe.

Pyelonephritis
  See: Urinary Infections

Pyorrhea (Periodontitis)
    Anger at the inability to make decisions. Wishy-washy people.

    I approve of myself, and my decisions are always perfect for me.

Quinsy (Peritonsillar Abscess)
  See: Sore Throat, Tonsillitis

    A strong belief that you cannot speak up for yourself and ask for your needs.

    It is my birthright to have my needs met. I now ask for what I want with love and with ease.

Rabies
    Anger. A belief that violence is the answer.

    I am surrounded and indwelled with peace.

Rash
  See: Hives

    Irritation over delays. Babyish way to get attention.

    I love and approve of myself. I am at peace with the process of life.

Rectum
  See: Anus

Respiratory Ailments
See: Bronchitis, Colds, Coughs, Influenza

Fear of taking in life fully.

I am safe. I love my life.

Rheumatism

Feeling victimized. Lack of love. Chronic bitterness. Resentment.

I create my own experiences. As I love and approve of myself and others, my experiences get better and better.

Rheumatoid Arthritis

Deep criticism of authority. Feeling very put upon.

I am my own authority. I love and approve of myself. Life is good.

Rickets

Emotional malnutrition. Lack of love and security.

I am secure and nourished by the love of the Universe itself.

Right Side of Body

Giving out, letting go, masculine energy, men, the father.

I balance my masculine energy easily and effortlessly.

Ringworm

Allowing others to get under your skin. Not feeling good enough or clean enough.

I love and approve of myself. No person, place, or thing has any power over me. I am free.

Root Canal
See: Teeth

Can't bite into anything anymore. Root beliefs being destroyed.

I create firm foundations for myself and for my life. I choose my beliefs to support me joyously.

Round Shoulders See: Shoulders, Spinal Curvature	Carrying the burdens of life. Helpless and hopeless.	I stand tall and free. I love and approve of me. My life gets better every day.
Sagging Lines	Sagging lines on the face come from sagging thoughts in the mind. Resentment of life.	I express the joy of living and allow myself to enjoy every moment of every day totally. I become young again.
Scabies	Infected thinking. Allowing others to get under your skin.	I am the living, loving, joyous expression of life. I am my own person.
Sciatica	Being hypocritical. Fear of money and of the future.	I move into my greater good. My good is everywhere, and I am secure and safe.
Scleroderma	Protecting the self from life. Not trusting yourself to be there and to take care of yourself.	I relax completely, for I now know I am safe. I trust Life, and I trust myself.
Scoliosis See: Round Shoulders, Spinal Curvature		

Problem	Probable Cause	New Thought Pattern
Scratches	Feeling life tears at you, that life is a rip-off. That you are being ripped off.	*I am grateful for life's generosity to me. I am blessed.*
Seasickness See: Motion Sickness	Fear. Fear of death. Lack of control.	*I am totally safe in the Universe. I am at peace everywhere. I trust Life.*
Seizures	Running away from the family, from the self, or from life.	*I am at home in the Universe. I am safe and secure and understood.*
Senility See: Alzheimer's Disease	Returning to the so-called safety of childhood. Demanding care and attention. A form of control of those around you. Escapism.	*Divine protection. Safety. Peace. The Intelligence of the Universe operates at every level of life.*
Shin(s)	Breaking down ideals. Shins represent the standards of life.	*I live up to my highest standards with love and with joy.*
Shingles (Varicella)	Waiting for the other shoe to drop. Fear and tension. Too sensitive.	*I am relaxed and peaceful because I trust the process of life. All is well in my world.*
Shoulders See: Joints, Round Shoulders	Represent our ability to carry out experiences in life joyously. We make life a burden by our attitude.	*I choose to allow all my experiences to be joyous and loving.*

Sickle Cell Anemia

A belief that one is not good enough, which destroys the very joy of life.

This child lives and breathes the joy of life and is nourished by love. God works miracles every day.

Sinus Problems (Sinusitis)

Irritation with one person, someone close.

I declare peace and harmony in-dwell me and surround me at all times. All is well.

Skeleton
See: Bones

Crumbling of structure. Bones represent the structure of your life.

I am strong and sound. I am well structured.

Skin

Protects our individuality. A sense organ.

I feel safe to be me.

Skin Problems
See: Hives, Psoriasis, Rash

Anxiety, fear. Old, buried guck. I am being threatened.

I lovingly protect myself with thoughts of joy and peace. The past is forgiven and forgotten. I am free in this moment.

Slipped Disc

Feeling totally unsupported by Life. Indecisive.

Life supports all of my thoughts; therefore, I love and approve of myself, and all is well.

Snoring

Stubborn refusal to let go of old patterns.

I release all that is unlike love and joy in my mind. I move from the past into the new and fresh and vital.

Solar Plexus	Gut reactions. Center of our in-tuitive power.	*I trust my inner voice. I am strong, wise, and powerful.*
Sore Throat See: Quinsy, Throat, Tonsillitis	Holding in angry words. Feeling unable to express the self.	*I release all restrictions, and I am free to be me.*
Sores	Unexpressed anger that settles in.	*I express my emotions in joyous, positive ways.*
Spasms	Tightening our thoughts through fear.	*I release, I relax, and I let go. I am safe in life.*
Spastic Colitis See: Colitis, Colon, Intestines, Mucus Colon	Fear of letting go. Insecurity.	*It is safe for me to live. Life will always provide for me. All is well.*
Spinal Curvature (Scoliosis Kyphosis) See: Round Shoulders, Spinal Misalignments: Special Section	The inability to flow with the support of Life. Fear and try-ing to hold on to old ideas. Not trusting life. Lack of integrity. No courage of convictions.	*I release all fears. I now trust the process of Life. I know that life is for me. I stand straight and tall with love.*

Spinal Meningitis	Inflamed thinking and rage at life.	I release all blame and accept the peacefulness and joy of life.
Spine See: Spinal Misalignments: Special Section	Flexible support of life.	I am supported by Life.
Spleen	Obsessions. Being obsessed about things.	I love and approve of myself. I trust the process of life to be there for me. I am safe. All is well.
Sprains	Anger and resistance. Not wanting to move in a certain direction in life.	I trust the process of life to take me only to my highest good. I am at peace.
Sterility	Fear and resistance to the process of life, OR not needing to go through the parenting experience.	I trust in the process of life. I am always in the right place, doing the right thing, at the right time. I love and approve of myself.
Stiff Neck See: Neck Problems	Unbending bullheadedness.	It is safe to see other viewpoints.
Stiffness	Rigid, stiff thinking.	I am safe enough to be flexible in my mind.

Stomach	Holds nourishment. Digests ideas.	*I digest life with ease.*
Stomach Problems See: Gastritis, Heartburn, Peptic Ulcer, Ulcers	Dread. Fear of the new. Inability to assimilate the new.	*Life agrees with me. I assimilate the new every moment of every day. All is well.*
Stroke (Cerebrovascular Accident/CVA)	Giving up. Resistance. "Rather die than change." Rejection of life.	*Life is change, and I adapt easily to the new. I accept life—past, present, and future.*
Stuttering	Insecurity. Lack of self-expression. Not being allowed to cry.	*I am free to speak up for myself. I am now secure in my own expression. I communicate only with love.*
Sty See: Eye Problems	Looking at life through angry eyes. Angry at someone.	*I choose to see everyone and everything with joy and love.*
Suicide	See life only in black and white. Refusal to see another way out.	*I live in the totality of possibilities. There is always another way. I am safe.*
Swelling See: Edema, Holding Fluids	Being stuck in thinking. Clogged, painful ideas.	*My thoughts flow freely and easily. I move through ideas with ease.*

Syphilis
See: Venereal Disease

Tapeworm

Strong belief in being a victim and unclean. Helpless to the seeming attitudes of others.

Others only reflect the good feelings I have about myself. I love and approve of all that I am.

Teeth

Represent decisions.

I decide to be me. I approve of myself as I am.

— Problems
See: Root Canal

Long-standing indecisiveness. Inability to break down ideas for analysis and decisions.

I make my decisions based on the principles of truth, and I rest securely knowing that only right action is taking place in my life.

Temporomandibular Joint
See: Jaw Problems

Testicles

Masculine principles. Masculinity.

It is safe to be a man.

Tetanus
See: Lockjaw

A need to release angry, festering thoughts.

I allow the love from my own heart to wash through me and cleanse and heal every part of my body and my emotions.

257

Throat

Avenue of expression. Channel of creativity.

I open my heart and sing the joys of love.

— Problems
See: Sore Throat

The inability to speak up for oneself. Swallowed anger. Stifled creativity. Refusal to change.

It's okay to make noise. I express myself freely and joyously. I speak up for myself with ease. I express my creativity. I am willing to change.

Thrush
See: Candida, Mouth, Yeast Infections

Anger over making the *wrong* decisions.

I lovingly accept my decisions, knowing I am free to change. I am safe.

Thymus

Master gland of the immune system. Feeling attacked by Life. *They are out to get me.*

My loving thoughts keep my immune system strong. I am safe inside and out. I hear myself with love.

Thyroid
See: Goiter, Hyperthyroidism, Hypothyroidism

Humiliation. "I never get to do what I want to do. When is it going to be my turn?"

I move beyond old limitations and now allow myself to express freely and creatively.

Tics, Twitches

Fear. A feeling of being watched by others.

I am approved of by all of Life. All is well. I am safe.

Tinnitus — Refusal to listen. Not hearing the inner voice. Stubbornness. — *I trust my Higher Self. I listen with love to my inner voice. I release all that is unlike the action of love.*

Toes — Represent the minor details of the future. — *All details take care of themselves.*

Tongue — Represents the ability to taste the pleasures of life with joy. — *I rejoice in all of my life's bountiful givingness.*

Tonsillitis
See: Quinsy, Sore Throat — Fear. Repressed emotions. Stifled creativity. — *My good now flows freely. Divine ideas express through me. I am at peace.*

Tuberculosis — Wasting away from selfishness. Possessive. Cruel thoughts. Revenge. — *As I love and approve of myself, I create a joyful, peaceful world to live in.*

Tumors — Nursing old hurts and shocks. Building remorse. — *I lovingly release the past and turn my attention to this new day. All is well.*

Ulcers
See: Heartburn, Peptic Ulcer, Stomach Problems — Fear. A strong belief that you are not good enough. What is eating away at you? — *I love and approve of myself. I am at peace. I am calm. All is well.*

Urethritis

Angry, emotions. Being pissed off. Blame.

I only create joyful experiences in my life.

Urinary Infections (Cystitis, Pyelonephritis)

Pissed off. Usually at the opposite sex or a lover. Blaming others.

I release the pattern in my consciousness that created this condition. I am willing to change. I love and approve of myself.

Urticaria
See: Hives

Uterus

Represents the home of creativity.

I am at home in my body.

Vaginitis
See: Female Problems, Leukorrhea

Anger at a mate. Sexual guilt. Punishing the self.

Others mirror the love and self-approval I have for myself. I rejoice in my sexuality.

Varicella
See: Shingles

Varicose Veins

Standing in a situation you hate. Discouragement. Feeling overworked and overburdened.

I stand in truth and live and move in joy. I love Life and circulate freely.

Vasovagal Attack
See: Fainting

Venereal Disease
See: AIDS, Gonorrhea, Herpes, Syphilis

Sexual guilt. Need for punishment. Belief that the genitals are sinful or dirty. Abusing another.

I lovingly and joyously accept my sexuality and its expression. I accept only thoughts that support me and make me feel good.

Vertigo
See: Dizziness

Viral Infections
See: Infection

Lack of joy flowing through life. Bitterness.

I lovingly allow joy to flow freely in my life. I love me.

Vitiligo

Feeling completely outside of things. Not belonging. Not one of the group.

I am at the very center of Life, and I am totally connected in Love.

Vomiting

Violent rejection of ideas. Fear of the new.

I digest life safely and joyously. Only good comes to me and through me.

Vulva

Represents vulnerability.

It is safe to be vulnerable.

Warts

Little expressions of hate. Belief in ugliness.

I am the love and the beauty of Life in full expression.

261

Weakness

A need for mental rest.

I give my mind a joyous vacation.

Whiteheads
See: Pimples

Hiding ugliness.

I accept myself as beautiful and loved.

Wisdom Tooth, Impacted

Not giving yourself mental space to create a firm foundation.

I open my consciousness to the expansion of life. There is plenty of space for me to grow and to change.

Wounds
See: Cuts, Injuries

Anger and guilt at the self.

I forgive myself, and I choose to love myself.

Wrist

Represents movement and ease.

I handle all my experiences with wisdom, with love, and with ease.

Yeast Infections
See: Candida, Thrush

Denying your own needs. Not supporting yourself.

I now choose to support myself in loving, joyous ways.

SPECIAL SECTION
Spinal Misalignments

So many people have back problems that are so diversified that I felt that it would be helpful to list the spine and all the vertebrae as a separate category. Please study the accompanying spinal chart with its information. Then cross-reference the chart with the mental equivalents listed below. As always, use your own wisdom to ascertain the meaning that is most helpful to you.

❖❖❖ ❖❖❖

CHART OF EFFECTS OF SPINAL MISALIGNMENTS

Vertebrae	Areas	Effects
1C	Blood supply to the head, pituitary gland, scalp, bones of the face, brain, inner and middle ear, sympathetic nervous system.	Headaches, nervousness, insomnia, head colds, high blood pressure, migraine headaches, nervous breakdowns, amnesia, chronic tiredness, dizziness.
2C	Eyes, optic nerves, auditory nerves, sinuses, mastoid bones, tongue, forehead.	Sinus trouble, allergies, crossed eyes, deafness, eye troubles, earache, fainting spells, certain cases of blindness.
3C	Cheeks, outer ear, face bones, teeth, trifacial nerve.	Neuralgia, neuritis, acne or pimples, eczema.
4C	Nose, lips, mouth, eustachian tube.	Hay fever, catarrh, hearing loss, adenoids.
5C	Vocal cords, neck glands, pharynx.	Laryngitis, hoarseness, throat conditions such as sore throat or quinsy.
6C	Neck muscles, shoulders, tonsils.	Stiff neck, pain in upper arm, tonsillitis, whooping cough, croup.
7C	Thyroid gland, bursae in the shoulders, elbows.	Bursitis, colds, thyroid conditions.
1T	Arms from the elbows down, including hands, wrists, and fingers; esophagus and trachea.	Asthma, cough, difficult breathing, shortness of breath, pain in lower arms and hands.
2T	Heart, including its valves and covering; coronary arteries	Functional heart conditions and certain chest conditions.
3T	Lungs, bronchial tubes, pleura, chest, breast.	Bronchitis, pleurisy, pneumonia, congestion, influenza.
4T	Gall bladder, common duct	Gall bladder conditions, jaundice, shingles.
5T	Liver, solar plexus, blood.	Liver conditions, fevers, low blood pressure, anemia, poor circulation, arthritis.
6T	Stomach.	Stomach troubles, including nervous stomach, indigestion, heartburn, dyspepsia.

NECK REGION

MID-BACK

ATLAS
AXIS
CERVICAL SPINE
1st THORACIC
THORACIC SPINE

Vertebra	Areas	Effects
7T	Pancreas, duodenum.	Ulcers, gastritis.
8T	Spleen.	Lowered resistance.
9T	Adrenal and supra-renal glands.	Allergies, hives.
10T	Kidneys.	Kidney troubles, hardening of the arteries, chronic tiredness, nephritis, pyelitis.
11T	Kidneys, ureters.	Skin conditions such as acne, pimples, eczema or boils.
12T	Small intestines, lymph circulation.	Rheumatism, gas pains, certain types of sterility.
1L	Large intestines, inguinal rings.	Constipation, colitis, dysentery, diarrhea, some ruptures or hernias.
2L	Appendix, abdomen, upper leg.	Cramps, difficult breathing, acidosis, varicose veins.
3L	Sex organs, uterus, bladder, knees.	Bladder troubles, menstrual troubles such as painful or irregular periods, miscarriages, bed wetting, impotency, change of life symptoms, many knee pains.
4L	Prostate gland, muscles of the lower back, sciatic nerve.	Sciatica, lumbago: difficult, painful, or too frequent urination: backaches.
5L	Lower legs, ankles, feet.	Poor circulation in the legs, swollen ankles, weak ankles and arches, cold feet, weakness in the legs, leg cramps.
SACRUM	Hip bones, buttocks.	Sacro-iliac conditions, spinal curvatures.
COCCYX	Rectum, anus.	Hemorrhoids (piles), pruritis (itching), pain at end of spine on sitting.

LOW BACK

PELVIS

1st LUMBAR

LUMBAR SPINE

SACRUM

COCCYX

Misalignments of spinal vertebrae and discs may cause irritation to the nervous system and affect the structures, organs, and functions which may result in the conditions shown above.

© Parker Chiropractic Research Foundation, 1975

SPINAL MISALIGNMENTS

VERTEBRAE	PROBABLE CAUSE	NEW THOUGHT PATTERN
Cervical Spine		
1-C	Fear. Confusion. Running from life. Feeling not good enough. "What will the neighbors say?" Endless inner chatter.	*I am centered and calm and balanced. The Universe approves of me. I trust my Higher Self. All is well.*
2-C	Rejection of wisdom. Refusal to know or understand. Indecision. Resentment and blame. Out of balance with life. Denial of one's spirituality.	*I am one with the Universe and all of life. It is safe for me to know and to grow.*
3-C	Accepting blame for others. Guilt. Martyrdom. Indecision. Grinding oneself down. Biting off more than one can chew.	*I am responsible only for myself and I rejoice in who I am. I can handle all that I create.*

	Problem	Affirmation
4-C	Guilt. Repressed anger. Bitterness. Bottled-up feelings. Stuffed tears.	I am clear in my communication with life. I am free to enjoy life right now.
5-C	Fear of ridicule and humiliation. Fear of expression. Rejecting one's good. Overburdened.	My communication is clear. I accept my good. I let go of all expectations. I am loved and I am safe.
6-C	Burdens. Overload. Trying to fix others. Resistance. Inflexibility.	I lovingly release others to their own lessons. I lovingly care for myself. I move with ease through life.
7-C	Confusion. Anger. Feeling helpless. Can't reach out.	I have a right to be me. I forgive the past. I know who I am. I touch others with love.

Thoracic Spine

	Problem	Affirmation
1-T	Fear of life. Too much to cope with. Can't handle it. Closing off from life.	I accept life and I take it in easily. All good is mine now.
2-T	Fear, pain, and hurt. Unwillingness to feel. Shutting the heart off.	My heart forgives and releases. It is safe to love myself. Inner peace is my goal.

3-T	Inner chaos. Deep, old hurts. Inability to communicate.	*I forgive everyone. I forgive myself. I nourish myself.*
4-T	Bitterness. A need to make others wrong. Condemnation.	*I give myself the gift of forgiveness and we are both free.*
5-T	Refusing to process the emotions. Dammed-up feelings, rage.	*I let life flow through me. I am willing to live. All is well.*
6-T	Anger at life. Stuffed negative emotions. Fear of the future. Constant worry.	*I trust life to unfold before me in positive ways. It is safe to love myself.*
7-T	Storing pain. Refusal to enjoy.	*I willingly let go. I allow sweetness to fill my life.*
8-T	Obsession with failure. Resisting your good.	*I am open and receptive to all good. The Universe loves me and supports me.*
9-T	Feeling let down by life. Blaming others. A victim.	*I claim my own power. I lovingly create my own reality.*
10-T	Refusal to take charge. Needing to be a victim. "It's your fault."	*I open myself to joy and love, which I give freely and receive freely.*

11-T	Low self-image. Fear of relationships.	*I see myself as beautiful and lovable and appreciated. I am proud to be me.*
12-T	Disowning the right to live. Insecure and fearful of love. Inability to digest.	*I choose to circulate the joys of life. I am willing to nourish myself.*

Lumbar Spine

1-L	A crying for love and a need to be lonely. Insecurity.	*I am safe in the Universe and all Life loves me and supports me.*
2-L	Stuck in childhood pain. See no way out.	*I grow beyond my parents' limitations and live for myself. It is my turn now.*
3-L	Sexual abuse. Guilt. Self-hatred.	*I release the past. I cherish myself and my beautiful sexuality. I am safe. I am loved.*
4-L	Rejection of sexuality. Financial insecurity. Fear of career. Feeling powerless.	*I love who I am. I am grounded in my own power. I am secure on all levels.*

5-L	Insecurity. Difficulty in communicating. Anger. Inability to accept pleasure.	I deserve to enjoy life. I ask for what I want and I accept with joy and pleasure.
Sacrum	Loss of power. Old stubborn anger.	I am the power and authority in my life. I release the past and claim my good now.
Coccyx	Out of balance with yourself. Holding on. Blame of self. Sitting on old pain.	I bring my life into balance by loving myself. I live in today and love who I am.

FURTHER COMMENTS

I've learned that children—and animals, too, because they're so open—may be largely influenced by the consciousness of the adults around them. Therefore, when working for children or pets, use the affirmations both for them and for also clearing the consciousness of the parent, teacher, relative, and so on, who may be surrounding and influencing them.

Remember, the word *metaphysical* means to go beyond the physical to the mental cause behind it. As an example, if you told me that you had a problem with constipation, I'd know that you had some sort of belief in limitation and lack and, therefore, were frightened to let go of anything out of fear of not being able to replace it. It could also mean that you were holding on to an old, painful memory of the past and wouldn't let go. You might have a fear of letting go of relationships that no longer nourish you, a job that's unfulfilling, or some possessions that are now unusable. You might even be stingy about money. Your dis-ease would give me many clues to your mental attitude.

I'd try to make you understand that a closed fist and a tight attitude cannot take in anything new. I'd help you develop more trust in the Universe (the power that supplies your breath) to provide for you so that you could flow with the rhythms of life. I'd help you release your patterns of fear and teach you how to create a new cycle of good experiences by using your mind in a different way. I might ask you to go home and clean out your closets, giving away all the useless stuff to make room for new things. And as you were doing this, I'd ask you to say aloud, "I am releasing the old and making room for the new." Simple, but effective. And as you began to understand the principle of release and letting go, the constipation, which is a form of gripping and holding on, would take care of itself. The body would freely release that which was no longer useful in a normal way.

Perhaps you've noticed how often I've used the concepts of *love, peace, joy,* and *self-approval*. When we can truly live from the loving space of the heart, approving of ourselves and trusting the Divine Power to provide for us, then peace and joy will fill our lives, and illness and uncomfortable experiences will cease to be in our experience. Our goal is to live happy, healthy lives, enjoying our own company. Love dissolves anger, love releases resentment, love dissipates fear, and love creates safety. When you can come from a space of totally loving yourself, then everything in your life must flow with ease, harmony, health, prosperity, and joy.

A good way to use this book when you have a physical problem is to:

1. Look up the mental cause. See if this could be true for you. If not, sit quietly and ask yourself: "What could be the thoughts in me that create this?"

2. Repeat to yourself (aloud, if you can): "I am willing to release the pattern in my consciousness that has created this condition."

3. Repeat the new thought pattern to yourself several times.

Whenever you think of the condition, repeat the steps.

❖❖❖ ❖❖❖

LOVING TREATMENT

This closing meditation is helpful to read daily, as it creates a healthy consciousness and, therefore, a healthy body.

DEEP AT THE CENTER OF MY BEING, there is an infinite well of love. I now allow this love to flow to the surface. It fills my heart, my body, my mind, my consciousness, my very being, and radiates out from me in all directions and returns to me multiplied. The more love I use and give, the more I have to give; the supply is endless. The use of love makes ME FEEL GOOD. It is an expression of my inner joy. I love myself; therefore, I provide a comfortable home for myself, one that fills all my needs and is a pleasure to be in. I fill the rooms with the vibration of love so that all who enter, myself included, will feel this love and be nourished by it.

I love myself; therefore, I work at a job that I truly enjoy doing, one that uses my creative talents and abilities, working with and for people whom I love and who love me, and earning a good income. I love myself; therefore, I behave and think in a loving way to all people, for I know that that which I give out returns to me multiplied. I only attract loving people in my world, for they are a mirror of what I am. I love myself; therefore, I forgive and totally release the past and all past experiences, and I am free. I love myself; therefore, I live totally in the now, experiencing each moment as good, and knowing that my future is bright, joyous, and secure. I am a beloved child of the universe, and the universe lovingly takes care of me now and forever more.

And so it is.

I love you.

❖❖❖ ❖❖❖

EPILOGUE

The last major revision of *Heal Your Body* was in 1988. I still get mail asking for the mental patterns for the latest dis-eases of the moment, such as fibromyalgia; however, I see no reason to add any more patterns.

I've learned that there are really just two mental patterns that contribute to dis-ease: fear and anger. Anger can show up as impatience, irritation, frustration, criticism, resentment, jealousy, or bitterness. These are all thoughts that poison the body. When we release this burden, all the organs in our body begin to function properly. Fear could be tension, anxiety, nervousness, worry, doubt, insecurity, feeling not good enough, or unworthiness. Do you relate to any of this stuff? We must learn to substitute faith for fear if we are to heal.

Faith in what? Faith in life. I believe that we live in a "Yes" Universe. No matter what we choose to believe or think, the Universe always says *yes* to us. If we think poverty, the Universe says *yes* to that. If we think prosperity, the Universe says *yes* to that. So we want to think and believe that we have the right to be healthy, that health is natural to us. The Universe will support and say *yes* to this belief. Be a "Yes" person, and know that you live in a "Yes" world, being responded to by a "Yes" Universe.

If you find yourself with some sort of dis-ease that's not listed in *Heal Your Body,* become your own investigator and healer. Ask yourself: *Is it one of the forms of fear, or is it one of the forms of anger?* Are you willing to release those thoughts? Are you willing to replace those thoughts with positive affirmations?* Loving yourself will also contribute greatly to healing your body, for love heals.

So how do you love yourself? First of all, and most important: Cease all criticism of yourself and others. Accept yourself as you are. Praise yourself as much as you can. Criticism breaks down the inner spirit; praise builds it up. Look into a mirror often, and simply say: *I LOVE YOU, I REALLY LOVE YOU.* It may be difficult at first, but keep practicing, and soon you will mean and feel what you say. Love yourself as much as you can, and all of life will mirror this love back to you.

By the way, fibromyalgia is fear showing up as extreme tension due to stress.

— Louise Hay, 2008

(*My book *I CAN DO IT*® will give you a lot of affirmations to get you started until you learn to create your own.)

The Power Is Within You

Dedication

I lovingly dedicate this book to all those who have attended my lectures, my staff at Hay House, all the wonderful people who have written to me over the years, and to Linda Carwin Tomchin, whose help and input into the creation of this book was indispensable. My heart has grown so much just knowing each and every one of you.

Preface

There is a great deal of information in this book. Do not feel you have to absorb it all at once. Certain ideas will leap out at you. Work with those ideas first. If I say anything that you disagree with, just ignore it. If you can get just one good idea out of this book and use it to improve the quality of your life, then I feel complete in writing it.

As you read you will become aware that I use many terms such as *Power, Intelligence, Infinite Mind, Higher Power, God, Universal Power, Inner Wisdom* . . . and so on. This is done to show you that there is no limitation on what you choose to call that Power that runs the Universe and is also within you. If any name disturbs you, then substitute another that feels right for you. In the past I have even crossed out words or names that did not appeal to me when I read a book and wrote in the word that I liked better. You could do the same.

You will also notice that I spell two words differently than they are normally spelled. *Disease* is spelled *dis-ease* and denotes anything that is not in harmony with you or your environment. *AIDS* is spelled in lower-case letters— *aids*—to diminish the power of the word, and therefore, the dis-ease. This idea was originally created by the Reverend Stephan Pieters. We at Hay House heartily endorse this concept, and urge our readers to do so as well.

This book was written as an extension of *You Can Heal Your Life*. Time has passed since the writing of that book and many new ideas have revealed themselves to me. Those ideas I wish to share with all of you who have been writing over the years asking for more information. I feel an important thing to be aware of is that the Power we are all seeking "out there" is also within us and readily available to us to use in positive ways. May this book reveal to you how very powerful you really are.

Introduction

I am not a healer. I do not heal anyone. I think of myself as a stepping stone on a pathway of self-discovery. I create a space where people can learn how incredibly wonderful they are by teaching them to love themselves. That's all I do. I'm a person who supports people. I help people take charge of their lives. I help them discover their own power and inner wisdom and strengths. I help them get the blocks and the barriers out of the way, so they can love themselves no matter what circumstances they happen to be going through. This doesn't mean that we will never have problems, but it is how we react to the problem that makes a tremendous difference.

After years of individual counseling with clients and conducting hundreds of workshops and intensive training programs across the country and around the world, I found that there is only one thing that heals every problem, and that is: *to love yourself*. When people start to love themselves more each day, it's amazing how their lives get better. They feel better. They get the jobs they want. They have the money they need. Their relationships either improve, or the negative ones dissolve and new ones begin. It's a very simple premise—*loving yourself*. I've been criticized for being too simplistic, and I have found that the simple things are usually the most profound.

Someone said to me recently, "You gave me the most wonderful gift—you gave me the gift of myself." So many of us hide from ourselves and we don't even know who we are. We don't know what we feel, we don't know what we want. Life is a voyage of self discovery. To me, to be enlightened is to go within and to know who and what we really are, and to know that we have the ability to change for the better by loving and taking care of ourselves. It's not selfish to love ourselves. It clears us so that we can love ourselves enough to love other people. We can really help the planet when we come from a space of great love and joy on an individual basis.

The Power that created this incredible Universe has often been referred to as *love*. *God is love*. We have often heard the statement: *Love makes the world go 'round*. It's all true. Love is the binding agent that holds the whole Universe together.

To me, love is a deep appreciation. When I talk about loving ourselves, I mean having a deep appreciation for who we are. We accept all the different parts of ourselves—our little peculiarities, the embarrassments, the things we may not do so well, and all the wonderful qualities, too. We accept the whole package with love. Unconditionally.

Unfortunately, many of us will not love ourselves until we lose the weight, or get the job, or get the raise, or the boyfriend, or whatever. We often put conditions on our love. But we can change. We *can* love ourselves as we are right now!

There is also a lack of love on this planet as a whole. I believe our whole planet has a dis-ease called aids, and more and more people are dying every day. This physical challenge has given us the opportunity to overcome barriers and go beyond our morality standards and differences of religion and politics and to open our hearts. The more of us who can do it, the quicker we are going to find the answers.

We are in the midst of enormous individual and global change. I believe that all of us who are living at this time chose to be here to be a part of these changes, to bring about change, and to transform the world from the old way of life to a more loving and peaceful existence. In the Piscean Age we looked "out there" for our savior: "Save me. Save me. Please take care of me." Now we are moving into the Aquarian Age, and we are learning to go within to find our savior. We are the power we have been seeking. We are in charge of our lives.

If you are not willing to love yourself today, then you are not going to love yourself tomorrow, because whatever excuse you have today, you'll still have tomorrow. Maybe you'll have the same excuse 20 years from now, and even leave this lifetime holding on to the same excuse. Today is the day you can love yourself totally with no expectations.

I want to help create a world where it is safe for us to love each other, where we can express who we are and be loved and accepted by the people around us without judgment, criticism, or prejudice. Loving begins at home. The bible says, *"Love thy neighbor as thyself."* Far too often we forget the last couple of words—*as thyself.* We really can't love anyone out there unless the love starts inside us. Self-love is the most important gift we can give ourselves, because when we love who we are, we will not hurt ourselves, and we will not hurt anyone else. With inner peace, there would be no wars, no gangs, no terrorists, and no homeless. There would be no dis-ease, no aids, no cancer, no poverty, and no starvation. So this, to me, is a prescription for world peace: *to have peace within ourselves*. Peace, understanding, compassion, forgiveness, and most of all, love. We have the power within us to effect these changes.

Love is something we can choose, the same way we choose anger, or hate, or sadness. We *can* choose love. It's always a choice within us. Let's begin right now in this moment to choose love. It's the most powerful healing force there is.

The information in this book, which has been a part of my lectures over the past five years, is yet another stepping stone on your pathway to self-discovery—an opportunity to know a little bit more about yourself and to understand the potential that is your birthright. You have an opportunity to love yourself more, so you can be a part of an incredible universe of love. Love begins in our hearts, and it begins with us. Let your love contribute to the healing of our planet.

Louise L. Hay

PART ONE

Becoming Conscious

When we expand our thinking and beliefs, our love flows freely. When we contract, we shut ourselves off.

Chapter 1

The Power Within

*The more you connect to the Power
within you, the more you can be free
in all areas of your life.*

Who are you? Why are you here? What are your beliefs about life? For thousands of years, finding the answers to these questions has meant *going within*. But what does that mean?

I believe there is a Power within each of us that can lovingly direct us to our perfect health, perfect relationships, perfect careers, and which can bring us prosperity of every kind. In order to have these things, we have to believe first that they are possible. Next, we must be willing to release the patterns in our lives that are creating conditions we say we do not want. We do this by going within and tapping the Inner Power that already knows what is best for us. If we are willing to turn our lives over to this greater Power within us, the Power that loves and sustains us, we can create more loving and prosperous lives.

I believe that our minds are always connected to the One Infinite Mind, and therefore, all knowledge and wisdom is available to us at any time. We are connected to this Infinite Mind, this Universal Power that created us, through that spark of light within, our Higher Self, or the Power within. The Universal Power loves all of Its creations. It is a Power for good and It directs everything in our lives. It doesn't know how to hate or lie or punish. It is pure love, freedom, understanding, and compassion. It is important to turn our lives over to our Higher Self, because through It we receive our good.

We must understand that we have the choice to use this Power in any way. If we choose to live in the past and rehash all of the negative situations and conditions that went on way back when, then we stay stuck where we are. If we make a conscious decision not to be victims of the past and go about creating new lives for ourselves, we are supported by this Power within, and new, happier experiences begin to unfold. I don't believe in two powers. I think there is One Infinite Spirit. It's all too easy to say, "It's the devil," or *them*. It really is only us, and either we use the power we have wisely or we misuse the power. Do we have the devil in our hearts? Do we condemn others for being different than we are? What are we choosing?

Responsibility Vs. Blame

I also believe that we contribute toward the creation of every condition in our lives, good or bad, with our thinking, feeling patterns. The thoughts we think create our feelings, and we then begin to live our lives in accordance with these feelings and beliefs. This is not to blame ourselves for things going *wrong* in our lives. There is a

difference between being responsible and blaming ourselves or others.

When I talk about responsibility, I am really talking
about having power. Blame is about giving away one's
power. Responsibility gives us the power to make changes
in our lives. If we play the victim role, then we are using
our personal power to be helpless. If we decide to accept
responsibility, then we don't waste time blaming somebody or something *out there*. Some people feel guilty for
creating illness, or poverty, or problems. They choose to
interpret responsibility as guilt. (Some members of the
media like to refer to it as *New Age Guilt*.) These people
feel guilty because they believe that they have failed in
some way. However, they usually accept everything as a
guilt trip in one way or another because it's another way
to make themselves wrong. That is not what I'm talking
about.

If we can use our problems and illnesses as opportunities to think about how we can change our lives, we have
power. Many people who come through catastrophic illness say that it was the most wonderful thing that ever
happened to them because it gave them a chance to go
about their lives differently. A lot of people, on the other
hand, go around saying, "I'm a victim, woe is me. Please,
doctor, fix me." I think these people will have a difficult
time even getting well or handling their problems.

Responsibility is our ability to respond to a situation.
We always have a choice. It does not mean that we deny
who we are and what we have in our lives. It merely
means that we can acknowledge that we have contributed
to where we are. By taking responsibility, we have the

power to change. We can say, "What can I do to make this different?" We need to understand that we all have personal power *all the time*. It depends on how we use it.

Many of us are now realizing that we come from dysfunctional homes. We carry over a lot of negative feelings about who we are and our relationship to life. My childhood was filled with violence, including sexual abuse. I was starved for love and affection and had no self-esteem at all. Even after leaving home at the age of 15, I continued to experience abuse in many forms. I hadn't yet realized that the thinking, feeling patterns I had learned early in life had brought this abuse upon me.

Children often respond to the mental atmosphere of the adults around them. So I learned early about fear and abuse and continued to recreate those experiences for myself as I grew up. I certainly didn't understand that I had the power to change all of this. I was unmercifully hard on myself because I interpreted lack of love and affection to mean I must be a bad person.

All of the events you have experienced in your lifetime up to this moment have been created by your thoughts and beliefs from the past. Let's not look back on our lives with shame. Look at the past as part of the richness and fullness of your life. Without this richness and fullness, we would not be here today. There is no reason to beat yourself up because you didn't do better. You did the best you knew how. Release the past in love, and be grateful that it has brought you to this new awareness.

The past only exists in our minds and in the way we choose to look at it in our minds. *This* is the moment we are living. *This* is the moment we are feeling. *This* is the moment we are experiencing. What we are doing right now is laying the groundwork for tomorrow. So *this* is the moment to make the decision. We can't do anything tomorrow, and we can't do it yesterday. We can only do it today. What is important is what we are choosing to think, believe, and say *right now*.

When we begin to take conscious charge of our thoughts and words, then we have tools that we can use. I know this sounds simple, but remember, *the point of power is always in the present moment.*

It is important for you to understand that your mind is not in control. *You* are in control of your mind. The Higher Self is in control. You can stop thinking those old thoughts. When your old thinking tries to come back and say, "It's so hard to change," take mental command. Say to your mind, "I now choose to believe it is becoming easy for me to make changes." You may have this conversation with your mind several times before it acknowledges that you are in charge and that you really mean what you say.

Imagine that your thoughts are like drops of water. One thought or one drop of water does not mean very much. As you repeat thoughts over and over, you first notice a stain on the carpet, then there is a little puddle, then a pond, and as these thoughts continue, they can become a lake, and finally an ocean. What kind of ocean are you creating? One that is polluted and toxic and unfit to swim in, or one that is crystal clear and blue and invites you to enjoy its refreshing waters?

People often tell me, "I can't stop thinking a thought." I always reply, "Yes, you can." Remember, how often have you refused to think a positive thought? You just have to tell your mind that that is what you are going to do. You have to make up your mind to stop thinking negatively. I'm not saying that you have to fight your thoughts when you want to change things. When the negative thoughts come up, simply say, "Thank you for sharing." In that way, you are not denying what is there, and you are not giving your power over to the negative thought. Tell yourself that you are not going to buy into the negativity anymore. You want to create another way of thinking. Again, you don't have to fight your thoughts. Acknowledge and go beyond them. Don't drown in a sea of your own negativity, when you can float on the ocean of life.

You are meant to be a wonderful, loving expression of life. Life is waiting for you to open up to it—to feel worthy of the good it holds for you. The wisdom and intelligence of the Universe is yours to use. Life is here to support you. Trust the Power within you to be there for you.

If you get scared, it is helpful to become aware of your breath as it flows in and out of your body. Your breath, the most precious substance of your life, is freely given to you. You have enough to last for as long as you live. You accept this precious substance without even thinking, and yet you doubt that life can supply you with the other necessities. Now is the time for you to learn about your own power and what you are capable of doing. Go within and find out who you are.

We all have different opinions. You have a right to yours and I have a right to mine. No matter what goes on in the world, the only thing you can work on is what is right for you. You have to get in touch with your inner guidance because it is the wisdom that knows the answers for you. It's not easy to listen to yourself when your friends and family are telling you what to do. Yet, all the answers to all the questions you are ever going to ask are within you now.

Every time you say, "I don't know," you shut the door to your own inner wisdom. The messages you get from your Higher Self are positive and supportive of you. If you start getting negative messages, then you are working from ego and your human mind level, and even perhaps your imagination, although positive messages often come to us through our imagination and our dreams.

Support yourself by making the right choices for you. When in doubt, ask yourself, *"Is this a decision that is loving for me? Is this right for me now?"* You may make another decision at some later point, a day, a week, or a month later. But ask yourself these questions in each moment.

As we learn to love ourselves and trust our Higher Power, we become co-creators with the Infinite Spirit of a loving world. Our love for ourselves moves us from being victims to being winners. Our love for ourselves attracts wonderful experiences to us. Have you ever noticed that people who feel good about themselves are naturally attractive? They usually have a quality about them that is just wonderful. They are happy with their lives. Things come to them easily and effortlessly.

I learned a long time ago that I am a being of oneness with the Presence and Power of God. Knowing this, that the wisdom and understanding of Spirit resides within me, and I am, therefore, divinely guided in all my dealings with others upon the planet. Just as all the stars and planets are in their perfect orbit, I am also in my divine right order. I may not understand everything with my limited human mind; however, on the cosmic level, I know I am in the right place, at the right time, doing the right thing. My present experience is a stepping stone to new awareness and new opportunities.

Who are you? What did you come here to learn? What did you come here to teach? We all have a unique purpose. We are more than our personalities, our problems, our fears, and our illnesses. We are far more than our bodies. We are all connected with everyone on the planet and with all of life. We are all spirit, light, energy, vibration, and love, and we all have the power to live our lives with purpose and meaning.

Chapter 2

Following My Inner Voice

*The thoughts we choose to think are
the tools we use to paint the canvas of
our lives.*

I remember when I first heard that I could change my life
if I was willing to change my thinking. It was quite a
revolutionary idea to me. I lived in New York and discovered the Church of Religious Science. (Often people
confuse the Church of Religious Science, or Science of
Mind, which was founded by Ernest Holmes, with the
Christian Science Church founded by Mary Baker Eddy.
They all reflect *new thought*; however, they are different
philosophies.)

The Science of Mind has ministers and practitioners
who carry on the teachings of the Church of Religious
Science (the Church). They were the very first people who
told me that my thoughts shaped my future. Even though
I didn't understand what they meant, this concept
touched what I call the *inner ding* within me, that place
of intuition that is referred to as the *voice within*. Over
the years, I've learned to follow it, because when that *ding*
goes "Yes," even if it seems a crazy choice, I know that
it's right for me.

So these concepts struck a cord in me. Something said, "Yes, they are right." And then I began the adventure of learning how to change my thinking. Once I accepted the idea and said "yes" to it, I went through the hows. I read a lot of books, and my home became like many of yours, filled with masses of spiritual and self-help books. I went to classes for many years, and I explored everything related to the subject. I literally immersed myself in *new thought* philosophy. It was the first time that I had really studied in my life. Up until then I didn't believe in anything. My mother was a lapsed Catholic, and my stepfather was an atheist. I had some strange idea that Christians either wore hair shirts or were eaten by lions, and neither appealed to me.

I really delved into the Science of Mind, because that was an avenue that was open for me at the time, and I found it really wonderful. At first it was sort of easy. I grasped a few concepts, and I started to think and talk a little bit differently. In those days I was a constant complainer and full of self-pity. I just loved to wallow in the pits. I didn't know that I was continually perpetuating more experiences in which to pity myself. But then again, I didn't know any better in those days. Gradually, I found that I was no longer complaining quite so much.

I started to listen to what I said. I became aware of my self-criticism, and I tried to stop it. I began to babble affirmations without quite knowing what they meant. I started with the easy ones, of course, and a few small changes began to take place. I got the green lights and the parking places, and boy, did I think I was hot stuff. Oh wow! I thought I knew it all, and I very soon became quite cocky and arrogant and dogmatic in my beliefs. I felt I knew all the answers. In hindsight, it was really my way of feeling safe in this new area.

When we start to move away from some of our old rigid beliefs, especially if we've previously been in total control, it can be very scary. It was very frightening for me, so I would grasp onto whatever would make me feel safe. It was a beginning for me, and I still had a long way to go. And still do.

Like most of us, I didn't always find the pathway easy and smooth because just babbling affirmations didn't work all the time, and I couldn't understand why. I asked myself, "What am I doing wrong?" Immediately, I blamed myself. Was this one more example of me not being good enough? That was a favorite old belief of mine.

At the time my teacher, Eric Pace, would look at me and refer to the idea of *resentment*. I didn't have the faintest idea what he was talking about. Resentment? Me? Surely, I didn't have any resentments. After all, I was on my pathway, I was spiritually perfect. How little I could see myself then!

I continued doing the best I could in my life. I studied metaphysics and spirituality and learned about myself as much as possible. I grasped what I could, and sometimes, I applied it. Often, we hear a lot of things, and sometimes we grasp them, but we don't always practice them. Time seemed to go by very quickly, and at that point, I had been studying Science of Mind for about three years and had become a practitioner of the Church. I began to teach the philosophy, but I wondered why my students seemed to be floundering. I couldn't understand why they were so stuck in their problems. I gave them so much good advice. Why weren't they using it and getting well? It never dawned on me that I was speaking the truth more than I was living it. I was like a parent who tells the child what to do but then does exactly the opposite.

Then one day, seemingly out of the blue, I was diagnosed with vaginal cancer. First, I panicked. Then, I had doubts that all this stuff I was learning was valid. It was a normal and natural reaction. I thought to myself, "If I was clear and centered, I wouldn't have the need to create the illness." In hindsight, I think when I was diagnosed, I felt safe enough at that point to let the illness surface so that I could do something about it, rather than having it be another hidden secret that I wouldn't know about until I was dead.

I knew too much by then to hide from myself any longer. I knew that cancer was a dis-ease of resentment that is held for a long time until it eats away at the body. When we stifle our emotions inside of us, they have to go somewhere in the body. If we spend a lifetime stuffing things down, they will eventually manifest somewhere in the body.

I became very aware that the resentment (which my teacher had referred to so many times) within me had to do with being physically, emotionally, and sexually abused as a child. Naturally, I would have resentment. I was bitter and unforgiving of the past. I had never done any work to change or release the bitterness and let it go. When I left home, it was all I could do to forget what happened to me; I thought I had put it behind me when in actuality I had simply buried it.

When I found my metaphysical pathway, I covered up my feelings with a nice layer of spirituality and hid a lot of garbage inside me. I put a wall around myself that kept me literally out of touch with my own feelings. I didn't know who I was or where I was. After my diagnosis, the real inner work of learning to know myself began. Thank God, I had tools to use. I knew I needed to go within myself if I was going to make any permanent changes. Yes, the doctor could give me an operation and perhaps take care of my illness for the moment, but if I didn't change the way I was using my thoughts and my words, I'd probably re-create it again.

It is always interesting to me to learn where in our bodies we put our cancers—on which side of the body are our tumors, the left or the right. The right side represents the masculine side, from where we give out. The left is the feminine side, the receptive part, from where we take in. Almost all of my life, when anything went wrong, it was always on the right side of my body. It was where I stored all the resentment toward my stepfather.

I was no longer content to get green lights and parking places. I knew that I had to go much, much deeper. I realized that I was not really progressing in my life the way

I wanted to because I hadn't really cleared out this old garbage from childhood, and I wasn't living what I was teaching. I had to recognize the inner child inside me and work with her. My inner child needed help because she was still in great pain.

I quickly began a self-healing program in earnest. I concentrated on *me* totally and did little else. I became very committed to getting well. Some of it was a little weird, yet I did it anyway. After all, this was my life on the line. It became almost a 24-hour-a-day job for the next six months. I began reading and studying everything I could find about alternative ways to heal cancer because I truly believed it could be done. I did a nutritional cleansing program that detoxified my body from all the junk foods I had eaten for years. For months, I seemed to be living on sprouts and pureed asparagus. I know I had more to eat, but that is what I remember the most.

I worked with my Science of Mind practitioner and teacher, Eric Pace, to clear the mental patterns so the cancer wouldn't return. I said affirmations and did visualizations and spiritual mind treatments. I did daily sessions in front of a mirror. The most difficult words to say were, "I love you, I really love you." It took a lot of tears and a lot of breathing to get through it. When I did, it was as if I took a quantum leap. I went to a good psychotherapist who was skilled in helping people express and release their anger. I spent a long period of time beating pillows and screaming. It was wonderful. It felt so good because I had never, ever had permission to do that in my life.

I don't know which method worked; maybe a little bit

of everything worked. Most of all I was really consistent with what I did. I practiced during all my waking hours. I thanked myself before I went to sleep for what I had done during the day. I affirmed that my healing process was taking place in my body while I slept, and that I would awaken in the morning bright and refreshed and feeling good. In the morning, I'd awaken and thank myself and my body for the work during the night. I would affirm that I was willing to grow and learn each day and make changes without seeing myself as a bad person.

I also worked on understanding and forgiveness. One of the ways was to explore my parents' childhoods as much as I could. I began to understand how they were treated as children, and I realized that because of the way they were brought up, they couldn't really have done anything differently than they did. My stepfather was abused at home, and he continued this abuse with his children. My mother was brought up to believe the man was always right and you stood by and let him do what he wanted. No one taught them a different approach. It was their way of life. Step by step, my growing understanding of them enabled me to start the forgiveness process.

The more I forgave my parents, the more willing I was to forgive myself. Forgiveness of ourselves is enormously important. Many of us do the same damage to the inner child that our parents did to us. We just continue the abuse, and it's very sad. When we were children and other people mistreated us, we didn't have many options, but when we grow up and we *still* mistreat the inner child, it's disastrous.

As I forgave myself, I began to trust myself. I found

that when we don't trust life or other people, it's really because we don't trust ourselves. We don't trust our Higher Selves to take care of us in all situations, so we say, "I'll never fall in love again because I don't want to get hurt," or "I'll never let this happen again." What we are really saying to ourselves is, "I don't trust you enough to take good care of me, so I'm going to stay away from everything."

Eventually, I began to trust myself enough to take care of me, and I found it easier and easier to love myself once I trusted myself. My body was healing, and my heart was healing.

My spiritual growth had come in such an unexpected way.

As a bonus, I began to look younger. The clients I now attracted were almost all people who were willing to work on themselves. They made enormous progress without me really saying anything. They could sense and feel that I was living the concepts I was teaching, and it was easy for them to accept these ideas. Of course, they had positive results. They began to improve the quality of their lives. Once we begin to make peace with ourselves on the inner level, life seems to flow much more pleasantly.

So what did this experience teach me personally? I realized that I had the power to change my life if I was willing to change my thinking and release the patterns that kept me living in the past. This experience gave me the inner knowledge that if we are really willing to do the work, we can make incredible changes in our minds, our bodies, and our lives.

No matter where you are in life, no matter what you've contributed to creating, no matter what's happening, you are always doing the best you can with the understanding and awareness and knowledge that you have. And when you know more, you will do it differently, as I did. Don't berate yourself for where you are. Don't blame yourself for not doing it faster or better. Say to yourself, "I'm doing the best I can, and even though I'm in a pickle now, I will get out of it somehow, so let's find the best way to do it." If all you do is tell yourself that you're stupid and no good, then you stay stuck. You need your own loving support if you want to make changes.

The methods I use are not my methods. Most of them I learned at Science of Mind, which is what I basically teach. Yet these principles are as old as time. If you read any of the old spiritual teachings you will find the same messages. I am trained as a minister of the Church of Religious Science; however, I do not have a church. I am a free spirit. I express the teachings in simple language so that they reach many people. This path is a wonderful way of getting your head together and really understanding what life is all about, and how you can use your mind to take charge of your life. When I started all this 20 or so years ago, I had no idea that I would be able to bring hope and help to the number of people that I do today.

Chapter 3

The Power of Your Spoken Word

*Every day declare for yourself what
you want in life. Declare it as though
you have it!*

The Law of Mind

There is a law of gravity, and there are several other physical laws, like physics and electricity, most of which I
don't understand. There are also spiritual laws, like the
law of cause and effect: *what you give out comes back.*
There is also a law of mind. I don't know how it works,
in much the same way that I don't know how electricity
works. I only know that when I flick the switch, the light
comes on.

I believe that when we think a thought or when we
speak a word or sentence, it somehow goes out from us
into a law of mind and comes back to us as experience.

We are now beginning to learn the correlation between
the mental and the physical. We are beginning to understand how the mind works and that our thoughts are creative. Our thoughts speed through our minds very quickly,
so it is difficult to shape them at first. Our mouths, on the

other hand, are slower. So if we can start editing our speech by listening to what we say and not letting negative things come out of our mouths, then we can begin to shape our thoughts.

There is tremendous power in our spoken words, and many of us are not aware just how important they are. Let us consider words as the foundation of what we continually create in our lives. We use words all the time, yet we babble away, seldom thinking about what we are truly saying or how we are saying it. We pay very little attention to the selection of our words. In fact, most of us speak in negatives.

As children we were taught grammar. We were taught to select words according to these rules of grammar. However, I have always found that the rules of grammar continually change, and what was improper at one time is proper at another time, or vice versa. What was slang in the past is considered common usage in the present. However, grammar does not take into consideration the meaning of words and how they affect our lives.

On the other hand, I was not taught in school that my choice of words would have anything to do with what I would experience in life. No one taught me that my thoughts were creative, or that they could literally shape my life. Nobody taught me that what I gave out in the form of words would return to me as experiences. The purpose of the golden rule was to show us a very basic law of life: *"Do unto others as you would do unto yourself."* What you give out comes back to you. It was never meant to cause guilt. No one ever taught me that I was worth loving or that I deserved good. And nobody taught me that life was here to support me.

I remember that as children, we would often call each other cruel and hurtful names and try to belittle one another. But why did we? Where did we learn such behavior? Look at what we were taught. Many of us were told repeatedly by our parents that we were stupid or dumb or lazy. We were a nuisance and not good enough. Sometimes we heard our parents say that they wished we had never been born. Maybe we cringed when we heard these words, but little did we realize how deeply imbedded the hurt and pain would become.

Changing Our Self-Talk

Too often, we accepted the early messages that our parents gave us. We heard, "Eat your spinach," "Clean your room," or "Make your bed," in order to be loved. You got the idea that you were only acceptable if you did certain things—that acceptance and love were conditional. However, that was according to somebody's idea of what was worthwhile and had nothing to do with your deep, inner self-worth. You got the idea that you could only exist if you did these things to please others, otherwise you did not have permission to even exist.

These early messages contribute to what I call our *self-talk*—the way we talk to ourselves. The way we talk to ourselves inwardly is really important because it becomes the basis of our spoken words. It sets up the mental atmosphere in which we operate and which attracts to us our experiences. If we belittle ourselves, life is going to mean very little to us. If we love and appreciate ourselves, then life can be a wonderful, joyous gift.

If our lives are unhappy, or if we are feeling unfulfilled, it's very easy to blame our parents, or *them*, and say it's all *their* fault. However, if we do, we stay stuck in our conditions, our problems, and our frustrations. Words of blame will not bring us freedom. Remember, there is power in our words. Again, our power comes from taking responsibility for our lives. I know it sounds scary to be responsible for our lives, but we really are, whether we accept it or not. If we want to be responsible for our lives, we've got to be responsible for our mouths. The words and phrases we say are extensions of our thoughts.

Start to listen to what you say. If you hear yourself using negative or limiting words, change them. If I hear a negative story, I don't go around repeating it to everyone. I think it has gone far enough, and I let it go. If I hear a positive story, however, I will tell everyone.

When you are out with other people, begin to listen to what they say and how they say it. See if you can connect what they say with what they are experiencing in life. Many, many people live their lives in *shoulds*. *Should* is a word that my ear is very attuned to. It is as if a bell goes off every time I hear it. Often, I will hear people use a dozen *shoulds* in a paragraph. These same people wonder why their lives are so rigid or why they can't move out of a situation. They want a lot of control over things that they cannot control. They are either making themselves wrong or making someone else wrong. And then they question why they aren't living lives of freedom.

We can also remove the expression *have to* from our vocabulary and our thinking as well. When we do, we will release a lot of self-imposed pressure on ourselves. We create tremendous pressure by saying, "I have to go to work. I have to do this. I have to . . . I have to . . . "Instead, let's begin to say, *choose to*. "I choose to go to work because it pays the rent right now." *Choose to* puts a whole different perspective on our lives. Everything we do is by choice even though it may not seem to be so.

A lot of us also use the word *but*. We make statements, then we say *but*, which heads us in two different directions. We give conflicting messages to ourselves. Listen to how you use the word *but* the next time you speak.

Another expression we need to be mindful of is *don't forget*. We're so used to saying, "Don't forget this or that," and what happens? We forget. We really want to remember and instead we forget, so we can begin to use the phrase *please remember* in place of *don't forget*.

When you wake up in the morning, do you curse the fact that you have to go to work? Do you complain about the weather? Do you grumble that your back or head hurts? What is the second thing and the third thing you think or say? Do you yell at the children to get up? Most people say more or less the same thing every morning. How does what you say start your day? Is it positive and cheerful and wonderful? Or is it whining and condemning? If you grumble and complain and moan, you're setting yourself up for such a day.

What are your last thoughts before going to bed? Are they powerful healing thoughts or poverty worry thoughts? When I speak of poverty thoughts, I don't only mean about the lack of money. It can be a negative way of thinking about anything in your life—any part of your life that is not flowing freely. Do you worry about tomorrow? Usually, I will read something positive before I go to sleep. I am aware that when I sleep I am doing a lot of clearing that will prepare me for the next day.

I find it very helpful to turn over to my dreams any problems or questions I may have. I know my dreams will help me take care of whatever is going on in my life.

I am the only person who can think in my mind, just like you are the only person who can think in your mind. Nobody can force us to think in a different way. We choose our thoughts, and these are the basis for our *self-talk*. As I experienced how this process worked more in my life, I began to live more of what I was teaching others. I really watched my words and my thoughts, and I constantly forgave myself for not being perfect. I allowed myself to be me, rather than struggling to be a super person who may only be acceptable in others' eyes.

When I began for the first time to trust life and to see it as a friendly place, I lightened up. My humor became less biting and more truly funny. I worked on releasing criticism and judgment of myself and other people, and I stopped telling disaster stories. We are so quick to spread bad news. It's just amazing. I stopped reading the newspaper and gave up the 11 o'clock news at night, because all the reports were concerned with disaster and violence and very little good news. I realized that most people don't want to hear good news. They love to hear bad news, so they have something to complain about. Too many of us keep recycling the negative stories until we believe that there is only bad in the world. For awhile there was a radio station that broadcast only good news. It went out of business.

When I had my cancer, I decided to stop gossiping, and to my surprise, I found I had nothing to say to anyone. I became aware that whenever I met a friend, I would immediately dish the latest dirt with them. Eventually, I discovered there were other ways of talking, although it wasn't an easy habit to break. Nonetheless, if I gossiped about other people, then other people probably gossiped about me, because what we give out we get back.

As I worked more and more with people, I really began to listen to what they said. I really began to hear the words, not just get the general drift. Usually, after ten minutes with a new client, I could tell exactly why they had a problem because I could hear the words they were using. I could understand them by the way they were talking. I knew that their words were contributing to their problems. If they were talking negatively, imagine what their *self-talk* was like? It must be more of the same negative programming—poverty thinking—as I called it.

A little exercise I suggest you do is to put a tape recorder by your telephone, and every time you make or get a call, push the record button. When the tape is full on both sides, listen to what you have been saying and how you say it. You will probably be amazed. You will begin to hear the words you use and the inflection of your voice. You will begin to become aware. If you find yourself saying something three times or more, write it down because it is a pattern. Some of the patterns may be positive and supportive, and you also may have some very negative patterns that you repeat over and over and over again.

The Power of the Subconscious Mind

In light of what I've been speaking of, I want to discuss the power of our subconscious minds. Our subconscious minds make no judgments. The subconscious mind accepts everything we say and creates according to our beliefs. It always says *yes*. Our subconscious minds love us enough to give us what we declare. We have choice, though. If we choose these poverty beliefs and concepts, then it is assumed that we want them. It will continue to give us these things until we are willing to change our thoughts and words and beliefs for the better. We are never stuck because we can always choose again. There are billions and billions of thoughts from which to choose.

Our subconscious minds don't know true from false or right from wrong. We don't want to deprecate ourselves in any way. We don't want to say something like, "Oh stupid, old me," because the subconscious mind will pick this *self-talk* up, and after a while you will feel that way.

If you say it enough times, it will become a belief in your subconscious.

The subconscious mind has no sense of humor, and it is important for you to know and understand this concept. You cannot make a joke about yourself and think it doesn't mean anything. If it is a put-down about yourself, even if you are trying to be cute or funny about it, the subconscious mind accepts it as true. I don't let people tell put-down jokes in my workshops. They can be raunchy but not put-downs of a nationality or sex or whatever.

So don't joke about yourself and make derogatory remarks about yourself because they will not create good experiences for you. Don't belittle others either. The subconscious mind doesn't distinguish between you and the other person. It hears the words, and it believes you are talking about yourself. The next time you want to criticize someone, ask why you feel that way about yourself. You only see in others what you see in yourself. Instead of criticizing others, praise them, and within a month, you will see enormous change within you.

Our words are really a matter of approach and attitude. Notice the way that lonely, unhappy, poor, sick people talk. What words do they use? What have they accepted as the truth for themselves? How do they describe themselves? How do they describe their work, their lives, their relationships? What do they look forward to? Be aware of their words, but please don't run around telling strangers that they are ruining their lives by the way they talk. Don't do it to your family and friends either because the information will not be appreciated. Instead, use this information to begin to make the connection for yourself, and practice it if you want your life to change, because even on the smallest level, if you change the way you talk, your experiences are going to change.

If you are a person with an illness who believes that it is fatal and that you are going to die and that life is no good because nothing ever works for you, then guess what?

You can choose to release your negative concept of life. Start affirming for yourself that you are a person who is lovable, and you are worth healing, and that you attract everything you need on the physical level to contribute to your healing. Know that you are willing to get well and that it is safe for you to get well.

Many people only feel safe when they are sick. They are usually the kind that have difficulty saying the word *no*. The only way they can say *no* is by saying, "I'm too sick to do it." It's a perfect excuse. I remember a woman at one of my workshops who had three cancer operations. She couldn't say *no* to anybody. Her father was a doctor, and she was Daddy's good little girl, so whatever daddy told her to do, she did. It was impossible for her to say *no*. No matter what you asked her, she had to say *yes*. It took four days to get her to literally shriek "No!" at the top of her lungs. I had her do it while shaking her fist. "No! No! No!" Once she got into it, she loved it.

I find that many women with breast cancer can't say *no*. They nourish everybody except themselves. One of the things I recommend to a woman with breast cancer is that she must learn to say, "No, I don't want to do it. No!" Two or three months of saying *no* to everything will begin to turn things around. She needs to nourish herself by saying, "This is what *I* want to do, not what *you* want me to do!"

When I used to work with clients privately, I would hear them argue on behalf of their limitations, and they would always want me to know why they were stuck because of one reason or another. If we believe we are stuck and accept that we are stuck, then we are stuck. We get "stuck" because our negative beliefs are being fulfilled. Instead, let's begin to focus on our strengths.

Many of you tell me that my tapes saved your lives. I want you to realize that no book or tape is going to save you. A little piece of tape in a plastic box is not saving your life. What you are doing with the information is what matters. I can give you plenty of ideas, yet what you do with them is going to count. I suggest that you listen to a particular tape over and over again for a month or more so that the ideas become a new habit pattern. I'm not your healer or savior. The only person who is going to make a change in your life is *you*.

Now, what are the messages you want to hear? I know I say this over and over again—*loving yourself is the most important thing you can do, because when you love yourself, you are not going to hurt yourself or anyone else.* It's the prescription for world peace. If I don't hurt me and I don't hurt you, how can we have war? The more of us who can get to that place, the better the planet will be. Let's begin to be conscious of what is going on by listening to the words we speak to ourselves and others. Then we can begin to make the changes that will help heal ourselves as well as the rest of the planet.

Chapter 4

Reprogramming Old Tapes

Be willing to take the first step, no
matter how small it is. Concentrate on
the fact that you are willing to learn.
Absolute miracles will happen.

Affirmations Do Work

Now that we understand a little bit more about how powerful our thoughts and words are, we have to retrain our thinking and speaking into positive patterns if we are going to get beneficial results. Are you willing to change your *self-talk* into positive affirmations? Remember, every time you think a thought, and every time you speak a word, you are saying an affirmation.

An affirmation is a beginning point. It opens the way to change. In essence you are saying to your subconscious mind, "I am taking responsibility. I am aware that there is something I can do to change." When I talk about *doing affirmations,* I mean to consciously choose sentences or words that will either help to eliminate something from your life or help to create something new in your life, and you do this in a positive way. If you say, "I don't want to be sick anymore," the subconscious mind hears *sick more.* You have to tell it clearly what you do want. That is, say: *'I am feeling wonderfully well. I radiate good health."*

The subconscious mind is very straightforward. It has no strategy or designs. What it hears is what it does. If you say, "I hate this car," it doesn't give you a wonderful new car, because it doesn't know what you want. Even if you get a new car, you will probably hate it soon, because that is what you have been saying about it. The subconscious only hears, *hate this car.* You need to clearly declare your desires in a positive way, as in: *'I have a beautiful new car that suits all my needs."*

If there is something in your life that you really dislike, I have found one of the quickest ways to release it is to *bless it with love. "I bless you with love and I release you and let you go."* This works for people, situations, objects, and living quarters. You could even try it on a habit you would like to be free of and see what happens. I had one man who said, "I bless you with love and release you from my life," to every cigarette he smoked. After a few days his desire for smoking was considerably less and in a few weeks the habit was gone.

You Deserve Good

Think for a moment. What is it you really want right now? What is it you want today in your life? Think about it, and then say, "I accept for myself _____ (whatever it is you want). This is where I find that most of us get stuck.

The bottom line is the belief that we don't deserve to have what we want. Our personal power lies in the way we perceive our deservability. Our not deserving comes from childhood messages. Again, we don't have to feel that we cannot change because of these messages. Often times, people will come up to me and say, "Louise, affirmations don't work." It really has nothing to do with the affirmations; it is the fact that we don't believe we deserve the good.

The way to find out if you believe that you deserve something is to say an affirmation and notice the thoughts that come up as you say it. Then write them down, because when you see them on paper, they will be very clear to you. The only thing that keeps you from deserving, or loving yourself, or whatever, is someone else's belief or opinion that you have accepted as truth.

When we don't believe that we deserve good, we will knock the pinnings out from under ourselves, which we can do in a variety of ways. We can create chaos, we can lose things, we can hurt ourselves, or have physical problems like falling, or have accidents. We have to start believing that we deserve all the good that life has to offer.

In order to reprogram the false or negative belief, what would be the first thought that you would need to begin to create this new "whatever" in your life? What would be the building block or the foundation that you would need to stand on? What would be the sort of thing that you would need to know for yourself? To believe? To accept?

Some good thoughts to start with would be:

- *"I am worthwhile."*
- *"I am deserving."*
- *"I love myself."*
- *"I allow myself to be fulfilled."*

These concepts form the very basis of beliefs on which you can build. Do your affirmations on top of these building blocks to create what you want.

Whenever I speak somewhere, somebody will come up at the end of the lecture or will write me a letter and tell me that he or she has had a healing take place while he or she was in the room. Sometimes it's very minor, and sometimes it's quite dramatic. A woman came up to me recently and told me that she had a lump in her breast, and it literally disappeared during the lecture. She heard something, and she decided to let something go. This is a good example of how powerful we are. When we are not ready to let something go, when we really want to hold on to something because it is serving us in some way, it doesn't matter what we do, it probably won't work. However, when we are ready to let it go, as this woman was, it's amazing how the smallest circumstance can help us release it.

If you still have a habit that you haven't released, ask yourself how it serves you. What do you get out of it? If you can't get an answer, ask in a different way. "If I no longer had this habit, what would happen?" Very often the answer is, "My life would be better." It comes back to the fact that we believe we don't deserve a better life in some way.

Ordering from the Cosmic Kitchen

When you first say an affirmation, it may not seem true. But remember, affirmations are like planting seeds in the ground. When you put a seed in the ground, you don't get a full-grown plant the next day. We need to be patient during the growing season. As you continue to say the affirmation, either you will be ready to release whatever you don't want, and the affirmation will become true; or it will open a new avenue to you. Or, you may get a brilliant brainstorm, or a friend may call you and say, "Have you ever tried this?" You will be led to the next step that will help you.

Keep your affirmations in the present tense. You can sing them and make a jingle out of them so they repeat over and over in your head. Remember that you cannot affect a specific person's actions with your affirmations. To affirm that "John is now in love with me," is a form of manipulation, and it is trying to have control over another persons' life. It will usually have a boomerang effect on you. You will become very unhappy when you don't get what you want. You can say, "I am now loved by a wonderful man who is . . . . ," and list the qualities you want in the relationship. That way you allow the Power within you to bring to you the perfect person to fill that bill, who may possibly be John.

You don't know what another person's spiritual lesson is, and you don't have a right to interfere in their life process. You certainly wouldn't want someone else doing it to you. If someone is ill, bless them and send them love and peace, don't demand that they get well.

I like to think of doing affirmations as placing our order in the *cosmic kitchen*. If you go to a restaurant and the waiter or waitress comes and takes your order, you don't follow them into the kitchen to see if the chef got the order or how he is going to prepare the food. You sit and drink your water or coffee or tea or you talk to your friend, and maybe eat your roll. You assume that your food is being prepared and will be out when it is ready. It's the same when we begin to do affirmations.

When we put our order into the *cosmic kitchen,* the great chef, our Higher Power, is working on it. So you go on with your life and know it is being taken care of. It's on order. It's happening. Now if the food comes out and it isn't what you ordered, and if you have self-esteem, you will send it back. If not, you will eat it. You also have a right to do that with the *cosmic kitchen*. If you don't get exactly what you want, you can say, "No, that's not quite it; this is what I want." Perhaps, you weren't clear in your ordering.

The idea here, too, is to let go. At the end of my treatments and meditations, I use the words, *And so it is*. It is a way of saying, "Higher Power, it's in your hands now, I release it to you." Spiritual mind treatment, which is taught by the Science of Mind, is very effective. You can obtain more information about it through your local Religious Science Church or through books by Ernest Holmes.

Reprogramming the Subconscious Mind

The thoughts we think accumulate, and when we are unaware, the old thought resurfaces. When we are reprogramming our minds, it is normal and natural that we go a little forward, we come a little back, and we go a little forward again. It is part of practicing. I don't think there is any new skill that you can learn absolutely 100 percent in the first 20 minutes.

Do you remember when you first learned how to use a computer, how frustrating it was? It took practice. You had to learn how it worked, to learn its laws and systems. I called my first computer my Magic Lady, for when I mastered her rules she did indeed deliver what seemed like magic to me. Yet, while I was learning, the way she would teach me I was off track or going in the wrong direction, was to devour pages of work that I would then have to do over again. Out of all the mistakes, I learned how to flow with the system.

To flow with the system of Life, you want to become aware that your subconscious mind is like a computer—garbage in, garbage out. If you put negative thoughts in, then negative experiences come out. Yes, it takes time and practice to learn the new ways of thinking. Be patient with yourself. When you are learning something new, and the old pattern returns, are you going to say, "Oh, I didn't learn anything?" Or are you going to say, "Okay, that's all right, come on, let's do it again the new way."

Or, say you cleared an issue and think you'll never have to deal with it again. How do you know if you've really worked it through unless you test yourself? So, you bring up the old situation one more time and watch how you react. If you jump right back into the old way of reacting to it, then you know you haven't really learned that particular lesson, and you need to do more work on it. That's all it means. You have to realize it's a little test to see how far you've come. If you begin to repeat your affirmations, the new statements of truth about yourself, you give yourself an opportunity to react differently. Whether it's a health problem, a financial one, or a relationship difficulty, if you react in a new way to the situation, then you're on your way to having another issue handled, and you can move on to other areas.

Remember, too, that we work on layers at a time. You can reach a plateau and think, "I've done it!" And then some old issue resurfaces and you injure yourself, or get sick, and you don't get better for some time. Look to see what the underlying beliefs are. It may mean you have some more work to do because you are going to the next deeper layer.

Don't feel that you *are not good enough*, because something you have worked to clear comes up again. When I discovered that I was not a *bad person* because once again

I was facing an old issue, it became much easier for me to keep going. I learned to say to myself, "Louise, you are doing very well. Look how far you have come. You just need more practice. And I love you."

I believe each one of us decides to incarnate upon this planet at particular points in time and space. We have chosen to come here to learn a particular lesson that will advance us on our spiritual, evolutionary pathway.

One of the ways to allow the process of life to unfold for you in a positive, healthy way is to declare your own personal truths. Choose to move away from the limiting beliefs that have been denying you the benefits you so desire. Declare that your negative thought patterns will be erased from your mind. Let go of your fears and burdens. For a long time now, I have been believing the following ideas, and they have worked for me:

- *"Everything I need to know is revealed to me."*
- *"Everything I need comes to me in the perfect time-space sequence."*
- *"Life is a joy and filled with love."*
- *"I am loving and lovable and loved."*
- *"I am healthy and filled with energy."*
- *"I prosper wherever I turn."*
- *"I am willing to change and to grow,"* and
- *"All is well in my world."*

I have learned that we don't always stay positive 100 percent of the time, and I include myself in this knowledge. As much as possible, I see life as a wonderful joyous experience. I believe that I am safe. I have made it a personal law for me.

I believe that everything I need to know is revealed to me, so I need to keep my eyes and ears open. When I had cancer, I remember thinking that a foot reflexologist would be very helpful for me. One evening I went to a lecture of some sort. Usually I sit in the front row because I like being close to the speaker; however that night I was compelled to sit in the back row. Right after I sat down, a foot reflexologist sat next to me. We began to talk and I learned that he even made house calls. I didn't have to look for him, he came to me.

I also believe that whatever I need comes to me in the perfect time-space sequence. When something goes wrong in my life, I immediately start to think, "All is well, it's okay, I know that this is all right. It's a lesson, an experience, and I'll pass through it. There is something here that is for my highest good. All is well. Just breathe. It's okay." I do the best I can to calm myself, so I can think rationally about whatever is going on, and, of course, I do work through everything. It may take a little time, but sometimes, things that seem to be great disasters really turn out to be quite good in the end, or at least, not the disasters that they seemed to be in the beginning. Every event is a learning experience.

I do a lot of positive *self-talk,* morning, noon and night. I come from a loving space of the heart, and I practice loving myself and others as much as I possibly can.

My love expands all the time. What I do today is much more than what I was doing six months or a year ago. I know a year from now my consciousness and my heart will have expanded, and I'll be doing more. I know that what I believe about myself becomes true for me, so I choose to believe wonderful things about myself. There was a time when I didn't, so I know I have grown, and I continue to work on myself.

I also believe in meditation. To me, meditation is when we sit down and turn off our inner dialogue long enough to hear our own wisdom. When I meditate, I usually close my eyes, take a deep breath and ask: *'What is it I need to know?'* I sit and listen. I might also ask, *'What is it I need to learn?'* or *'What is the lesson in this?'* Sometimes, we think we're supposed to *fix* everything in our lives, and maybe we're really only supposed to *learn* something from the situation.

When I first began to meditate, I had violent headaches the first three weeks. Meditation was so unfamiliar and against all my usual inner programming. Nevertheless, I hung in there, and the headaches eventually disappeared.

If you are constantly coming up with a tremendous amount of negativity when you meditate, it may mean that it *needs* to come up, and when you quiet yourself, it starts to flow to the surface. Simply see the negativity being released. Try not to fight it. Allow it to continue as long as it needs to.

If you fall asleep when you meditate, that's all right. Let the body do what it needs to do, it will balance out in time.

Reprogramming your negative beliefs is very powerful. A good way to do it is by making a tape *with your own voice* saying your affirmations. Play it as you go to sleep. It will have a great deal of value for you because you will be listening to your own voice. An even more powerful tape would be your mother's voice telling you how wonderful you are and how much she loves you. Once you have the tape, it's good to relax the body before you begin reprogramming. Some people like to start from the tips of their toes and move up to the top of their head, tensing and relaxing. However you do it, release the tension. Let the emotions go. Get to a state of openness and receptivity. The more relaxed you are, the easier it is to receive the new information. Remember, you are always in charge, and you are always safe.

It is wonderful to listen to tapes or read self-awareness books, and do your affirmations. But, what are you doing for the other 23 hours and 30 minutes of the day? You see, that is what really matters. If you sit down and meditate and then get up and rush to work and scream at someone, that counts, too. Meditation and affirmations are wonderful, yet the other times are just as important.

Treat Doubt as a Friendly Reminder

I am often asked questions about whether people are doing affirmations correctly or whether they are even working. I'd like you to think of *doubt* a little differently than you may have been. I believe that the subconscious mind resides in the solar plexus area of the body, where you carry those *gut feelings*. When something sudden happens don't you immediately get a strong feeling in your gut? It is where you take everything in and store it.

Ever since we were little children, every message we have received, everything we have done, all the experiences we have had, all that we have said, have all gone into the filing cabinet right there in the solar plexus area. I like to think that there are little messengers in there, and when we think thoughts or have experiences, the messages go in, and the messengers file them in the appropriate files. For many of us we have been building up files labeled: *I'm not good enough. I'll never make it. I don't do it right.* We have gotten absolutely buried under these files. Suddenly we do affirmations such as: *I'm wonderful and I love myself.* The messengers pick them up and say, "What's this??? Where does it go? We've never seen this one before!"

So the messengers call *Doubt*. "Doubt! Come over here and see what's going on." So *Doubt* picks up the message and asks the conscious mind, "What's this? You have always been saying these other things." On a conscious level we can react in two ways. We can say, "Oh you're right, I'm terrible. I'm no good. I'm sorry. That's not the right message," and go back to our old ways. Or we can say to *Doubt*, "That was the old message. I have no need for it now. This is the new message." Tell *Doubt* to start a new file because there will be lots of these loving messages coming through from now on. Learn to treat doubt as a friend, not the enemy, and thank it for questioning you.

It doesn't matter what you do in this world. It doesn't matter if you are a bank president or a dishwasher, a housewife or a sailor. You have wisdom inside of you that is connected to Universal Truth. When you are willing to look within and ask a simple question such as, "What is this experience trying to teach me?" and if you are willing to listen, then you will have the answer. Most of us are so busy running around creating the soap opera and drama we call our lives that we don't hear anything.

Don't give your power over to other people's pictures of right and wrong. They only have power over us when we give our power to them. Groups of people give their power over to others. It happens in a lot of cultures. Women in our culture give their power to men. They say things like, "My husband won't allow me to." Well that's certainly giving your power away. If you believe it, you box yourself into a place where you can't do anything unless you are given permission by another person. The more open-minded you are, the more you learn, and the more you can grow and change.

A woman once shared with me that when she got married she was very unassertive because that was the way she was brought up. It took years for her to realize that her conditioning kept her locked in a corner. She blamed everyone—her husband and her in-laws—for her problems. Eventually, she divorced her husband, however, she still blamed him for so many things that were not right in her life. It took her ten years to relearn her patterns and to take her power back. In hindsight, she realized that *she* was responsible for not speaking up and for not standing up for herself—not her husband or her in-laws. They were there to reflect back to her what she felt inside—a sense of powerlessness.

Don't give your power away based on what you read either. I remember years ago I read some articles in a well known magazine and I happened to know something about each subject described in the articles. In my opinion, the information was totally erroneous. The magazine lost all credibility for me, and I didn't read it again for many years. You are the authority in your life, so don't think that because something is in print that it's always the truth.

Inspirational speaker Terry Cole-Whittaker wrote a wonderful book called *What You Think Of Me Is None Of My Business*. It's true. What you think of me *is* none of my business—it's *your* business. In the end, what you think of me is going out from you in vibrations and will come back.

When we have illumination, when we become conscious of what we are doing, we can begin to change our lives. Life is really here for *you*. You need only ask. Tell life what you want, and then allow the good to happen.

PART TWO

Dissolving the Barriers

We want to know what is going on inside us, so we can know what to let go. Instead of hiding our pain, we can release it totally.

Chapter 5

Understanding the Blocks That Bind You

Chronic patterns of self-hate, guilt, and self-criticism raise the body's stress levels and weaken the immune system.

Now that we understand a little more about the power that we have within us, let's take a look at what keeps us from using it. I think that almost all of us have barriers of some kind or another. Even when we do a lot of work on ourselves, and clear out the blocks, new layers of old barriers still keep coming up.

Many of us feel so flawed that we believe that we are not good enough and never will be. And, if we find something wrong with us, then we are going to find something wrong with other people as well. If we are still continuing to say, "I can't do this because my mother said . . . , or my father said . . . ," then we have not yet grown up.

So now you want to let your barriers go, and perhaps learn something different that you didn't know before now. Perhaps one sentence here will trigger a new thought.

Can you imagine how wonderful it would be if every day you learned a new idea that would help you let go of the past and create harmony in your life? When you become aware and understand the individual process of life, you will know what direction to take. If you put your energies into learning about yourself, you will eventually see those problems and issues that you need to dissolve.

We all have challenges in life. Everybody does. Nobody goes through life without them; otherwise, what would be the purpose of coming to this particular school called Earth? For some, there are health challenges, and for other people there are relationship challenges, or career or financial challenges. Some have a little or a lot of everything.

I think one of our biggest problems is that most of us haven't the faintest idea of what it is we want to let go. We know what is not working and we know what we want in our life, yet we don't know what's holding us back. So let's take this time to look at the blocks that bind us.

If you think for a moment about your own patterns and problems and the things that hold you back, which categories do they fall into—*criticism, fear, guilt, or resentment*? I call these categories, *The Big Four*. Which is your favorite one? Mine was a combination of criticism and resentment. Maybe you are like me and have two or three. Is it fear that always comes up, or guilt? Are you very, very critical or resentful? Let me point out that resentment is anger that is stuffed down. So if you believe you are not allowed to express your anger, then you have stored a lot of resentment.

We cannot deny our feelings. We cannot conveniently ignore them. When I had my cancer diagnosis, I had to look very clearly at myself. I had to acknowledge some nonsense that I didn't want to admit about myself. For instance, I was a very resentful person, and I carried a lot of bitterness from the past. I said, "Louise, you have no time to indulge in that anymore. You really must change." Or as Peter Mc Williams says, "You can no longer afford the luxury of a negative thought."

Your experiences always reflect your inner beliefs. You can literally look at your experiences and determine what your beliefs are. Maybe it's disturbing to consider, but if you look at the people in your life, they are all mirroring some belief you have about yourself. If you are always being criticized at work, it is probably because you are critical and have become the parent who once criticized the child. Everything in our lives is a mirror of who we are. When something is happening out there that is not comfortable, we have an opportunity to look inside and say, "How am I contributing to this experience? What is it within me that believes I deserve this?"

We all have family patterns, and it is very easy for us to blame our parents, or our childhood, or our environment, but that keeps us stuck. We don't become free. We remain victims, and we perpetuate the same problems over and over again.

So it really doesn't matter what anybody else did to you or what they taught you in the past. Today is a new day. You are now in charge. Now is the moment in which you are creating the future in your life and your world. It really doesn't matter what I say either, because only *you* can do the work. Only you can change the way you think and feel and act. I'm just saying that you *can*. You definitely can because you have a Higher Power within you that can help break you free from these patterns if you allow It.

You can remind yourself that when you were a little baby, you loved yourself for who you were. There is not one little baby who criticizes its body and thinks, "Oh, my hips are too big." Babies are thrilled and delighted just because they have bodies. They express their feelings. When a baby is happy, you know it, and when a baby is angry, the whole neighborhood knows it. They are never afraid to let people know how they feel. They live in the moment. You were like that once. As you grew up, you listened to people around you, and learned about fear and guilt and criticism from them.

If you grew up in a family where criticism was the norm, then you are going to be critical as an adult. If you grew up in a family where you were not allowed to express anger, then you are probably terrified of anger and confrontation, and you swallow it and let it reside in your body.

If you were raised in a family where everybody was manipulated by guilt, then you are probably going to be the same way as an adult. You are probably a person who runs around saying "I'm sorry" all the time, and can never ask for anything outright. You feel you have to be manipulative in some way in order to get what you want.

As we grow up, we begin to pick up these false ideas and lose touch with our inner wisdom. So we really need to release these ideas and return to the purity of spirit where we truly love ourselves. We need to re-establish the wonderful innocence of life and the moment-by-moment joy of existence, the same joy that a baby feels in its blissful state of wonder.

Think of what you want to become true for yourself. State them in positive, not negative affirmations. Now, go to the mirror and repeat your affirmations. See what obstacles are in your way. When you begin to state an affirmation like, *"I love and approve of myself,"* really pay attention to what negative messages come up because as you recognize them they become the treasures that will unlock the door to your freedom. Usually, the messages are one of the four I mentioned earlier—criticism, fear, guilt, or resentment. And, most likely you learned these messages from people "back there."

Some of you have chosen some difficult tasks to handle in this lifetime, and it is my belief that we really come here to love ourselves in spite of what *they* say or do. We can always go beyond our parents' or our friends' limitations. If you were a good little girl or boy, you learned your parents' limited way of looking at life. You see, you are not bad; you are ideal children. You learned exactly what your parents taught you. Now that you are grown up, you're doing the same thing. How many of you hear yourself saying what your parents used to say? Congratulations! They were very good teachers and you were very good students, but now it is time for you to begin to think for yourself.

A lot of us may face resistance when we look in the mirror and repeat our affirmations. However, resistance is the first step to change. Most of us want our lives to change, but when we are told that we have to do something different, we say, "Who me? I don't want to do that."

Others may experience feelings of despair. Often, if you look at the mirror and say, "I love you," the little child inside says, "Where have you been all this time? I've been waiting for you to notice me." Waves of sadness come up because you have been rejecting the little child for a long, long time.

When I did this exercise in one of my workshops, a woman said she was very, very scared. I asked her what frightened her, and she shared the fact that she was an incest survivor. Many of us have had this experience called incest and we are learning to come through it. It's interesting that it occurs so often on our planet. We read so much about incest these days, yet I don't think it is happening any more now than it ever did. We have advanced to a state where we now feel that children have rights and we are allowing ourselves to see this ugly sore in society. In order to release the problem, we have to first recognize it and then we can work through it.

Therapy is so important for incest survivors. We need a safe space where we can work through these feelings. When we have let the anger and rage and shame out then we move to the space where we can love ourselves. No matter what we are working on we want to remember that the feelings that come up are *just* feelings. We are not in the experience anymore. We need to work on making the inner child feel safe. We have to thank ourselves for having had the courage to survive this experience. Sometimes when we are dealing with an issue such as incest, it's difficult to accept that the other person was doing the best he or she could at the time with the understanding and awareness and knowledge that they had. Acts of violence always come from people who were violated themselves. We all need healing. When we learn to love and cherish who we are, we will no longer harm anyone.

Stop All Criticism

When we are dealing with criticism, we are usually criticizing ourselves all the time for the same things over and over. When are we going to wake up and learn that criticism doesn't work? Let's try another tactic. Let's approve of ourselves as we are right now. Critical people often attract a lot of criticism because it is their pattern to criticize. What we give out, we get back. They may also need to be perfect at all times. Who's perfect? Have you ever met a perfect person? I haven't. If we complain about another person, we are really complaining about some aspect of ourselves.

Everyone is a reflection of us, and what we see in another person, we see in ourselves. Many times we don't want to accept parts of who we are. We abuse ourselves with alcohol or drugs or cigarettes or overeating or whatever. These are ways of beating up on ourselves for not being perfect—but, being perfect for who? Whose early demands and expectations are we still trying to meet? Be willing to let that go. Just *be*. You will find that you are wonderful just as you are this very moment.

If you have always been a critical person who sees life through very negative eyes, it is going to take time for you to turn yourself around to be more loving and accepting. You will learn to be patient with yourself as you practice letting go of the criticism which is only a habit, not the reality of your being.

Can you imagine how wonderful it would be if we could live our lives without ever being criticized by anyone? We would feel totally at ease, totally comfortable. Every morning would be a wonderful new day because everyone would love you and accept you and nobody would criticize you or put you down. You can give this happiness to yourself by becoming more accepting of the things that make you unique and special.

The experience of living with yourself can be the most wonderful experience imaginable. You can wake up in the morning and feel the joy of spending another day with you.

When you love who you are, you automatically bring out the best in you. I'm not saying you will be a better person because that implies that you are not good enough now. However, you will find more positive ways to fulfill your needs, and to express more of who you really are.

Guilt Makes Us Feel Inferior

Many times people give you negative messages because it is the easiest way to manipulate you. If someone is trying to make you feel guilty, ask yourself, "What do they want? Why are they doing this?" Ask these questions instead of inwardly agreeing, "Yes, I'm guilty, I must do what they say."

Many parents manipulate their children with guilt because they were raised the same way. They tell lies to their children to make them feel *less than*. Some people are still manipulated by their relatives and friends when they grow up because, first of all, they don't respect themselves, otherwise they wouldn't let it happen. Secondly, they are manipulative themselves.

Many of you live under a cloud of guilt. You always feel *wrong*, or that you are not doing the right thing, or apologizing to someone for something. You will not forgive yourself for something you did in the past. You berate yourself for a lot that goes on in your life. Let the cloud dissipate. You don't need to live that way any longer.

Those of you who feel guilty can now learn to say *no* and call people on their nonsense. I'm not saying to be angry with them, but you don't have to play their game anymore. If saying "no" is new to you, say it very simply: "No. No, I cannot do that." Don't give excuses or the manipulator will have ammunition to talk you out of your decision. When people see that manipulating you doesn't work, they will stop. People will only control you as long as you allow them to. You may feel guilty the first time you say no; however, it gets easier the next few times.

A woman at one of my lectures had a baby who was born with congenital heart dis-ease. She felt guilty because she believed that it was her fault—she did something to the baby. Unfortunately, guilt does not solve anything. In her case, no one did anything wrong. I told her that I thought it could have been a soul choice for the baby, and a lesson for both the mother and baby. My answer was for her to love the baby and love herself and stop feeling that she did something wrong. That sort of guilt would not heal anyone.

If you do something that you are sorry about, stop doing it. If you did something in the past that you still feel guilty about, forgive yourself. If you can make amends, do it, and don't repeat the action again. Every time guilt comes up in your life, ask yourself, "What do I still believe about myself?" "Who am I trying to please?" Notice the childhood beliefs that come up.

When someone comes to me who has been involved in a car accident, there is usually guilt on a deep-seated level and a need for punishment. There can also be a lot of repressed hostility because we feel we don't have the right to speak up for ourselves. Guilt seeks punishment, so we can literally become our own judge, jury, and executioner—condemning ourselves to a self-imposed prison. We punish ourselves, and there is no one around to come to our defense. It's time to forgive ourselves and set ourselves free.

One elderly lady at one of my seminars felt enormous guilt about her middle-aged son. He was an only child who grew up to be a very withdrawn person. She felt guilty because she was very strict with him while he was growing up. I explained that she had done the best she knew how to do at the time. I believe he chose her as a mother before he incarnated into this lifetime, so on a spiritual level, he knew what he was doing. I told her that she was wasting all her energy feeling guilty about something that she couldn't change. She sighed, "It's such a shame that he's this way, and I'm sorry I did a bad job."

You see, that's wasted energy because it doesn't help her son now, and it certainly doesn't help her. Guilt becomes a very heavy burden and makes people feel inferior.

Instead, I told her that every time the feeling came up, she could say something like, "No, I don't want to feel that anymore. I'm willing to learn to love myself. I accept my son exactly as he is." If she continued to do this, the pattern would start to shift.

Even if we don't know how to love ourselves, the fact that we are *willing* to love ourselves will create the difference. It's just not worth it to hold on to these patterns. The lesson is always *love yourself*. Her lesson was not to heal her son, but to love herself. He came into this life to love himself. She can't do it for him, and he can't do it for her.

Organized religions are often really good at making people feel guilty. Many of them do some heavy numbers to keep people in line, especially when they are young. However, we aren't little children anymore, and we don't have to be kept in line. We are adults who can decide what we want to believe. The child in us feels the guilt, but there is also the adult in us who can teach the child otherwise.

When you hold your emotions down, or hold things in, you create havoc within you. Love yourself enough to allow yourself to feel your emotions. Allow your feelings to come to the surface. You may find yourself crying for days or getting angry a lot. You may have to process quite a bit of old stuff. I suggest you do affirmations that make going through the process easier, smoother, and more comfortable:

- *"I now release with ease all old negative beliefs."*
- *"It's comfortable for me to change."*
- *"My pathway is now smooth."*
- *"I am free of the past."*

Don't also add judgment to your feelings. That only pushes the feelings down even more. If you are going through incredible dilemmas or crises, affirm that you are safe and that you are willing to feel. Affirming these positive feelings will bring about beneficial changes.

Chapter 6

Letting Your Feelings Out

A tragedy can turn out to be our greatest good if we approach it in ways from which we can grow.

Releasing Anger in Positive Ways

Everyone deals with anger at one time or another in their lives. Anger is an honest emotion. When it is not expressed or processed outwardly, it will be processed inwardly, in the body, and usually develops into a dis-ease or dysfunction of some sort.

Like criticism, we usually get angry about the same things over and over again. When we are angry, and we feel we don't have a right to express it, we swallow it down, which causes resentment, bitterness, or depression. So, its good to *handle* our anger when it comes up.

There are several ways to deal with anger in positive ways. One of the best ways is to talk openly to the person with whom you are angry and to release the pent-up emotions. You can say, "I am angry with you because _____." When we feel like screaming at someone, then the anger has been building up for a long time.

Often, it is because we feel we cannot speak to the other person. So, the second best way to let the anger out is to talk to the person in the mirror.

Find yourself a place where you will feel safe and will not be disturbed. Look into your own eyes in the mirror. If you find that you cannot, then concentrate on your mouth or nose. See yourself and/or the person who you believe has done something wrong to you. Remember the moment when you became angry and let yourself feel the anger come through you. Begin to tell this person exactly what you are so angry about. Show all the anger you feel. You could say something like:

- *"I am angry at you because* _____*."*
- *"I am hurt because you did* _____*."*
- *"I am so afraid because you* _____*."*

Get all your feelings out. If you feel like expressing yourself physically, then get some pillows and start hitting them. Don't be afraid to let your anger take its natural course. You have already kept your feelings bottled up too long. There is no need to feel any guilt or shame. Remember, our feelings are thoughts in action. They serve a purpose, and when you let them loose from your mind and body, you allow space inside for other, more positive, experiences.

When you have finished expressing your anger to the person or persons, do your best to forgive them. Forgiveness is an act of freedom for yourself because you are the one who will benefit from it. If you can't forgive someone, then the exercise is just a negative affirmation and is not healing for you. There is a difference between *releasing* and just *rehashing* old angers. You may want to say something like:

> *"Okay, that situation is over. That is in the past now. I don't approve of your action, and yet I understand that you were doing the best you could with the knowledge and understanding you had at the time. I am done with this. I release you and let you go. You are free and I am free."*

You may want to do this exercise several times before you truly feel that you have gotten rid of all of your anger. You may also want to work on one anger issue or several. Do what feels right for you.

There are other methods we can use to release the anger. We can scream into a pillow, we can kick pillows, we can beat the bed or a punching bag. We can write a *hate letter* and then burn it. We can scream in our cars with the windows rolled up. We can play tennis or go to the golf range and just hit balls one after the other. We can exercise, swim, or run around the block several times. We can write or draw our feelings using our nondominant hand— the creative process is a natural release for emotions.

One man at my seminar said he used an egg timer as he began screaming into a pillow. He gave himself ten minutes to let out all his frustrations and anger about his father. After five minutes, he was exhausted, and every thirty seconds, he would look at the egg timer and realize he still had a few more minutes to go.

I used to beat the bed and make a lot of noise. I can't do that now because my dogs get frightened and think I am angry at them. Now I find it very effective to scream in the car, or dig a hole in the garden.

As you can see, you can become quite creative when releasing your feelings. I recommend that you do something physically to release charged-up emotions—in a safe way. Don't be reckless or dangerous to yourself or others. Remember, also, to communicate with your Higher Power. Go within and know that there is an answer to your anger and that you will find it. It is very healing to meditate and visualize your rage flowing freely out of your body. Send love to the other person, and see your love dissolve whatever disharmony there is between you. Be willing to become harmonious. Perhaps the anger you feel is reminding you that you aren't communicating well with others. By recognizing it, you can correct it.

It's amazing how many people tell me how much happier they have become once they release anger towards another person. It is as though a huge burden has been dropped. One of my students had a difficult time letting her anger out. Intellectually, she understood her feelings, yet she couldn't express them outwardly. Once she allowed herself this expression, she kicked and screamed and called her mother and alcoholic daughter all sorts of names. She felt a tremendous weight lift from her. When her daughter visited her afterwards, she couldn't stop hugging her. She allowed room for love to come inside where all the repressed anger had been.

Maybe you have been a person who's been angry for a major part of your life. You have, what I call, *habitual anger.* Something happens and you get angry. Something else happens and you get angry again. Once more it happens, and you keep getting angry, but you never go beyond getting angry. Habitual anger is childish—you always want your own way. It would be helpful to ask yourself:

- *"Why am I choosing to be angry all the time?"*
- *"What am I doing to create situation after situation that angers me?"*
- *"Is this the only way I can react to life?"*
- *"Is this what I want?"*
- *"Who am I still punishing? Or loving?"*
- *"Why do I want to be in this state?"*
- *"What am I believing that causes all these frustrations?"*
- *"What am I giving out that attracts in others the need to irritate me?"*

In other words, why do you believe that to get your way, you need to get angry? I'm not saying that there are no injustices, and there aren't times when you have a right to feel angry. However, habitual anger is not good for your body because it lodges in there.

Notice what you focus on most of the time. Sit in front of a mirror for ten minutes and look at yourself. Ask: *'Who are you? What is it that you want? What makes you happy? What can I do to make you happy?'* Now is the time to do something else. Create a new space inside yourself for loving, optimistic, and cheerful patterns.

People often get angry while they are driving their cars. People often express their frustrations about the other lousy drivers on the road. Long ago, I got over the fact that I was going to be upset because of someone else's inability to follow the rules of the road. So the way I handle driving my car is: first, I put love into the car when I get in. Next, I know and affirm that I'm always surrounded by wonderful, competent, happy drivers. Everyone around me is a good driver. Because of my beliefs and affirmations whenever I'm on the road, I have very few poor drivers around me. They're off bothering the person who's shaking his fist and screaming.

Your car is an extension of you, just like everything and everyone are extensions of you, so put some love into your car, and then send love out to everyone around you on the streets and the highways. I believe, that the parts of your car are similar to the parts of your body.

For instance, one of my workers felt that she had "no vision," she could not see where her life was going or where she wanted it to go. One morning she woke up and found her windshield smashed. Another person, an acquaintance of mine, felt that he was "stuck" in his life. He was not moving forward or moving backwards but was not moving at all. His tire became flat and he couldn't move anywhere. I know it may sound silly at first, but it's fascinating to me that the terminology that these two people used to describe their current mental state also related to their car. "Having no vision" means that you can't see in front of you. The windshield is a perfect metaphor, likewise "being stuck" is a perfect example of a flat tire. The next time something happens to your car, make a note as to what you feel the broken part represents and see if you can connect it to how you are feeling at that particular moment. You may be surprised at the results. One day I will write a little book and call it *Heal Your Automobile.*

There was a time when people did not understand the body/mind connection. Now it is time for us to expand our thinking even more and to understand the machinery/mind connection. Every situation in your life is a learning experience and can be handled so that it works for you.

There is nothing new or unique about anger. No one escapes the experience. The key is in recognizing it for what it is and taking that energy in a healthier direction. If you get sick, don't get angry over it. Instead of putting anger into your body, fill it with love and forgive yourself. Those of you who are caregivers for sick people can remember to take care of yourselves, too. If you don't, you won't be any good to yourself or your friends and family. You will burn out. Do something to let your feelings out as well. Once you learn to deal with anger in a positive way that readily benefits you, you will find many wonderful changes occurring in the quality of your life.

Resentment Causes a Variety of Ills

Resentment is anger that has been buried for a long time. The main problem with resentment is that it lodges in the body, usually in the same place, and in time, it seethes and eats away at the body and often turns into tumors and cancers. Therefore, repressing anger and letting it settle in our bodies is not conducive to good health. Again, it's time to let these feelings out.

Many of us were raised in families where we weren't allowed to be angry. Women, in particular, were taught that to be angry was something *bad*. Anger was not acceptable, except for one person, usually a parent. So we learned to swallow our anger rather than express it. Again, we can now realize that we are the ones who are holding on to it. Nobody else is involved at all.

An oyster takes a grain of sand, and it builds layer after layer after layer of calcite over it until it becomes a beautiful pearl. Similarly, we take our emotional hurts and nurse them over and over again, by what I call, running the old movie over and over in our minds. If we want to be free from our hurts, if we want to get out of them, then it's time to go beyond them.

One of the reasons women create cysts and tumors in the uterus is through, what I call, the *he done me wrong syndrome*. The genitals represent either the most masculine part of the body, the masculine principle, or the most feminine part of the body, the feminine principle. When people have emotional episodes, usually in relationships, they take it to one of these areas. With women, they may take it to their female organs, their most feminine part, and nurse the hurt until it becomes a cyst or tumor.

Since resentment is buried deeply inside us, we may have to do a lot of work to dissolve it. I received a letter from a woman who was working on her third cancer tumor. She still had not dissolved the resentment pattern and kept creating new tumors in her body. I could tell she felt very self-righteous about her bitterness. It was easier for her to let the doctor remove the latest tumor than to work on forgiveness. It would have been good if she was able to do both. Doctors are good at removing growths, only we can keep them from re-appearing.

Sometimes we would rather die than change our patterns. And we do. I have noticed many people would rather die than change their eating habits. And they do. This is very disturbing when it happens to someone we love and we are aware of alternative choices they could make.

No matter what choices we make, they are always right for us and there is no blame, even if we leave the planet. We will all leave the planet in time and we will all find a way to do it at the right time for us.

Again, we don't have to blame ourselves for failing or doing it wrong. We don't have to feel guilty. There is no blame. No one has done it *wrong*. A person does the best he or she knows how to with the understanding and awareness that is available. Remember, we all have the Power within us, and we have all come here to learn certain lessons. Our Higher Selves know our destiny in this lifetime and what we learn in order to move forward in our evolutionary process. There is never any wrong way, there just *is*. We are all on an endless journey through eternity, and we have lifetime after lifetime. What we don't work out in this life, I believe we will work out in another.

Suppressed Feelings Lead to Depression

Depression is anger turned inward. It is also anger that you feel you do not have a right to have. For instance you may not feel it's okay to be angry at your parent or spouse or employer or best friend. Yet you are angry. And you feel stuck. That anger becomes depression. Far too many people today suffer from depression, even chronic depression. By the time we feel that depressed, it is very difficult to get out of it. It feels so hopeless that it becomes an effort to do anything.

I don't care how spiritual you are, you have got to wash your dishes every now and then. You can't let the sink pile up with dirty dishes and say, "Oh, I'm metaphysical." The same with your feelings, if you want to have a mind that flows freely then clean up your inner mental *dirty dishes*.

One of the best ways is to give yourself permission to express some of your anger so that you don't have to stay so depressed. There are now therapists that specialize in anger releasing. Having a session or two with one of them could be most helpful.

It's my personal opinion that we all need to beat the bed once a week whether we feel we're angry or not. There are some therapies that encourage you to get into your anger; however, I think they often keep you immersed in the anger process too long. Anger, like any emotion that surfaces, lasts only a few minutes. Babies move in and out of their emotions very quickly. It is our reaction to the emotion that causes us to hold and repress it.

Author Elisabeth Kübler-Ross uses a wonderful exercise in her seminars, she calls *externalization*. She has you take a piece of rubber hose and some old phone books, and you beat them over and over again, letting all sorts of emotions emerge.

When you are releasing anger, it's okay to be embarrassed about it, especially if it was against your family rules to get angry. It will be embarrassing the first time you do it, but when you get into it, it can be such fun and very powerful. God is not going to hate you for being angry. Once you have released some of this old anger, you will be able to see your situation in a new light and find new solutions.

Another one of the suggestions I would make for a person who is depressed is to work with a good nutritionist and really get your diet cleaned up. Its amazing how that can help the mind. People who are depressed often eat very poorly which adds to the problem. We all want to make the best choices so that the food we are taking in is good for our body. Also, many times we find there is a chemical imbalance in the body that is further aggravated by the intake of medication of some sort.

Rebirthing is another wonderful process for releasing your feelings because it goes beyond the intellect. If you have never had a rebirthing session, I recommend that you try it. It has been very helpful for many people. It's a breathing modality that helps you connect with old issues so that you can release them in a positive way. Some rebirthers have you repeat your affirmations as you are going through the process.

Then there is body work, such as Rolfing, a process of deep connective-tissue manipulation, developed by Ida Rolf. Or Heller work, or Trager work. They are all excellent ways to release restrictive patterns in the body. Different processes work differently for each person. One process may be good for one, yet not for another. We can only find what is best for ourselves by trying different avenues.

Self Help sections in book stores are excellent places to read about different alternatives. Health Food stores often have bulletin boards that list meetings and classes. When the student is ready, the teacher appears.

Fear Is Not Having Trust

Fear is rampant on the planet. You can see and hear about it in the news every day in the form of wars, murders, greed, and more. Fear is a lack of trust in ourselves. Because of that we don't trust Life. We don't trust that we are being taken care of on a higher level, so we feel we must control everything from the physical level. Obviously, we are going to feel fear because we can't control everything in our lives.

Trust is what we learn when we want to overcome our fears. It's called taking the *leap-of-faith*. Trust in the Power within that is connected to Universal Intelligence. Trust in that which is invisible, instead of trusting only in the physical, material world. I'm not saying that we do nothing, yet if we have trust, we can go through life much easier. If you recall what I said earlier, I believe that everything I need to know is revealed to me. I trust that I am being taken care of, even though I am not physically in control of everything that is happening around me.

When a fearful thought comes up, it really is trying to protect you. I suggest that you say to the fear, "I know you want to protect me. I appreciate that you want to help me. And I thank you." Acknowledge the fearful thought; it's there to take care of you. When you become physically frightened, your adrenalin pumps through your body to protect you from danger. It's the same with the fear you manufacture in your mind.

Observe your fears and recognize that you are not them. Think of fear the way you view images on a movie screen. What you see on the screen is really not there. The moving pictures are just frames of celluloid, and they change and disappear very rapidly. Our fears will come and go as rapidly as those pictures, unless we insist on holding on to them.

Fear is a limitation of our minds. People have so much fear about getting sick or about becoming homeless or whatever. Anger is fear that becomes a defense mechanism. It protects you and yet it would be much more powerful for you to do affirmations so you can stop recreating fearful situations in your minds, and love yourself through the fear. Again, nothing comes from outside of us. We are at the center of everything that happens in our lives. Everything is inside—every experience, every relationship, is the mirror of a mental pattern that we have inside us.

Fear is the opposite of love. The more we are willing to love and trust who we are, the more we attract these qualities to ourselves. When we are on a streak of really being frightened or upset or worried or not liking ourselves, isn't it amazing how everything goes wrong in our lives? One thing after another. It seems it will never stop.

Well, it is the same when we really love ourselves. Everything starts to go on a winning streak and we get the "green lights" and the "parking places." All of the things that make life so wonderful—the big and the little. We get up in the morning, and the day flows beautifully.

Love yourself so that you can take care of yourself. Do everything you can to strengthen your heart, your body, and your mind. Turn to the Power within you. Find a good spiritual connection, and really work on maintaining it.

If you are feeling threatened or fearful, consciously breathe. We often hold our breath when we are frightened. So take a few deep breaths. Breathing opens the space inside you that is your power. It straightens your spine. It opens your chest and gives your heart room to expand. By breathing you begin to drop the barriers and open up. You expand rather than contract. Your love flows. Say: "*I am one with the Power that created me. I am safe. All is well in my world.*"

Cleaning Up Our Addictions

One of the primary ways we mask our fears is through addictions. Addictions suppress the emotions, so that we don't feel. However, there are many kinds of addictions besides the chemical ones. There are also, what I call, pattern addictions—patterns we adopt to keep us from being present in our lives. If we don't want to deal with what's in front of us, or if we don't want to be where we are, we have a pattern that keeps us out of touch with our lives. For some people, it is a food addiction or a chemical addiction. There may be a genetic disposition for alcoholism, however, the choice to stay sick is always an individual one. So often, when we talk about something being hereditary, it is really the little child's acceptance of the parents' ways of handling fear.

For others, there are emotional addictions. You can be addicted to finding fault in people. No matter what happens, you will always find someone to blame. "It's their fault, they did it to me."

Maybe you are addicted to running up bills. There are many of you addicted to being in debt; you do everything to keep yourselves over your heads in debt. It doesn't seem to have anything to do with the amount of money you have.

You can be addicted to rejection. Everywhere you go, you attract others who reject you. You will find them. However, the rejection on the outside is a reflection of your own rejection. If you don't reject yourself, nobody else will either, or if they do, it certainly won't matter to you. Ask yourself, "What am I not accepting about myself?"

There are plenty of people addicted to illness. They are always catching something or worrying about getting sick. They seem to belong to the "Illness of the Month Club."

If you're going to be addicted to anything, why not be addicted to loving yourself? You can be addicted to doing positive affirmations or doing something that is supportive of you.

Compulsive Overeating

I receive a lot of letters from people with weight problems. They go on diets that last two or three weeks, then they stop. They feel guilty about falling off their diets, and instead of recognizing that they did what they could at the time, they get angry at themselves and feel guilty. Then to punish themselves, because guilt always seeks punishment, they go out and eat foods that are not good for their bodies. If they could acknowledge that for the two weeks they followed a particular regime they were doing something wonderful for their bodies and stop laying guilt trips on themselves, they would begin to break the pattern. They could also begin to say: *"I used to have a problem with weight, now I allow myself to be the perfect weight for me,"* and the pattern would start to shift inside. Yet we don't want to concentrate on the food issue too much for that is *not* where the problem lies.

Overeating has always meant a need for protection. When you feel insecure or frightened, you pad yourself with a layer of safety. Weight has nothing to do with food. Most of you spend a lifetime being angry at yourselves for being fat. What a waste of energy. Instead, realize there is something going on in your life that is making you feel unsafe and insecure. It could be your work, your spouse, your sexuality, or your life in general. If you are overweight, put the food/weight issue aside and work on the pattern that says, "I need protection because I'm insecure."

It's amazing how our cells respond to our mental patterns. When the need for protection is gone, or when we start feeling secure, the fat will melt off. I have noticed in my own life that when I am not feeling safe, I will gain some weight. When my life is going so fast, and I'm doing so much, and I'm spreading myself all over the place, I feel a need for protection, a need for security. So I say, "Okay, Louise, it's time to work on safety. I want you to really know that you are safe, and it's okay, and you can do all this stuff, and you can be at all these places, and you can have all that is happening right now, and you are safe, and I love you."

Weight is only the outer effect of a fear that is inside you. When you look in the mirror and see the fat person staring back, remember that you are looking at the result of your old thinking. When you start to change your thinking, you are planting a seed for what will become true for you. What you choose to think today will create your new figure tomorrow. One of the best books on releasing excess weight is *The Only Diet There Is* by Sondra Ray. It's all about dieting from negative thinking. She shows you step by step how to do it.

Self Help Groups

Self Help Groups have become the new social form. I see this as a very positive move. These programs do tremendous good. People with similar problems getting together not to whine and complain, but to find ways to work through these issues and improve the quality of their lives. There is now a group for almost every problem you can think of. Many of them are listed in the phone book under *Community Services* in the front of your Yellow Pages or see Appendix B in the back of this book (page 233). I know you can find one that is right for you. Many churches now hold group meetings.

You could even go to the local health food store, one of my favorites, and see what is listed on their bulletin board. If you are serious about changing your life, you will find the way.

The 12-Step Programs are everywhere. 12-Step Programs have been around for some time and they have developed a format that really works and bring about wonderful results. Their Al-Anon program for people who live with, or were raised by, addicted people is one of the best groups for all sorts of people.

Feelings Are Our Inner Gauge

When growing up in a troubled or dysfunctional family, we learn to avoid conflict whenever possible, and this results in the denial of our feelings. We often do not trust others to meet our needs so we don't even ask for help. We are convinced that we must be strong enough to handle things ourselves. The only problem is that we fail to be in touch with our own feelings. Feelings are our most helpful link to our relationship with ourselves, others and the world around us, and they are an indication of what's working or not working in our lives. Shutting them off only leads to more complex problems and physical illnesses. What you can feel, you can heal. If you don't allow yourself to feel what is going on inside of you, you won't know where to begin the healing process.

On the other hand, many of us seem to go through life always feeling guilty or jealous or fearful or sad. We develop habit patterns that keep perpetuating the same experiences that we say we don't want to have. If you keep feeling angry, or sad, or fearful, or jealous and don't get in touch with the underlying cause, you will continue to create more anger, sad, fear, et cetera. When we stop feeling like victims, we are able to take our power back. We must be willing to learn the lesson so the problem can disappear.

When we trust the process of life and our spiritual connection with the Universe, we can dissolve our angers and fears as soon as they appear. We *can* trust in life and know that everything is happening in divine right order and the perfect time-space sequence.

Chapter 7

Moving Beyond the Pain

*We are far more than our bodies and
personalities. The inner spirit is always
beautiful and lovable, no matter how
our outer appearances may change.*

The Pain of Death

It's wonderful to be positive. It's also wonderful to acknowledge what you are feeling. Nature has given you
feelings to get you through certain experiences and to
deny them causes more pain. Remember, death is not a
failure. Everyone dies, it's part of the process of life.

When someone you love dies, the mourning process
takes at least one year. So give yourself that space. It's difficult to have to go through all the holidays and seasons—
Valentine's Day, your birthday, your anniversary, Christmas, et cetera, so be very gentle with yourself and let
yourself grieve. There are no rules, so don't make any for
yourself.

It's also okay to get angry and have hysterics when
someone dies. You can't pretend it doesn't hurt. You
want to give your feelings an outlet. Let yourself cry.
Look in the mirror and scream, "It isn't fair," or whatever

you feel inside. Again, let it out, otherwise, you will create problems for your body. You have to take care of yourself the best you can, and I know it's not easy.

Those of us who have been working with people with aids find that the grieving process becomes on-going. It is the same as the grieving process in war time. There are too many onslaughts to the emotional/nervous system to handle. Many times I reach out to special friends and dissolve into hysterics when it all becomes too much. It was much easier when my mother died. I felt the natural completion of her ninety-one year cycle. Though I grieved, I had no anger or rage at injustice or untimeliness. Wars and epidemics bring up tremendous frustration at the seeming unfairness of it all.

Although grieving takes time, sometimes you feel like you're in a bottomless pit. If you are still grieving after a few years, then you are wallowing in it. You need to forgive and release the other person and yourself. Remember, we don't lose anyone when they die because we never owned them in the first place.

If you are having a difficult time letting go, there are several things you can do. First of all, I suggest you do some meditations with the person who is gone. No matter what he or she thought or did while they were alive, when they leave the planet, a veil lifts and they see life very clearly. So they no longer have the fears and the beliefs that they had when they were here. If you are grieving a lot, they would probably tell you not to worry because all is well. In your meditations, ask the person for help to get you through this period, and tell him or her that you love them.

Don't judge yourself for not being with the person or doing enough for the person while he or she was alive. That's just adding guilt to your grief. Some of you use this time as an excuse for not getting on with your own life. Some of you would like to leave the planet, too. Or, for some of you, the death of someone you know and love brings up your own fear of death.

Use this time to do inner work on yourself so you can release some of your own stuff. A lot of sadness comes to the surface upon the death of a loved one. Let yourself feel the sadness. You need to get to a point where you feel safe enough to let the old pains come up. If you would allow yourself two or three days of crying, much of the sadness and guilt would disappear. If you need to, find a therapist or a group to help you feel safe enough so that you can release the emotions. Another suggestion is to say affirmations like: "*I love you and I set you free. You are free and I am free.*"

One woman at one of my workshops was having a very difficult time letting go of the anger she felt towards an aunt who was very ill. She was terrified that her aunt would pass away and she would not be able to communicate how she really felt about the past. She didn't want to speak with the aunt because she felt all choked up inside. I suggested to her that she work with a therapist, for one-on-one work can be so helpful. When we are stuck in any area, it is an act of love for ourselves to reach out for help.

There are many types of therapists all over who are experienced in these situations. You don't need to go for a long time, just a short while so that you can get through your difficult period. There are also many grief support groups. It might be helpful for you to join one because it would assist you as you go through the process.

Understanding Our Pain

Many of us live from day to day with unrelieved pain. It may be a small, inconsequential part of our lives, or it may take up a large, unbearable portion of it. But what is pain? Most of us agree that it is something we would like to be free of. Let's look at what we can learn from it. Where does it come from? What is it trying to tell us?

The dictionary defines pain as an "unpleasant or distressing sensation due to bodily injury or disorder," as well as a "mental or emotional suffering or torment." Since pain is an outgrowth of both mental and physical dis-ease, it is clear that both the mind and the body are susceptible to it.

I recently witnessed a wonderful example to illustrate this point as I watched two little girls playing in a park. The first child raised her hand to playfully slap her friend on the arm. Before she was able to connect, the other little girl said, "Ow!" The first little girl looked at her and said, "Why did you say 'Ow'? I haven't even touched you yet." To which her friend quickly replied, "Well, I *knew* it was gonna hurt." In this instance, the mental pain presumed the expected physical pain.

Pain comes to us in many forms. A scratch. A bump. A bruise. Dis-ease. Uneasy sleep. A threat. A knotty feeling in your stomach. A numbing sensation in your arm or leg. Sometimes it hurts a lot, sometimes only a little, but we know it's there. In most cases, it is trying to tell us something. At times, the message is obvious. A sour stomach experienced during the work week, but not on the weekend, may indicate a need for a job change. And many of us know the significance of the pain that occurs after a night of excessive drinking.

Whatever the message, we must remember that the human body is a wonderfully constructed piece of machinery. It tells us if there are problems but only if we are willing to listen. Unfortunately, many of us do not take or make the time to listen.

Pain is actually one of the body's "last-resort" messages to tell us that something is wrong in our lives. We're really off-track somewhere. The body is always aspiring for optimum health no matter what we do to it. However, if we abuse our bodies tremendously, we contribute to the conditions of our dis-ease.

When we first feel pain, what do we do? We usually

run to the medicine cabinet or to the drugstore, and we take a pill. In effect, we say to the body, "Shut up, I don't want to hear you." The body will quiet down for a little bit, then the whisperings return, this time a little louder. Maybe we go to the doctor for an injection or a prescription, or we do something else. At some point, we have to pay attention to what is going on because we may have a full-blown dis-ease of some sort. Even at that point, some people still want to play victim and still don't listen. Others awaken to what's going on and are willing to make changes. It's okay. We all learn in different ways.

The answers may be as simple as getting a good night's sleep, or not going out seven nights a week, or not pushing yourself at work. Allow yourself to listen to your body because it *does* want to get well. Your body wants to be healthy, and you can cooperate with it.

When I first feel pain or discomfort, I quiet myself. I trust that my Higher Power will let me know what needs to be changed in my life, so I can be free from this dis-ease. In these quiet times, I visualize the most perfect natural setting with my favorite flowers growing in abundance all around me. I can feel and smell the sweet, warm air as it blows gently across my face. I concentrate on relaxing every muscle in my body.

When I feel that I have reached a state of complete relaxation, I simply ask my Inner Wisdom, *"How am I contributing to this problem? What is it that I need to*

know? What areas of my life are in need of change?"
Then I let the answers pour over me. The answers may
not come at that moment but I know that they will be revealed to me soon. I know that whatever changes are
needed are the right ones for me and that I will be completely safe no matter what unfolds before me.

Sometimes you wonder how you can accomplish such
changes. "How will I live? What about the children? How
will I pay my bills?" Again, trust your Higher Power to
show you the means to live a plentiful, pain-free life.

I also suggest that you make changes one step at a time.
Lao-Tse said, *'The journey of a thousand miles begins
with one step."* One small step added to another can create significant, major advancements. Once you go about
making your changes, please remember that pain does not
necessarily disappear overnight, and yet it may. It has
taken time for pain to surface; therefore, it may take some
time to recognize it is no longer needed. Be gentle to yourself. Don't gauge your progress by someone else's. You
are unique and have your own way of handling your life.
Put your trust in your Higher Self in order to free yourself of all physical and emotional pain.

Forgiveness Is the Key to Freedom

I often ask clients, "Would you rather be right or would
you rather be happy?" We all have opinions on who was
right and who was wrong according to our own percep-
tions, and we can all find ways to justify our feelings. We
want to punish others for what they did to us; however,

we are the ones running the story over and over in our own minds. It is foolish for us to punish ourselves in the present because someone hurt us in the past.

To release the past, we want to be willing to forgive, even if we don't know *how*. Forgiveness means giving up our hurtful feelings and just letting the whole thing go. A state of nonforgiveness actually destroys something within ourselves.

No matter what avenue of spirituality you follow you will usually find that forgiveness is an enormous issue at any time, but most particularly when there is an illness. When we are ill we really need to look around and see who it is we need to forgive. And usually the very person who we think we will never forgive is the one we need to forgive the most. Not forgiving someone else doesn't harm the person in the slightest, but it plays havoc with us. The issues aren't theirs; the issues are ours.

The grudges and hurts you feel have to do with forgiving yourself, not someone else. Affirm that you are totally willing to forgive everyone. *"I am willing to free myself from the past. I am willing to forgive all those who may ever have harmed me and I forgive myself for having harmed others."* If you think of anyone who may have harmed you in any way at any point in your life, bless that person with love and release him or her, then dismiss the thought.

I wouldn't be where I am today if I hadn't forgiven the

people who have hurt me. I would not want to punish myself today for what they did to me in the past. I'm not saying that it would be easy. It's just that now I can look back at that stuff and say, "Oh yes, that's something that happened." However, I don't live there anymore. It is not the same thing as condoning their behavior.

If you feel ripped-off by another, know that nobody can take anything from you that is rightfully yours. If it belongs to you, it will return to you at the right time. If something doesn't come back to you, it wasn't meant to. You need to accept it and go on with your life.

To become free, you need to get out of your self-righteous resentment and off your *pity pot*. I love this expression, which originated with Alcoholics Anonymous, because it is such a wonderful, accurate description. When you are sitting on your *pity pot*, you are this helpless person who has no power at all. In order to have power, you have to stand on your own two feet and take responsibility.

Take a moment and close your eyes and imagine a beautiful stream of water in front of you. Take the old painful experience, the hurt, and the unforgiveness, and put the whole incident in the stream. See it begin to dissolve and drift downstream until it totally dissipates and disappears. Do this as often as you can.

This is a time for compassion and healing. Go within and connect with that part of yourself that knows how to heal. You are incredibly capable. Be willing to go to new levels to find capabilities of which you were not aware, not to just cure dis-ease, but to truly heal yourself on all possible levels. To make yourself whole in the deepest sense of the word. To accept every part of yourself and every experience you have ever had, and to know that it is all part of the tapestry of your life this time around.

I love *Emmanuel's Book*. There is a passage in it which has a good message.

The question to Emmanuel is:
"How do we experience painful circumstances without becoming embittered by them?'

And Emmanuel's reply is:
"By seeing them as lessons and not as retribution. Trust life, my friends. However far afield life seems to take you, this trip is necessary. You have come to traverse a wide terrain of experience in order to verify where truth lies and where your distortion is in that terrain. You will then be able to return to your home center, your soul self, refreshed and wiser."

If only we could understand that all of our so-called problems are just opportunities for us to grow and to change, and that most of them come from the vibrations that we have been giving off! All we really need to do is change the way we think, be willing to dissolve the resentment, and be willing to forgive.

PART THREE

Loving Yourself

Can you remember the last time you were in love? Your heart went ahhhh. *It was such a wonderful feeling. It's the same thing with loving yourself except that you will never leave. Once you have your love for yourself, it's with you for the rest of your life, so you want to make it the best relationship you can have.*

Chapter 8

How to Love Yourself

When you forgive and let go, not only does a huge weight drop off your shoulders, but the doorway to your own self-love opens.

For many of you who have been working on loving your-selves and for those of you who are just beginning, I am going to explore some ways to help you learn how to love yourselves. I call it my *Ten Steps*, and I have sent thou-sands of people this list over the years.

Loving yourself is a wonderful adventure; it's like learn-ing to fly. Imagine if we all had the power to fly at will? How exciting it would be! Let's begin to love ourselves now.

Many of us seem to suffer from a lack of self-esteem at one level or another. It is very difficult for us to love our-selves because we have all these so-called faults inside us that we feel make it impossible to love ourselves exactly as we are. We usually make loving ourselves conditional, and then when we are involved in relationships, we make loving the other person conditional also. We've all heard that we really can't love someone else until we love our-selves. So now that we have seen the barriers we have set up for ourselves, how do we catapult to the next step.

10 Ways to Love Yourself

1. Probably the most important key is to **stop criticizing yourself.** I talked about criticism in chapter five. If we tell ourselves that we are okay, no matter what is going on, we can make changes in our lives easily. It is when we make ourselves *bad* that we have great difficulty. We all change—everyone. Every day is a new day, and we do things a little differently than we did the day before. Our ability to adapt and flow with the process of life is our power.

Those who have come from dysfunctional homes often have become super-responsible and have gotten in the habit of judging themselves unmercifully. They have grown up amidst tension and anxiety. The message they get as children of dysfunctional homes is: "There must be something wrong with me." Think for a moment about the words you use when scolding yourself. Some of the phrases people tell me are: stupid, bad boy, bad girl, useless, careless, dumb, ugly, worthless, sloppy, dirty, et cetera. Are these the same words you use now when describing yourself?

There is a tremendous need to build self-worth and value in ourselves, because when we feel *not good enough*, we find ways to keep ourselves miserable. We create illness or pain in our bodies; we procrastinate about things that would benefit us; we mistreat our bodies with food, alcohol, and drugs.

We are all insecure in some ways because we are human. Let us learn not to pretend that we are perfect. Having to be perfect only puts immense pressure on ourselves, and it prevents us from looking at areas of our lives that need healing. Instead, we could discover our creative distinctions, our individualities, and appreciate ourselves for the qualities that set us apart from others. Each one of us has a unique role to play on this earth, and when we are critical of ourselves, we obscure it.

2. We must also **stop scaring ourselves**. Many of us terrorize ourselves with frightful thoughts and make situations worse than they are. We take a small problem and make it into a big monster. It's a terrible way to live, always expecting the worst out of life.

How many of you go to bed at night creating the worst possible scenario of a problem? That is like a little child who imagines monsters under the bed and then gets terrified. It's no wonder you can't sleep. As a child you needed your parent to come and soothe you. Now as an adult you know you have the ability to soothe yourself.

People who are ill do this a lot. Often they visualize the worst or they are immediately planning their funerals. They give their power to the media and see themselves as statistics.

You may also do this in relationships. Someone doesn't call and you immediately decide that you are totally unlovable and you'll never have another relationship again. You feel abandoned and rejected.

You do the same thing with your job. Someone makes a remark at work, and you begin to think you're going to be fired. You build these paralyzing thoughts in your mind. Remember, these frightening thoughts are negative affirmations.

If you find yourself habitually reviewing a negative thought or situation in your mind, find an image of something you really would like to replace it with. It could be a beautiful view, or a sunset, flowers, a sport, or anything you love. Use that image as your *switch-to* image every time you find that you are scaring yourself. Say to yourself, "No, I'm not going to think about that anymore. I'm going to think about sunsets, or roses, or Paris, or yachts, or waterfalls," whatever your image is. If you keep doing this, you will eventually break the habit. Again, it takes practice.

3. Another way is **be gentle and kind and patient with yourself.** Oren Arnold humorously wrote, *"Dear God—I pray for patience. And I want it right now!* Patience is a very powerful tool. Most of us suffer from the expectation of immediate gratification. We must have it now. We don't have the patience to wait for anything. We get irritable if we have to wait in lines or are stuck in traffic. We want all the answers and all the goodies right now. Too often, we make other people's lives miserable by our own impatience. Impatience is a resistance to learning. We want the answers without learning the lesson or doing the steps that are necessary.

Think of your mind as if it were a garden. To begin with, a garden is a patch of dirt. You may have a lot of brambles of self-hatred and rocks of despair, anger, and worry. An old tree, called fear, needs pruning. Once you get some of these things out of the way, and the soil is in good shape, you add some seeds or little plants of joy and prosperity. The sun shines down on it, and you water it and give it nutrients and loving attention.

At first, not much seems to be happening. But you don't stop, you keep taking care of your garden. If you are patient, the garden will grow and blossom. The same with your mind—you select the thoughts that will be nurtured, and with patience they grow and contribute to creating the garden of experiences you want.

We All Make Mistakes

It's okay to make mistakes while you are learning. As I said, so many of you are cursed with perfectionism. You won't give yourselves a chance to really learn anything new because if you don't do it perfectly in the first three minutes, you assume you are not good enough.

Anything you are going to learn takes time. When you first begin doing something, it usually doesn't feel right. To show you what I mean, take a moment right now and clasp your hands together. There is no right or wrong way to do this. Clasp your hands and notice which thumb is on top. Now open your hands and then clasp your hands again with the other thumb on top. It probably feels strange, odd, maybe even wrong. Clasp them again the first way, then the second, and the first again, and the second way and hold it. How does it feel? Not so odd. Not so bad. You're getting used to it. Maybe you can even learn to do it both ways.

It's the same when we are doing something a new way. It may feel different, and we immediately judge it. Yet, with a little bit of practice, it can become normal and natural. We're not going to love ourselves totally in one day, but we can love ourselves a little bit more every day.

Each day, we give ourselves a little bit more love, and in two or three months, we will have come so much further in loving ourselves.

So mistakes are your stepping stones. They are valuable because they are your teachers. Don't punish yourself for making a mistake. If you are willing to learn and grow from the mistake, then it serves as a step toward fulfillment in your life.

Some of us have been working on ourselves for a very long time and wonder why we still have issues that come up for us. We need to keep reinforcing what we know, not resisting by throwing our hands up in the air and saying, "What's the use?" As we learn new ways, we need to be gentle and kind to ourselves. Remember the garden above. When the negative weeds grow, pluck them out as quickly as you can.

4. We must **learn to be kind to our minds**. Let's not hate ourselves for having negative thoughts. We can think of our thoughts as *building* us up rather than *beating* us up. We don't have to blame ourselves for negative experiences. We can learn from these experiences. Being kind to ourselves means we stop all blame, all guilt, all punishment, and all pain.

Relaxation can help us as well. Relaxation is absolutely essential for tapping into the Power within, because if you are tense and frightened, you shut off your energy. It only takes a few minutes a day to allow the body and the mind to let go and relax. At any moment you can take a few deep breaths, close your eyes, and release whatever tension you're carrying. As you exhale, become centered and say to yourself silently: *"I love you. All is well."* You will notice how much calmer you feel. You are building messages that say you don't have to go through life tense and frightened all the time.

Meditate on a Daily Basis

I also recommend quieting your mind and listening to your own inner wisdom. Our society has made meditation into something mysterious and difficult to achieve, and yet meditation is one of the oldest and simplest processes there is. All we need to do is get into a relaxed state and repeat silently to ourselves words like *love* or *peace* or anything meaningful to us. *OM* is an ancient sound that I use at my workshops and it seems to work very well. We could even repeat: *I love myself*, or *I forgive myself*, or *I am forgiven*. Then listen for a while.

Some people think that if they meditate, they have to stop their minds from thinking. We really can't stop the mind, but we can slow down our thoughts and let them flow through. Some people sit with a pad and pencil and write down their negative thoughts because they seem to dissipate more easily. If we can get to a state where we are watching our thoughts float by—"Oh, there's a fear thought, and some anger, now there is a love thought, and now a disaster, there's an abandonment thought, a joy thought"—and don't give them importance, we begin to use our tremendous power wisely.

You can begin meditation anywhere and allow it to become a habit. Think of meditation as focusing on your

Higher Power. You become connected with yourself and your inner wisdom. You can do it in whatever form you like. Some people go into a kind of meditation while they are jogging or walking. Again, don't make yourself wrong for doing it differently. I love to get on my knees in the garden and dig in the dirt. It's a great meditation for me.

Visualize Optimistic Outcomes

Visualization is also very important, and there are many techniques you can use. Dr. Carl Simonton, in his book, *Getting Well Again*, recommends a lot of visualization techniques for people with cancer and they often yield excellent results.

With visualization you create a clear, positive image that enhances your affirmation. Many of you have written to me about the kinds of visualizations you do along with your affirmations. The important thing to remember about visualizations is that they must be compatible with the kind of person you are. Otherwise, your visualizations will not work.

For instance, a woman with cancer pictured the *good killer cells* in her body attacking the cancer and killing it. At the end of the visualization, she doubted whether she had done it correctly and didn't feel that it was working for her. So I asked her, "Are you a killer person?" I personally don't feel good about creating a war in my body. I suggested that she change her visualization to one that was a little more gentle. I think it's better to use images like the sun melting the sick cells, or a magician transforming them with his magic wand. When I had my cancer, I used the visualization of cool, clear water washing the dis-eased cells out of my body. We need to do visualizations that are not so offensive to us on the subconscious level.

Those of us who have family or friends who are sick do them an injustice by continually seeing them sick. Visualize them well. Send them good vibrations. However, remember that getting well is really up to them. There are many good audiotapes with guided visualizations and meditations that you can give them to help them through this process if they are open. If not, just send them love.

Everyone can visualize. Describing your home, having a sexual fantasy, imagining what you would do to a person who hurt you are all visualizations. It is amazing what the mind can do.

5. The next step is to **praise yourself**. Criticism breaks down the inner spirit, and praise builds it up. Acknowledge your Power, your God self. We are all expressions of the Infinite Intelligence. When you berate yourself, you belittle the Power that created you. Begin with little things. Tell yourself that you are wonderful. If you do it once and then stop, it doesn't work. Keep at it, even if it's one minute at a time. Believe me, it does get easier. The next time you do something new, or different, or something you are just learning and you're not too adept at it, be there for yourself.

It was a big thrill the first time I spoke at the Church of Religious Science in New York. I remember it vividly. It was a Friday noon meeting. People wrote questions and put them in a basket for me, the speaker. I brought the basket to the podium and answered the questions and did a small treatment after each. After I finished, I walked away from the podium and said to myself, "Louise, you were fantastic considering this was the first time out. By the time you do this about six times, you are going to be a pro." I didn't berate myself and say, "Oh, you forgot to say this or that." I didn't want to have the second time be something that would frighten me.

If I beat myself up the first time, I would beat myself up the second time, and I would dread speaking in the end. After a couple of hours, I thought of what I could change to improve. I never made myself wrong. I was very careful to praise myself and congratulate myself for being wonderful. By the time I had conducted six meetings, I was a pro. I think we can apply this method in all areas of our lives. I continued speaking at the meetings for quite some time. It was a wonderful training ground because it taught me how to think on my feet.

Allow yourself to accept *good* whether you think you deserve it or not. I've discussed how believing that we are not deserving is our unwillingness to accept good in our lives. It's what stops us from having what we want. How could we say anything good about ourselves if we think we don't deserve to be good.

Think about the laws of deserving in your home. Did you feel good enough, smart enough, tall enough, pretty enough, whatever? And what do you have to live for? You know you are here for a reason, and it's not to buy a new car every few years. What are you willing to do to fulfill yourself? Are you willing to do affirmations, visualizations, treatments? Are you willing to forgive? Are you willing to meditate? How much mental effort are you willing to exert to change your life and make it the life you want?

6. Loving yourself means supporting yourself. Reach out to friends and allow them to help you. You really are being strong when you ask for help when you need it. So many of you have learned to be so self-reliant and self-sufficient. You can't ask for help because your ego won't let you. Instead of trying to do it all yourself and then getting angry at yourself because you can't make it, try asking for help next time.

There are support groups in every city. There are 12-Step Programs for almost every problem, and in some areas there are healing circles and church-affiliated organizations. If you can't find what you want, you can start your own group. It's not as scary as you might think. Gather together two or three friends who have the same issues that you have, and set up a few guidelines to follow. If you do it with love in your heart, your little group will grow. People will be attracted like a magnet. Don't worry if it starts to grow and your meeting space gets too small. The Universe always provides. If you don't know what to do, write to my office, and we'll send you guidelines on how to conduct a group. You really can be there for each other.

I started *The Hayride* in Los Angeles in 1985 with six men with aids in my living room. We didn't know what we were going to do about this intense crisis. I told them we weren't going to sit around playing "ain't it awful" because we already knew that. We did what we could on a positive level to support each other. We're still meeting today, and we have about 200 people coming every Wednesday night to West Hollywood Park.

It's an extraordinary group for people with aids, and everyone is welcome. People come from all over the world to see how this group functions and because they feel supported. It's not only me, it's the group. Everyone contributes to making it effective. We meditate and do visualizations. We network and share information about alternative therapies and the latest medical methods. There are energy tables at one end of the room where people can lie down, and others share healing energies by laying on hands or praying for them. We have Science of Mind Practitioners they can talk to. At the end we sing and hug one another. We want people to go out feeling better than they came in, and sometimes people receive a positive lift that lasts for several days.

Support groups have become the new social form and they are very effectual tools in this complex day and age. Many "new thought" churches such as Unity and Religious Science have ongoing weekly support groups. Many groups are listed in new age magazines and newspapers.

Networking is so important. It sparks you and gets you going. I suggest that people who have similar ideas share time with one another on a regular basis.

When people work together on a common goal, they bring their pain, confusion, anger, or whatever, and come together, not to moan, but to find a way to go beyond, to rise above, and grow up in a way.

If you are very dedicated, very self-disciplined, and very spiritual, you can do a lot of work on yourself by yourself. When you are with a group of people doing the same thing, you can make quantum leaps because you learn from one another. Every single person in the group is a teacher. So if you have issues that need working on, I would suggest, if possible, that you get into a group of some sort where you can work them through.

7. Love your negatives. They are all part of your creation, just as we are all part of God's creation. The Intelligence that created us doesn't hate us because we make mistakes or get angry at our children. This Intelligence knows that we are doing the best we can and loves all of Its creation, as we can love ours. You and I have all made negative choices, and if we keep punishing ourselves for them, it becomes a habit pattern and we'll find it very tiresome to let them go and move on to more positive choices.

If you keep repeating, "I hate my job. I hate my house. I hate my illness. I hate this relationship. I hate this. I hate that," very little new good can come into your life.

No matter what negative situation you are in, it's there for a reason; otherwise you wouldn't have it in your life. Dr. John Harrison, the author of *Love Your Disease*, says that patients are never to be condemned for having multiple operations or illnesses. Actually, patients can congratulate themselves for finding a safe way to have their needs met. We have to understand that whatever issue or problem we have, we contributed to creating it in order to handle certain situations. Once we realize this, then we can find a positive way to fulfill our needs.

Sometimes people with cancer or other terminal illnesses have such a hard time saying "no" to an authoritative figure in their life, that on an unconscious level they will create a major dis-ease to say "no" for them. I knew a woman who, when she realized the illness she was creating for herself was just to be able to refuse her father's demands, decided to begin to live for herself for once. She began to say "no" to him. And while it was difficult for her at first, as she continued to stand up for herself she was delighted to find herself getting well.

Whatever our negative patterns are, we can learn to fulfill those needs in more positive ways. That's why it's so important to ask yourself the question, "What is the payoff from this experience? What am I getting that's positive?" We don't like to answer that question. However if we really look within and are honest with ourselves we will find that answer.

Perhaps your answer would be, "It's the only time I get loving attention from my spouse." Once realized, you can begin to look for more positive ways to achieve this.

Humor is another potent tool—it helps us release and lighten up during stressful experiences. At the *Hayride*, we set time aside for jokes. Sometimes we have a guest speaker called the "the laugh lady". She has a contagious laugh and puts everyone on a laughter cycle. We can't always take ourselves too seriously, and laughter is very healing. I also recommend watching old comedies such as those of Laurel and Hardy when you are feeling low or down.

When I did private counseling I would do my best to get people to begin to laugh at their problems. When we can see our lives as a stage play with soap opera and drama and comedy, we get a better perspective and we are on the way to healing. Humor enables us to pull back from the experience and to see it in a larger perspective.

8. Take care of your body. Think of it as this marvelous house in which you live for a while. You would love your house and take care of it, wouldn't you? So, watch what you put into your body. Drug and alcohol abuse is so prevalent because they are two of the most popular methods of escape. If you are into drugs it doesn't mean you are a bad person; it means you haven't found a more positive way of fulfilling your needs.

Drugs beckon to us: "Come and play with me, and we'll have a good time." It's true. They can make you feel wonderful. However, they alter your reality so much, and although it isn't evident at first, you have to pay a terrible price in the end. After taking drugs for a while, your health deteriorates immensely, and you feel awful most of the time. Drugs affect your immune system, which can lead to numerous physical ailments. Also, after repeated use, you develop an addiction, and you have to wonder what made you start taking drugs in the first place. Peer pressure may have compelled you to take them in the beginning, but continued and repeated use is another story.

I've yet to meet anyone who really loves him or herself

and who is hooked on drugs. We use drugs and alcohol to escape our childhood feelings of not being good enough and when they wear off, we feel worse than before. Then we usually have a load of guilt, too. We have to know that it's safe to feel our feelings and acknowledge them. The feelings pass, they don't stay.

Stuffing food into our bodies is another way to hide our love. We can't live without food because it fuels our bodies and helps to create new cells. Even though we may know the basics of good nutrition, often we still use food and diets to punish ourselves and create obesity.

We've become a nation of junk food addicts. We have been on what I call the *Great American Diet* for decades, filling ourselves with processed foods of every sort. We've allowed the food companies and their advertising gimmicks to influence our eating habits. Doctors aren't even taught nutrition in medical schools, unless they take it as an extracurricular subject. Most of what we consider conventional medicine, at the moment, concentrates on drugs and surgery, so if we really want to learn about nutrition, it's an issue that we must take into our own hands. It's an act of loving ourselves to become aware of what we put into our mouths and how it makes us feel.

If you eat lunch, and an hour later, you start feeling sleepy, you might ask yourself, "What did I eat?" You may have consumed something that isn't good for your body at that particular time. Start noticing what gives you energy and what depletes you and brings you down. You can do it by trial and error, or you could find a good nutritionist who can answer some of your questions.

Remember that what's right for one person isn't necessarily right for another—our bodies are different. A macrobiotic diet is wonderful for many people. So is Harvey and Marilyn Diamond's *Fit For Life* method. They are totally different concepts, and yet they both work. Every body is different from every other body, so we can't say that only one method works. You have to find out which way works best for you.

Find exercise that you enjoy, that is fun to do. Create a positive mental attitude about your exercise. Often, you create obstacles in your bodies primarily as a result of what you absorb from other people. Again, you need to forgive yourself and stop putting anger and resentment into your body if you want to create changes. Combining affirmations with your exercise is a way to reprogram negative concepts about your body and its shape.

We are in a time now where new technologies for health are multiplying, and we are learning to combine some ancient healing methods such as Ayurvedic medicine with sound wave technology. I have been studying how sound can stimulate our brain waves and accelerate our learning and healing. There is research that shows that we can cure illness by mentally changing our DNA structure. I think between now and the end of the century, we are going to explore a range of possibilities that will be enormously beneficial to much of the populace.

9. I often emphasize the importance of **mirror work** in order to find out the cause of an issue that keeps us from loving ourselves. There are several ways that you can practice mirror work. I like to look in the mirror the first thing in the morning and say: *"I love you. What can I do for you today? How can I make you happy?"* Listen to your inner voice, and start following through with what you hear. You may not get any messages to begin with because you're so used to scolding yourself, and you don't know how to respond with a kind, loving thought.

If something unpleasant happens to you during the day, go to the mirror and say: *"I love you anyway."* Events come and go, but the love that you have for yourself is constant, and it is the most important quality you possess in your life. If something wonderful happens, go to the mirror and say, "Thank you." Acknowledge yourself for creating this wonderful experience.

You can forgive in the mirror, too. Forgive yourself and forgive others. You can talk to other people in the mirror, especially when you are afraid to talk to them in person. You can clean up old issues with people—parents, bosses, doctors, children, lovers. You can say all sorts of things that you would be afraid to say otherwise, and remember to end by asking them for their love and approval because that is what you really want.

People who have problems loving themselves are almost always people who are not willing to forgive because not forgiving shuts that particular door. When we forgive and let go, not only does a huge weight drop off our shoulders, but the doorway to our own self-love opens up. People will say, "Oh, such a load has dropped off!" Well, of course it has, because we've been carrying this burden forever. Dr. John Harrison states that forgiveness of both the self and the parents, coupled with the release of past hurts, cures more illness than any antibiotic ever could.

It takes a lot to make children stop loving their parents, but when they do, it takes even more for them to forgive them. When we won't forgive, when we won't let go, we're binding ourselves to the past, and when we are stuck in the past, we cannot live in present time, and if we are not living in the present, how can we create our glorious future? Old garbage from the past just creates more garbage for the future.

Affirmations performed in front of a mirror are advantageous because you learn the truth of your existence. When you do an affirmation and you immediately hear a negative response such as, "Who are you kidding? It can't be true. You don't deserve that," then you have received a gift to use. You cannot make the changes you want until you are willing to see what is holding you back. The negative response you have just discovered is like a gift in that it becomes the key to freedom. Turn that negative response into a positive affirmation such as: *"I now deserve all good. I allow good experiences to fill my life."* Repeat the new affirmation until it does become a new part of your life.

I have also seen families change enormously when just one person does affirmations. Many people at the *Hayride* come from estranged families. Their parents literally will not talk to them. I've had them repeat the affirmation, *"I have wonderful, loving, warm, open communication with every member of my family, including my mother,"* or whoever the problem person was. Every time that person or the family comes to mind, I suggest that they go to the mirror and say the affirmation over and over again. It is amazing to see the parents actually show up at the meeting three, or six, or nine months later.

10. Finally, **love yourself** *now*—don't wait until you get it right. Dissatisfaction with yourself is a habit pattern. If you can be satisfied with yourself now, if you can love and approve of yourself now, then when good comes into your life, you will be able to enjoy it. Once you learn to love yourself, you can begin to love and accept other people.

We can't change other people, so leave them alone. We spend a lot of energy trying to make others different. If we used half that energy on ourselves, we could make ourselves different, and when *we* are different, others respond differently to us.

You can't learn life for another person. Everyone has to learn his or her particular lessons. All you can do is learn for yourself, and loving yourself is the first step, so you are not brought down by other people's destructive behaviors. If you are in a situation where you are with a really negative person who doesn't want to change, you need to love yourself enough to move away from that.

One woman at one of my lectures told me that her husband was very negative, and she didn't want him to be a bad influence on her two little children. I suggested that she start affirming that her husband was a wonderful, supportive man who really is working on himself and is bringing out his best qualities. I told her to affirm what she would like to have happen, and every time he was negative, simply run the affirmation through her mind. However, if the relationship continued negatively no matter what affirmations she said, then that might be an answer in itself—the relationship simply wouldn't work.

Because of the increasing divorce rate in our country, I think a question that many women need to ask themselves before they have children is: "Am I really willing to support these children totally on my own?" Being a single parent has become more and more the norm, and it's almost always the woman who acquires the added responsibility of raising children by herself. There was a time when marriages lasted a lifetime, but times have changed, so it's definitely a situation to be considered.

Far too often, we stay in abusive relationships and allow ourselves to be put down. What we are saying is, "I'm not worth loving, so I will stay here and accept this behavior because I must deserve it and I am sure nobody else would want me."

I know that I sound simplistic and repeat the same expressions over and over again, but I truly do believe that the quickest way to change any problem is to love who we are. It is amazing how the loving vibrations we send out will attract to us people who are loving.

Unconditional love is the goal I think we have come here to attain. It begins with self-acceptance and self-love.

You are not here to please other people or to live your lives their way. You can only live it your own way and walk your own pathway. You have come to fulfill yourself and express love on the deepest level. You are here to learn and grow and to absorb and project compassion and understanding. When you leave the planet, you don't take your relationship or your automobile or your bank account or your job with you. The only thing you take is your capacity to love!

Chapter 9

Loving the Child Within

*If you can't get close to other people,
it is because you don't know how to
be close to your own inner child. The
child in you is scared and hurting. Be
there for your child.*

One of the core issues that we want to begin to explore is healing the forgotten child within. Most of us have ignored our inner child for far too long.

It doesn't matter how old you are, there is a little child within you who needs love and acceptance. If you're a woman, no matter how self-reliant you are, you have a little girl who's very tender and needs help; and if you are a man, no matter how macho you are, you still have a little boy inside of you who craves warmth and affection.

Every age that you have been is within you—within your consciousness and memory. As children, when something went wrong, you tended to believe that there was something wrong with you. Children develop the idea that if they could only do it right, then parents or whoever would love them, and they wouldn't beat them or punish them.

So whenever the child wants something and doesn't get it, he or she believes, "I'm not good enough. I'm defective." And, as we grow older, we reject certain parts of ourselves.

At this point in our lives—right now—we need to begin to make ourselves whole and accept every part of who we are—the part that did all the stupid things, the part that was funny looking, the part that was scared, the part that was very foolish and silly, the part that had egg on its face. Every single part of ourselves.

I think that we often turn off or tune out around the age of five. We make that decision because we think that there is something wrong with us, and we're not going to have anything to do with the child anymore.

There is a parent inside, as well. You have a child and you have a parent, and most of the time, the parent scolds the child, almost on a nonstop basis. If you listen to your inner dialogue, you can hear the scolding. You can hear the parent tell you what you are doing wrong or how you are not good enough.

Consequently, we begin a war with ourselves, and we start to criticize ourselves the way our parents have been criticizing us. "You're stupid. You're not good enough. You don't do it right. Screwed up again!" It becomes a habit pattern. When we become adults, most of us totally ignore the child within us, or we criticize the child in the same way we used to be criticized. We continue the pattern over and over again.

I once heard John Bradshaw, author of several marvelous books on healing the inner child, say that each of us has 25,000 hours of parent tapes within us by the time we are adults. How many hours of those tapes, do you think, are telling you how wonderful you are? How much says that you are loved or that you are bright and intelligent? Or that you could do anything you wanted to and would grow up to be the greatest person? In reality, how many hours of those tapes are saying "No, No, No," in all its many forms?

It's no wonder we say *no* to ourselves or *should* all the time. We are responding to those old tapes. However, they are only tapes and are not the reality of your being. They are not the truth of your existence. They are just tapes you carry within, and they can be erased or rerecorded.

Every time you say that you are scared, realize it is the child in you who's scared. The grown-up really isn't afraid, yet the adult isn't being there for the child. The adult and the child need to develop a relationship with each other. Talk to each other about everything you do. I know it may sound silly, but it works. Let the child know that no matter what happens, you will never turn away or run away. You will always be there for it and love it.

For instance, if, when you were very young, you had a bad experience with a dog; that is, maybe it scared you or even bit you, the little child inside could still be frightened of dogs even though now you are a great, big adult. You may see a dog on the street that is teeny, but the little child inside you reacts in a total panic. It says, "DOG!!! I'm going to be hurt!" This is a wonderful opportunity for the parent inside of you to say to the child, "It's okay, I'm grown up now. I will take care of you. I won't let the dog hurt you. You don't have to be frightened anymore." Start parenting your own child in this way.

Healing the Hurts of the Past

I have found that working with the inner child is most valuable in helping to heal the hurts of the past. We are not always in touch with the feelings of the frightened little child within us. If your childhood was full of fear and battling, and you now mentally beat yourself up, you are continuing to treat your inner child in much the same way. The child inside, however, has no place to go. You need to go beyond your parents' limitations. You need to connect with the little lost child inside. He or she needs to know that you care.

Take a moment now and tell your child that you care, "I care. I love you. I really love you." Maybe you've been saying this to the big person, the adult inside you. So start talking to the little child. Visualize that you are taking him or her by the hand and go everywhere together for a few days, and see what wonderfully joyous experiences you can have.

You need to communicate with that part of yourself. What are the messages you want to hear? Sit down quietly, close your eyes, and talk to your child. If you haven't talked to her or him in 62 years, it may take a few times before the child will believe that you really want to talk to it. Be persistent: *"I want to talk to you. I want to see you. I want to love you."* You will eventually connect. You may see the child inside you, you may feel it, or you may hear it.

One of the first statements that you can make when you first talk to your child is an apology. Say you are sorry that you haven't talked to it in all these years, or that you are sorry for scolding it for so long. Tell the child that you want to make up for all the time spent apart from one another. Ask it how you can make it happy. Ask the child what frightens him or her. Ask how you can help, and ask what it wants from you.

Start out with simple questions; you will get the answers. *"What can I do to make you happy? What would you like today?"* For instance, you can say to the child, "I want to jog, what do you want to do?" He or she may answer, "Go to the beach." The communication will have begun. Be consistent. If you can take just a few moments a day to begin to connect with the little person inside of you, life is going to be a lot better.

Communicating with Your Inner Child

Some of you may already be doing inner-child work. There are many books on the subject, and many workshops and lectures are given about it. I've listed some books at the end for further study.

Self-Parenting, by John Pollard III, is excellent, and it's filled with wonderful exercises and activities that you can do with your inner child. If you are serious about doing practical work with your inner child, I recommend that you pick up this book. As I said before, there is a lot of help offered in this area. You are not alone and helpless, but you need to reach out and ask for help so that you can get assistance.

Another suggestion I have is to find a photograph of yourself as a child. Really look at the photograph. Do you see a miserable little kid? Do you see a happy child? Whatever you see, connect with it. If you see a frightened child, ask it why it was frightened, and start doing something to make it feel better. Find several photos of your younger self, and talk to the child in each photo.

It helps to talk to your child in the mirror. If you had a nickname as a child, use that name. Have a box of tissues handy. I suggest that you sit down in front of the mirror because if you are standing, as soon as it gets difficult, you will run out the door. Instead, sit down with your box of tissues, and start talking.

Another exercise you can do is to communicate through writing. Again, lots of information will surface. Use two different colored pens or felt markers. With one colored pen in your dominant hand, write a question. With the other colored pen in your nondominant hand, let your child write the answer. It's a very fascinating exercise. When you are writing the question, the adult thinks it knows the answer, but by the time you pick up the pen with the awkward hand, the answer often comes out quite differently than expected.

You can draw together, too. Many of you probably loved drawing and coloring when you were little children until you were told to be neat and not to draw out of the lines. So begin drawing again. Use your nondominant hand to draw a picture about an event that just happened. Notice how you feel. Ask your child a question, and just let it draw with the nondominant hand and see what it shows.

If you can get together with others in small core groups, or support groups, you can work on these ideas together. You can all let your inner children draw pictures, then you can sit around and carefully discuss what the pictures mean. The information you receive can be surprisingly insightful.

Play with your little child. Do things that your child likes to do. When you were little, what did you really like to do? When was the last time you did it? Too often, the parent inside us stops us from having fun because it's not the adult thing to do. So, take the time to play and have fun. Do the silly things you did when you were young, such as jumping in piles of leaves and running under the hose spray. Watch other children at play. It will bring back memories of the games you played.

If you want more fun in your life, make the connection with your inner child and come from that space of spontaneity and joy. I promise that you will start having more fun in your life.

Were you welcomed as a child? Were your parents really glad you were born? Were they delighted with your sexuality, or did they want the opposite sex? Did you *feel* you were wanted as a child? Was there a celebration when you arrived? Whatever the responses are, welcome your child now. Create a celebration. Tell it all the wonderful things you would tell a little baby who was welcomed into its new life.

What is it you always wanted your parents to tell you when you were a child? What was it they never said that you wanted to hear? All right, tell your child that very thing. Tell it to your child every day for a month while looking in the mirror. See what happens.

If you had alcoholic or abusive parents as a child, you can meditate and visualize them as sober, gentle people. Give your child what it wants. It has probably been deprived for too long. Start visualizing the sort of life you would like to have with this child. When the child feels safe and happy, it can trust you. Ask: *"What do I need to do so that you can trust me?"* Again, you will be amazed at some of the answers.

If you had parents who were not loving at all, and it's really hard for you to relate to them, find a picture of what you think a loving father or a loving mother looks like. Put the pictures of the loving parents around the photo of yourself as a child. Create some new images. Re-write your childhood if you must.

The beliefs that you learned when you were little are still inside the child. If your parents had rigid ideas, and you're very hard on yourself or tend to build walls, your child is probably still following your parents' rules. If you continue to pick on yourself for every mistake, it must be very scary for your inner child to wake up in the morning. "What is she or he going to yell at me about today?"

What our parents did to us is in the past was their consciousness. We are the parents now. We are using our consciousness. If you are still refusing to take care of the little child, you are stuck in self-righteous resentment. Invariably, it means that there is still someone to forgive. So what is it you haven't forgiven yourself for? What do you need to let go of? Well, whatever it is, just let it go.

If we are not giving the child praise and attention now, our parents aren't the blame. They were doing what they thought was right in that particular space and time. However, now, in the present moment, we know what we can do to nourish the child within us.

Those of you who had or have a pet know what it's like to come home and have the pet greet you at the door. It doesn't care what you are wearing. It doesn't care how old you are or if you have wrinkles or how much money you made today. The animal only cares that you're there. It loves you unconditionally. Do that for yourself. Be thrilled that you are alive and that you are here. You are the one person you are going to live with forever. Until you are willing to love the inner child, it's very hard for other people to love you. Accept yourself unconditionally and open-heartedly.

I find that it is often very helpful to create a meditation to make your child feel safe. Since I was a child of incest, I invented a wonderful imagery for my little girl.

First of all, she has a fairy godmother who looks just like Billie Burke in *The Wizard of Oz* because that's what really appeals to her. I know that when I'm not with her, she is with her fairy godmother, and she is always safe. She also lives in a penthouse way up high, with a doorman and two large dogs, so she knows that no one will ever hurt her again. When I can make her feel absolutely safe, then I, as the adult, can help her to release the painful experiences.

There was a time recently when I got off-center and cried for two hours. I realized that the little child in me suddenly felt very hurt and unprotected. I had to tell her that she wasn't bad or wrong. Rather, that she was reacting to something that had happened. So as quickly as I was able to, I did some affirmations and meditated, knowing that there was a Power far greater that would support and love me. After that, the little girl didn't feel so afraid and alone.

I'm also a great believer in teddy bears. When you were very little, often your teddy bear was your very first friend. It was your confidante because you could tell all your troubles and secrets to it, and it never snitched on you. It was always there for you. Take your teddy bear out of the closet now, and let your child have it once again.

It would also be marvelous for hospitals to supply teddy bears in all the beds, so that when the little child in us feels alone and frightened in the middle of the night, he or she can have a teddy bear to hug.

The Many Parts of You

Relationships are wonderful, marriages are wonderful, but the reality is, they are all temporary. However, your relationship with *you* is eternal. It goes on forever. Love the family within you—the child, the parent, and the youth-in-between.

Remember that there is a teen inside you, too. Welcome the teenager. Work with the teen as you work with the little child. What were all the difficulties that you went through as a teenager? Ask your teen the questions that you ask your child. Help the teenager through the intimidating episodes and apprehensive moments of puberty and beyond. Make these times okay. Learn to love your teen as you learn to love your child.

We can't love and accept each other until we love and accept that lost child within us. How old is the little lost child within you? Three, four, five? Usually, the child is less than five years old because that is generally when the child shuts down out of the need to survive.

Take your child by the hand, and love it. Create a wonderful life for you and your child. Say to yourself: *"I'm willing to learn to love my child. I am willing."* The Universe will respond. You will find ways to heal your child and yourself. If we want to heal, we must be willing to feel our feelings and move through them to the other side for the healing. Remember, our Higher Power is always available to support us in our efforts.

No matter what your early childhood was like, the best or the worst, you and only you are in charge of your life now. You can spend your time blaming your parents or your early environment, but all that accomplishes is to keep you stuck in victim patterns. It never helps you get the good you say you want.

Love is the biggest eraser I know. Love erases even the deepest and most painful memories because love goes deeper than anything else. If your mental images of the past are very strong, and you keep affirming, "It's all their fault," you stay stuck. Do you want a life of pain or one of joy? The choice and power are always within you. Look into your eyes, and love you and the little child within.

Chapter 10

Growing Up and Getting Old

*Be as understanding with your parents
as you want them to be with you.*

Communicating with Our Parents

When I was growing up, my teenage years were the most difficult of all. I had so many questions, but I did not want to listen to those who thought they had the answers, especially adults. I wanted to learn everything by myself because I did not trust the information that grown-ups gave me.

I felt particular animosity towards my parents because I was an abused child. I could not understand how my stepfather could treat me the way he did, nor could I understand how my mother could simply ignore what he was doing to me. I felt cheated and misunderstood, and I was certain that my family, specifically, and the world, in general, were against me.

Through my many years spent in the counseling of others, particularly young people, I have found that many people share the same feelings about their parents that I had about mine. Some of the words I hear teenagers use to describe how they feel are: *trapped*, *judged*, *watched*, and *misunderstood.*

Of course, it would be great to have parents who would be accommodating in any given situation; however, in most cases, that is not possible. Although our parents are merely human beings like the rest of us, we often feel that they are being unfair and unreasonable and have no understanding of what we are going through.

One young man I counseled had a very difficult time relating to his father. He felt that they had nothing in common, and when his father spoke to him, it was simply to utter some negative or belittling comment. I asked the young man if he knew how his grandfather had treated his father, and he admitted that he didn't. His grandfather had died before the young man was born.

I suggested that he ask his father about his own childhood and how it affected him. At first the young man was hesitant, because it was uncomfortable to talk to his father without feeling he would be ridiculed or judged. However, he took the plunge and agreed to approach his father.

The next time I saw him, the young man seemed more at ease. "Wow," he exclaimed, "I didn't realize what kind of a childhood my own father had." Apparently his grandfather had insisted that all of his children address him as *Sir,* and they lived by the old standard that children were to be seen but not heard. If they dared to utter one contrary word, they were severely beaten. No wonder his father was critical.

When we grow up, many of us have the good intentions of treating our children differently than the way we were treated. However, we learn from the world around us, and sooner or later, we begin to sound and act just like our parents.

In the case of this young man, his father inflicted the same kind of verbal abuse on his son that his own father had heaped on him. He may not have intended to do so; he was merely acting in a way consistent with his own upbringing.

However, the young man came to understand a little more about his father, and as a result, they were able to communicate more freely. Although it would take some effort and patience on both their parts before their level of communication would be ideal, at least they were both moving in a new direction.

I strongly believe that it is very important for all of us to take the time to find out more about our parents' childhoods. If your parents are still alive, you can ask them: *"What was it like when you were growing up? What was love like in your family. How did your parents punish you? What kind of peer pressure did you have to face in those days? Did your parents like the people you dated? Did you have a job while you were growing up?"*

By learning more about our parents, we can see the patterns that have shaped who they are, and, in turn, see why they treat us as they do. As we learn to empathize with our parents, we will see them in a new, more loving light. You may be able to open doors to a more communicative, loving relationship—one that has mutual respect and trust.

If you have difficulty even talking with your parents, first start in your mind or in front of the mirror. Imagine yourself telling them, "There's something I want to speak to you about." Go through this process several days in a row. It will help you decide what you want to say and how to say it.

Or, do a meditation and in your mind, talk to each of your parents and clean up your old issues. Forgive them and forgive yourself. Tell them you love them. Then, prepare to tell them the same things in person.

At one of my groups, a young man told me that he had a lot of anger and that he didn't trust others. He recycled this pattern of distrust over and over again in all his relationships. When we got to the root of the problem, he told me that he was so angry with his father for not being the person he wanted him to be.

Again, when we are on a spiritual pathway, it's not up to us to change the other person. First of all, we need to release all the pent-up feelings we harbor against our parents, and then we need to forgive them for not being who we wanted them to be. We always want everybody else to be like us, to think like us, to dress like us, to do what we do. However, as you know we are all so very different.

In order to have the space to be ourselves, we need to give that space to others. By forcing our parents to be something that they are not, we cut off our own love. We judge our parents just the way that they judge us. If we want to share with our parents, we need to begin by eradicating our own preconceived judgments of them.

Many of you continue to have power-struggle games with your parents as you grow older. Parents push a lot of buttons, so if you want to stop playing the game, you are going to have to stop taking a part in it. It is time for you to grow up and decide what you want. You can begin by calling your parents by their first names. Calling them Mommy and Daddy when you are in your 40s only keeps you stuck in the little child role. Start becoming two adults instead of parent and child.

Another suggestion is to write an affirmative treatment that details the kind of relationship you want with your mother and/or father. Begin declaring these words for yourself. After a while, you can tell him or her face to face. If your mother or father is still pushing your buttons, you are not letting either of them know how you really feel. You have a right to have the life you want. You have a right to be an adult. It may not be easy, I know. First, decide what it is that you need, and then tell your mother or father what that is. Don't make them wrong. Ask, "How can we work this out?"

Remember, with understanding comes forgiveness, and

with forgiveness comes love. When we progress to the point where we can love and forgive our parents, we will be well on our way to being able to enjoy fulfilling relationships with everyone in our lives.

Teens Need Self-Esteem

It alarms me that the rate of suicide among our teenagers is so on the rise. It seems that more and more young people feel overwhelmed by the responsibilities of life and would just as soon give up rather than to persevere and experience the multitude of adventures that life has to offer. Much of this problem has to do with the way we, as adults, expect them to respond to life situations. Do we want them to react as we would? Do we bombard them with negativity?

The period between age 10 and 15 can be a very critical time. Children in that age group have the tendency to conform, and they will do anything to be accepted by their peers. In their need for acceptance, they often hide their true feelings for fear they will not be accepted and loved for whom they really are.

The peer pressure and societal stress that I experienced when I was young pale in comparison to that which today's young people must endure, and yet, when I was 15, due to physical and mental abuse, I left school and home to be on my own. Think how jarring it must be for the child of today to have to deal with drug abuse, physical abuse, sexually transmitted dis-eases, peer pressure and gangs, family problems; and on a global level, nuclear war, environmental upheavals, crime and so much more.

As a parent, you can discuss the differences between negative and positive peer pressure with your teen. Peer pressure is all around us from the moment we are born until the day we leave the planet. We must learn how to deal with it and not let it control us.

Similarly, it is important for us to gain some knowledge and understanding of why our children are shy, mischievous, sad, slow in school, destructive, et cetera. Children are strongly influenced by the thinking, feeling patterns established in the home, and he or she makes daily choices and decisions from that belief system. If the home environment is not conducive to trusting and loving, the child will seek trust, love, and compassion elsewhere. Many gangs are a place where children feel safe. They form a family bond, no matter how dysfunctional it is.

I truly believe that a lot of hardships could be avoided if we could only get young people to ask themselves one important question before they act: *"Will this make me feel better about myself?"* We can help our teenagers see their choices in each situation. Choice and responsibility put power back into their hands. It enables them to do something without feeling like victims of the system.

If we can teach children that they are not victims and that it is possible for them to change their experiences by taking responsibility for their own lives, we will begin to see major breakthroughs.

It is vitally important to keep the lines of communication open with children, especially when they are in their teen years. Usually what happens when children start to talk about their likes and dislikes is that they are told over and over again, "Don't say that. Don't do that. Don't feel that. Don't be that way. Don't express that. Don't, don't, don't." Eventually, children stop communicating and sometimes leave home. If you want to have your children around as you grow older, keep the lines of communication open when they are younger.

Applaud your child's uniqueness. Allow your teenagers to express themselves in their own style, even if you think it's just a fad. Don't make them wrong, or tear them down. Goodness knows, I have been through many, many fads in my lifetime, and so will you and your teenagers.

Children Learn from Our Actions

Children never do what we tell them to do; they do *what* we do. We can't say, "Don't smoke," or "Don't drink," or "Don't do drugs," if *we* do them. We have to serve as examples and live the sort of life we want our children to express. When parents are willing to work on loving themselves, it's amazing to see the harmony that is achieved within the family. Children respond with a new sense of self-esteem and start to value and respect who they are.

An exercise in self-esteem that you and your children can do together is to make a list of some goals you would like to achieve. Ask your children to write down how they see themselves in ten years, in one year, in three months. What kind of lives do they want to have? What kind of friends would be most beneficial? Have them list their goals with short descriptions of each as well as how they can make their dreams come true. You do the same.

All of you might keep the lists nearby to remind yourselves of your goals. In three months' time, go over the lists together. Have the goals changed? Don't let your children beat themselves up if they didn't get as far as they wanted. They can always revise their lists. What is most important to give young people something positive to look forward to!

Separation and Divorce

If there is separation and/or divorce in the family, it is important that each parent be supportive. It's very stressful for a child to be told that the other parent is no good.

As the parent, you have to love yourself through the fears and anger to experience as much as possible. The children will pick up feelings from you. If you're going through a lot of turmoil and pain, they will surely pick that up from you. Explain to your children that your "stuff" has nothing to do with them and their inner worth.

Don't let them get the idea that anything that's happened is their fault because that is what most children think. Let them know that you love them very much and will always be there for them.

I suggest that you do mirror work with your children every morning. Do affirmations that will get you through the trying times easily and effortlessly so that everyone will be okay. Release your painful experiences with love, and affirm happiness for all concerned.

There is a wonderful group called *The California State Task Force to Promote Self-Esteem and Personal and Social Responsibility*. It was created in 1987 by Assembly-man John Vasconcellos. Among the appointed members are Jack Canfield and Dr. Emmett Miller. I support its efforts in researching and making recommendations to the government to bring self-esteem programs into schools. Other states are following suit by including self-esteem curriculum in the classroom.

I believe that we are on the brink of some major changes in our society, especially with regard to understanding our own self-worth. If teachers, especially, can get their own self-worth on the right track, they will help our children tremendously. Children reflect the social and economic pressures with which we are faced. Any program having to do with self-esteem will need to encompass students, parents, and teachers, as well as businesses and organizations.

Growing Older Graciously

So many of us fear growing old and looking old. We make growing old so terrible and unattractive. Yet, it is a normal and natural process of living. If we can't accept our inner child and be comfortable with who we were and who we are, how can we accept the next stage?

If you don't grow old, what is the alternative? You leave the planet. As a culture, we have created, what I call, "youth worship." It's all very well and good to love ourselves at certain ages, but why can't we love ourselves as we get older? We will eventually go through every age of life.

Many women feel a lot of anxiety and fear when they think about getting old. The gay community also deals with a lot of issues having to do with youth and looks and loss of beauty. Getting old may mean getting wrinkles and gray hair and saggy skin, and, yes, I want to grow old. That's all part of being here. We are on this planet to experience every part of life.

I can understand that we don't want to get old and sick, so let's separate these two ideas. Let's not imagine or envision ourselves getting sick as a way to die. I do not personally believe that we have to die with illness.

Instead, when it is our time to leave, when we have accomplished what we came here to do, we can take a nap, or go to bed at night, and leave peacefully. We don't have to become deathly ill. We don't have to be hooked to machines. We don't have to lie suffering in a nursing home in order to leave the planet. There is a tremendous amount of information available on how to stay healthy. Don't put it off, do it now. When we get older, we want to feel wonderful, so we can continue to experience new adventures.

I read something a while ago that intrigued me. It was an article about a San Francisco medical school that had discovered that the way we age is not determined by genes, but by something they call the *aging set point*—a biological time clock that exists in our minds. This mechanism actually monitors when and how we begin to age. The set point, or aging clock, is regulated in great part by one important factor: our attitudes toward growing old.

For instance, if you believe that 35 is middle aged, that belief triggers biological changes in your body that cause it to accelerate the aging process when you reach 35. Isn't it fascinating! Somewhere, somehow, we decide what is middle age and what is old age. Where are you setting that *aging set point* within you? I have this image in my mind that I am going to live to 96 years and still be active, so, it's very important that I keep myself healthy.

Remember, too, what we give out, we get back. Be aware of how you treat older people, because when you get old, that will be the way you are treated. If you believe certain concepts about old people, again, you are forming ideas that your subconscious will respond to. Our beliefs, our thoughts, our concepts about life and about ourselves, always become true for us.

Remember, I believe that you choose your parents before you were born in order to learn valuable lessons. Your Higher Self knew the experiences that were necessary for you to proceed on your spiritual course. So whatever you came to work out with your parents, get on with it. No matter what they say or do, or said or did, you are here ultimately to love yourself.

As parents, allow your children to love themselves by giving them the space to feel safe to express themselves in positive, harmless ways. Remember, too, just as we chose our parents, our children also chose us. There are important lessons for all of us to work out.

Parents who love themselves will find it easier to teach their children about self-love. When we feel good about ourselves, we can teach our children self-worth by example. The more we work on loving ourselves, the more our children will realize that it's an okay thing to do.

PART FOUR

Applying Your Inner Wisdom

All the theories in the world are useless unless there is action, positive change, and finally, healing.

Chapter 11

Receiving Prosperity

*When we get frightened, we want to
control everything, and then we shut
off the flow of our good. Trust life.
Everything we need is here for us.*

The Power within us is willing to give us our fondest
dreams and enormous plenty instantaneously. The problem is that we are not open to receiving it. If we want
something, our Higher Power doesn't say, "I'll think
about it." It readily responds, and sends it through, but
we have to be ready for it. If not, it goes back into the
storehouse of unfulfilled desires.

Many people come to my lectures and sit with their
arms folded across their bodies. I think, "How are they
going to let anything in?" It's a wonderful symbolic ges-
ture to open our arms wide so the Universe notices and
responds. For many it's very scary, because if they open
themselves up, they think they may get terrible things; and
they probably will, until they change whatever it is inside
them that believes they will attract doom and gloom.

When we use the term *prosperity*, a lot of people immediately think of money. However, there are many other concepts that come under the auspices of prosperity, such as: time, love, success, comfort, beauty, knowledge, relationships, health, and, of course, money.

If you are always feeling rushed because there isn't enough time to do everything you want, then you have lack of time. If you feel that success is beyond your reach, then you are not going to get it. If you feel life is burdensome and strenuous, then you will always feel uncomfortable. If you think you don't know very much, and you're too dumb to figure things out, you will never feel connected to the wisdom of the Universe. If you feel a lack of love and have poor relationships, then it will be difficult for you to attract love into your life.

What about beauty? There is beauty all around us. Do you experience the beauty that is abundant on the planet, or do you see everything as ugly and wasteful and dirty? How is your health? Are you sick all the time? Do you catch cold easily? Do you get many aches and pains? Finally, there is money. Many of you tell me that there is never enough money in your lives. What do you let yourself have? Or perhaps you feel you are on a fixed income. Who fixed it?

None of the above has anything to do with receiving. People always think, "Oh I want to get this and that and whatever." However, abundance and prosperity is about allowing yourself to accept. When you're not *getting* what you want, on some level you are not allowing yourself to accept. If we are stingy with life, then life will be stingy with us. If we steal from life, life will steal from us.

Being Honest With Ourselves

Honesty is a word we use a lot, not always understanding the true significance of what it means to be honest. It has nothing to do with morality or being a goodie-goodie. Being honest really has little to do with getting caught or going to jail. It is an act of love for ourselves.

The main value of honesty is that whatever we give out in life we will get back. The law of cause and effect is always operating on all levels. If we belittle or judge others, then we, too, are judged. If we are always angry, then we encounter anger wherever we go. The love we have for ourselves keeps us in tune with the love life has for us.

For instance, imagine that your apartment has just been burglarized. Do you immediately think that you are a victim? "My apartment was just ripped off! Who did this to me?" It is a devastating feeling when something like that happens; however, do you stop to think of how and why you attracted the experience?

Again, taking responsibility for creating our own experiences is not an idea that many of us want to accept all the time, perhaps just some of the time. It is so much easier to blame something outside of ourselves, yet our spiritual growth cannot occur until we recognize that there is little of value outside of us—everything comes from within.

When I hear that someone has just been robbed or experienced some kind of loss, the first question I ask is, "Whom did you steal from lately?" If a curious look comes over his or her face, I know I have touched a tender spot. When we think back to a time when we took something, and then think of what we lost shortly thereafter, the connection between the two experiences can be an eye-opener.

When we take something that isn't ours, we almost always lose something of greater value. We might take money or some object, and then we might lose a relationship. If we steal a relationship, we might lose a job. If we lift stamps and pens from the office, we might miss a train or a dinner date. The losses almost always hurt us in some important area of our lives.

It is unfortunate that many people steal from large companies, department stores, restaurants, or hotels and so on, rationalizing that these businesses can afford it. This type of rationalization does not work; the law of cause and effect continues to operate for each one of us. If we take, we lose. If we give, we get. It cannot be otherwise.

If there are many losses in your life or many things are going wrong, you might examine the ways in which you are taking. Some people, who would not dream of stealing things, will self-righteously rob another person of time or self-esteem. Each time we make another person feel guilty, we are stealing self-worth from him or her. To be truly honest on all levels takes a great deal of self-examination and self-awareness.

When we take something that does not belong to us, we are, in effect, instructing the Universe that we don't feel worthy of earning; we aren't good enough; we want to be stolen from; or there is not enough to go around. We believe that we must be sneaky and grab to get our good. These beliefs become effective walls around us that prevent us from experiencing abundance and joy in our lives.

These negative beliefs are not the truth of our being. We are magnificent and deserve the very best. This planet is abundantly plentiful. Our good always comes to us by the right of consciousness. The work we do in consciousness is always one of refining what we say and think and do. When we clearly understand that our thoughts create our reality, then we use our reality as a feedback mechanism to let us know what we need to change next. Being absolutely honest, down to the last paper clip, is a choice we make out of love for ourselves. Honesty helps to make our lives run more smoothly and more easily.

If you go to a store and they don't charge you for something you've bought and you know it, then it's your spiritual obligation to tell them so. If you are aware, you call it to their attention. If you don't know it, or only realize it when you get home or two days later, then that is something different.

If dishonesty brings disharmony into our lives, imagine what love and honesty can create. The good in our lives, the wonderful surprises we have—these, too, we have created. As we look within ourselves with honesty and unconditional love, we will discover so much about our power. What we can learn to create with our own consciousness has far greater value than any amount of money we could possibly steal.

Your Home Is Your Sanctuary

Everything is a reflection of what you believe you deserve. Look at your home. Is it a place that you really love to live in? Is it comfortable and joyous, or cramped, dirty, and always messy? The same with your car—do you like it? Does it reflect the love you have for yourself?

Are your clothes a bother and a nuisance and something you have to deal with? Your clothes are a reflection of how you feel about yourself. Again, the thoughts we have about ourselves can be changed.

If you want to find a new home, begin by opening yourself up to finding the right place, and affirm that it is waiting for you. When I was looking for a new home in Los Angeles, I couldn't believe that I would only find appalling places. I kept thinking that this is Los Angeles, and it's filled with wonderful apartments, so where are they?

It took me six months to find the one I wanted, and it was magnificent. During the time I was looking, the building was being constructed, and when it was finished, I found it waiting for me. If you look for something, but you are not finding it, there is probably a reason.

If you want to move from where you are because you don't like it, thank your present home for being there. Appreciate it for sheltering you from the weather. If it's difficult to like it, start with one part of the house that you like—it may be a corner of your bedroom. Don't say, "I hate this old place," because you are not going to find something that you love.

Love where you are, so you can be open to receiving a wonderful new home. If your home is messy and cluttered, then start cleaning it up. Your home is a reflection of who you are.

Loving Relationships

I am a great admirer of Dr. Bernie Siegel, the Connecticut oncologist, who has written, *Love, Medicine & Miracles.* Dr. Siegel has learned much from his cancer patients, and I would like to share what he says about unconditional love:

"Many people, especially cancer patients, grow up believing that there is some terrible flaw at the center of their being. A defect they must hide if they are to have any chance for love. Feeling unloved and unlovable and condemned to loneliness if their true selves became known. Such individuals set up defenses against sharing their innermost feelings with anyone. Because such people feel a profound emptiness inside they come to see all relationships and transactions in terms of getting something to fill the vaguely understood void within. They give love only on condition that they get something for it. And this leads to an ever deeper sense of emptiness which keeps the vicious cycle going."

Whenever I give a lecture and allow my audience the opportunity to ask questions, I can always count on being asked one thing in particular: "How can I create healthy, lasting relationships?"

All relationships are important because they reflect how you feel about yourself. If you are constantly beating yourself up by thinking that everything that goes wrong is your fault, or that you are always a victim, then you are going to attract the type of relationships that reinforce those beliefs in you.

One woman told me that she was in a relationship with a very caring and loving man, yet she had a need to test his love. So I asked her, "Why would you test his love?" She said she felt unworthy of his love because she wasn't loving herself enough. So I suggested that three times a day she stand with her arms opened, and say, "I am willing to let the love in. It's safe to let the love in." Then I told her to look into her own eyes and say, "I deserve. I am willing to *have* even if I don't *deserve.*"

Too often, you deny your good because you don't believe you can have it. For instance, you want to get married or have a long-lasting relationship. The person you go out with has four of the qualities you want in a partner. You know you're on your way. You want a little more of this or want to add something new to your list. Depending upon how much you believe you deserve to be loved, you may have to go through a dozen people before you get what you really want.

Likewise, if you believe that a Higher Power has surrounded you with truly loving people, or that everyone you meet or know brings only good into your life, then those are the types of relationships you will ultimately draw to yourself.

Codependent Relationships

Personal relationships always seem to be the first priority for many of us. Perhaps you are always searching for love. Hunting for love doesn't bring the right partner because the reasons for wanting love are unclear. We think, "Oh, if I only had someone who loved me, my life would be all better." That's not the way it works.

One exercise that I recommend is to write down the qualities you want from a relationship, such as fun, intimacy, open and positive communication, et cetera. Look at your list. Are these standards impossible to fulfill? Which of the requirements could you supply yourself?

There's a big difference between the *need for love*, and being *needy for love*. When you are *needy for love*, it simply means that you are missing love and approval from the most important person you know—yourself. You become involved in relationships that are codependent and ineffectual for both partners.

When we need someone else to fulfill us, we are codependent. When we rely on another to take care of us, so we don't have to do it ourselves, we become codependent. Many of us from dysfunctional families have learned codependency from the way we grew up. I believed for years that I was not good enough, and I sought love and approval wherever I went.

If you are always telling the other person what to do,

then you are probably trying to manipulate the relationship. On the other hand, if you are working to change your own inner patterns, then you are allowing things to happen in their right course.

Take a moment to stand in front of a mirror, and think about some of your own negative childhood beliefs that have been affecting your relationships. Can you see how you are still recreating the same beliefs? Think of some positive childhood beliefs. Do they hold the same charge for you as the negative ones?

Tell yourself that the negative beliefs no longer serve you and replace it with new, positive affirmations. You may want to write the new beliefs down and place them where you can see them every day. Again, be patient with yourself. Persevere with the new belief as much as you did with the old one. There were many times when I slipped back into old patterns before my new beliefs took root.

Remember, when you are able to contribute to the fulfillment of your own needs, then you will not be so *needy*, so codependent. It all begins with how much you love yourself. When you truly love yourself, you stay centered, calm, and secure, and your relationships at home as well as at work are wonderful. You will find yourself reacting to various situations and people differently. Matters that once may have been desperately important won't be quite as important anymore. New people will enter your life, and perhaps some old ones will disappear, which can be scary at first, and also wonderful, refreshing, and exciting.

Once you know what you want in a relationship, you must go out and be with people. No one is going to suddenly appear at your doorstep. A good way to meet people is in a support group or a night class. It enables you to connect with people who are like-minded or who are involved in the same interests. It's amazing how quickly you can meet new friends. There are many groups and classes available in cities all around the world. You need to seek these groups out. It helps when you associate with people traveling a similar path. An affirmation I suggest is: *"I am open and receptive to wonderful, good experiences coming into my life."* It's better than saying, "I'm looking for a new lover." Be open and receptive, and the Universe will respond for your highest good.

You will find that as your self-love grows, so will your self-respect, and any changes that you find yourself needing to make will be easier to accomplish when you know that they are the right ones for you. Love is never outside yourself—it is always within you. As you are more loving, you will be more lovable.

Beliefs About Money

Having fear about the issue of money comes from our early childhood programming. A woman at one of my workshops said that her wealthy father had always had a fear of going broke, and he passed on the fear that money would be taken away. She grew up being afraid that she wouldn't be taken care of. Her freedom with money was tied to the fact that her father manipulated his family through guilt. She had plenty of money all her life, and her lesson was to let go of the fear that she couldn't take care of herself. Even without all the money, she still could take care of herself.

Many of our parents grew up in the Depression, and many of us have inherited beliefs when we were young, such as, "We may starve," or "We may never find work," or "We may lose our home, our car," whatever.

Very few children say, "No that's nonsense." Children accept it and say, "Yes, that's right."

Make a list of your parents' beliefs about money. Ask yourself if you are still choosing to believe them now. You will want to go beyond your parents' limitations and fears because your life is not the same now. Stop repeating these beliefs to yourself. Begin transforming the pictures in your mind. When an opportunity comes up, don't echo your past history of lack. Begin proclaiming the new message for today. You can begin now to affirm that it's okay to have money and riches and that you will use your money wisely.

It is also normal and natural for us to have more money at certain times than others. If we can trust the Power within to always take care of us no matter what, we can easily flow through the lean times, knowing that we will have more in the future.

Money isn't the answer, although many of us think that if we have a lot of money, everything will be fine; we won't have any more problems or worries. But money is truly not the answer. Some of us have all the money that we could ever need, and we still aren't happy.

Be Grateful for What You Have

A gentleman I knew told me that he felt guilty because he couldn't pay back his friends for the kindness and gifts they gave him when he was not doing so well. I told him that there are times when the Universe gives to us, in whatever form we may need, and we may not be able to give back.

In whatever way the Universe has decided to respond to your need, be grateful. There *will* come a time when you will help somebody else. It may not be with money, but with time or compassion. Sometimes we don't realize that these things can be more valuable than money.

I can think of many people during the early days of my life who helped me enormously at a time when there was no way for me to pay them back. Years later, I have taken the opportunity to help others. Too often we feel we must exchange prosperity. We must reciprocate. If somebody takes us to lunch, we immediately have to take them to lunch; or somebody gives us a gift, and we immediately have to buy one for them.

Learn to receive with thanks. Learn to accept because the Universe perceives our openness to receive as not just exchanging prosperity. Much of our problem stems from our in-ability to receive. We can give but it's so difficult to receive.

When someone gives you a gift, smile, and say thank you. If you say to the person, "Oh, it's the wrong size or the wrong color," I guarantee the person won't ever give you another gift. Accept graciously, and if it really isn't right for you, give it to somebody else who can use it.

We want to be grateful for what we do have, so that we can attract more good to us. Again, if we focus on lack, then we will draw it to us. If we are in debt, we need to forgive ourselves, not berate ourselves. We need to focus on the debt being paid off by doing affirmations and visualizations.

The best thing we can do for people who are having money problems is to teach them how to create it in consciousness, because then it's lasting. It's much more lasting than handing them some money. I'm not saying, don't give your money away, but don't give it away because you feel guilty. People seem to say, "Well I have to help other people." You're a *people*, too. You are somebody, and you're worthy of prosperity. Your consciousness is the best bank account you can have. When you put in worthwhile thoughts, you will reap large dividends.

Tithing Is a Universal Principle

One of the ways to attract money into your life is to tithe. Tithing 10% of you income has long been an established principle. I like to think of it as *giving back to Life*. When we do that we seem to prosper more. The churches have always wanted you to tithe to them. It is one of their principle ways of gathering income. In current years that has expanded to tithing to where you get your spiritual food.

Who or what has nourished you on your quest for improving the quality of your life? That could be the perfect place for you to tithe. If tithing to a church or a person doesn't appeal to you, there are many wonderful non-profit organizations that could benefit others by your contributions. Investigate and find the one that is right for you.

People often say, "I will tithe when I have more money." Of course then they never do. If you are going to tithe, start now and watch the blessings flow. However if you only tithe to *get more,* then you have missed the point. It must be freely given or it won't work. I feel that life has been good to me and I gladly give to life in various ways.

There is so much abundance in this world just waiting for you to experience it. If you would know that there is more money than you could ever spend, or more people than you could ever meet, and more joy than you could imagine, you would have everything you need and desire.

If you ask for your highest good, then trust the Power within to provide it to you. Be honest with yourself and others. Don't cheat, not even a little, it will only come back to you.

The Infinite Intelligence that permeates all says "Yes!" to you. When something comes into your life, don't push it away, say "Yes!" to it. Open yourself to receiving good. Say "Yes!" to your world. Opportunity and prosperity will increase a hundredfold.

Chapter 12

Expressing Your Creativity

When our inner vision opens, our
horizons expand.

Our Work Is a Divine Expression

When people ask me about my purpose in life, I tell them that my work is my purpose. It is very sad to know that most people hate their jobs and even worse, that they don't know what they want to do. Finding your life's purpose, finding work that you love to do, is loving who you are.

Your work serves as your expression of creativity. You need to go beyond your feelings of not being good enough or not knowing enough. Allow the creative energy of the Universe to flow through you in ways that are deeply satisfying to you. It doesn't matter what you do, as long as it is satisfying to your being and it fulfills you.

If you hate where you work or hate what you're doing, you will always feel the same about your job unless you change inside. If you go to a new job with your same old work beliefs, you will only feel the same way again in time.

447

Part of the problem is that many people ask for what they want in a negative way. One woman had a very difficult time stating what she wanted in a positive way. She kept repeating, "I don't want this to be a part of the job," or "I don't want this to happen," or "I don't want to feel the negative energy there." Can you see that she was not declaring what she did want? We need to be clear on what we want!

Sometimes it's troublesome to ask for what we want. It's so easy to say what we don't want. Start declaring what you want your work to be. *"My work is deeply fulfilling. I help people. I am able to be aware of what they need. I work with people that love me. I feel safe at all times."* Or perhaps, *"My work allows me to express my creativity freely. I earn good money doing things I love."* Or, *"I am always happy at work. My career is filled with joy and laughter and abundance."*

Always declare in the present tense. What you declare, you will get! If you don't, then there are beliefs within you that are refusing to accept your good. Make a list of *What I believe about work*. You may be amazed at the negative beliefs within you. You won't prosper until you change those beliefs.

When you work at a job you hate, you are shutting down the ability of your Power to express itself. Think of the qualities you want in a job—what it would feel like if you had the perfect job. It is essential that you are clear about what you do want. Your Higher Self will find a job that is right for you. If you don't know, be willing to know. Open yourself to the wisdom that is inside you.

I learned early through Science of Mind that my job was to express Life. Every time I was presented with a problem, I knew it was an opportunity to grow and that the Power that created me had given me everything I needed to solve that problem. After my initial panic, I would quiet my mind and turn within. I gave thanks for the opportunity to demonstrate the Power of the Divine Intelligence working through me.

A woman at one of my workshops wanted to be an actress. Her parents persuaded her to attend law school, and she was under a lot of pressure from everyone around her to go into law. However, she stopped going after one month. She decided to take an acting class because that is what she always wanted to do.

Soon after, she started having dreams that she was going nowhere in her life, and she became miserable and depressed. She was having a problem letting go of her doubts and had reservations about making the biggest mistake in her life, which she feared she could never go back and change.

I asked her, "Whose voice is that in there?" She said those were the words that her father had told her several times.

There are many people who can relate to this young woman's story. She wanted to act, and her parents wanted her to be a lawyer. She got to a point of confusion, not knowing what to do. She needed to understand that it was her father's way of saying, "I love you." If she became a lawyer, he felt she would be safe and secure. That's what he wanted. However, it's not what *she* wanted.

She had to do what was right for her life even if it did not meet her fathers' expectations. I told her to sit in front of the mirror and look into her eyes and say, *"I love you, and I support you in having what you really want. I'm going to support you in every way that I can."*

I told her to take the time to listen. She needed to connect to her inner wisdom and realize that she didn't have to please anyone other than herself. She could love her father and still fulfill herself. She had the right to feel worthy and able to do it. And she could tell her father, "I love you and I don't want to be a lawyer—I want to be an actress," or whatever. It is one of our challenges to do what is right for us even when those who care about us have other ideas. We are not here to fulfill other peoples expectations.

When we have strong beliefs that we don't deserve, we have problems doing what we want. If other people tell you that you can't have, and then you deny yourself, the child inside you doesn't believe it deserves anything good. Again, it comes back to learning and practicing ways to love yourself more each day.

I repeat, do begin by writing down everything you believe about work and failure and success. Look at all the negatives, and realize that those are the beliefs that keep you from flowing in this area. You may find you have many beliefs that say you deserve to fail. Take each negative statement and turn it into a positive one. Begin to shape in your mind what you want your fulfilling work to be.

Your Income Can Come from Many Sources

How many of us believe that we have to work hard to earn a good living? Especially in this country, there is a work ethic that implies that one must work hard to be a good person, and in addition to that, work is drudgery.

I have found that if you work at what you love, you can usually create a good income for yourself. If you continually say, "I hate this job," you will get nowhere. Whatever you are doing, bring love and a positive attitude into it. If you are in an uncomfortable situation, look within to see what is the best lesson for you to learn from it.

One young woman told me that her belief system allowed money to come to her from all sorts of unexpected sources. Her friends criticized her ability to draw wealth to her in her unique way and insisted that she had to work hard to earn money. She said that they knew she didn't work hard at all. So she began to run the fear that if she didn't work hard, that meant that she didn't deserve the money she had.

Her consciousness was on the right track originally. She needed to thank herself instead of becoming fearful. She understood how to manifest abundance, and her life was working in that area without any struggle. However, her friends wanted to pull her down because they all worked hard and they didn't have as much money as she did.

Many times I reach out my hand to others, and if they take it and want to learn new things and go places, it's wonderful. If they try and drag me down, I say goodbye, and I work with somebody who really wants to come up out of the mud.

If your life is filled with love and joy, don't listen to some miserable, lonely person who tells you how to run your life. If your life is rich and abundant, don't listen to someone who is poor and in debt tell you how to run it. Very often, our parents are the ones telling us how to do things. They come from a place of burden and hardship and misery and then try to tell us how to run our lives!

Many people worry about the economy and believe they will either earn or lose money due to the economic situation at present. However, the economy is always moving up and down. So, it doesn't matter what is happening out there, or what others do to change the economy. We are not stuck because of the economy. No matter what is happening "out there" in the world, it only matters what you believe about yourself.

If you have a fear about becoming homeless, ask yourself, "Where am I not at home within my self? Where do I feel abandoned? What do I need to do to experience inner peace?" All outer experiences reflect inner beliefs.

I have always used the affirmation, *"My income is constantly increasing."* Another affirmation I like is, *"I go beyond my parents' income level.* You have a right to earn more than your parents' did. It's almost a necessity since things cost more now. Women, especially, experience a lot of conflict with this one. Often they find it difficult to earn more than their fathers are earning. They need to go beyond their feelings of not deserving and accept the abundance of financial wealth that is their divine right.

Your job is only one of many channels of an infinite source of money. Money is not the object of your right work. Money can come to you in many ways and from many avenues. No matter how it comes, accept it with joy as a gift from the Universe.

A young lady was complaining that her in-laws were buying her new baby all sorts of nice things and she could not afford to buy anything. I reminded her that the Universe wanted that baby to be well supplied with an abundance of all good and used the in-laws as a channel to supply it. She then could be grateful and appreciate the way in which the Universe was providing for her baby.

Relationships on the Job

The relationships we create at work are similar to the relationships we have as a family. They can be healthy or they can be dysfunctional.

A woman once asked me, "As a person who is usually positive, how do I deal with people in a work environment who are constantly negative?"

First of all, I thought it interesting that she was in a

work environment where everybody was negative when she said she was positive. I wondered why she was attracting negativity to her, perhaps there was negativity within her that she did not recognize.

I suggested that she start to believe for herself that she always worked in an area where it was peaceful and joyful, where people really appreciated each other and life as a whole. Where there was respect on all sides. Instead of complaining how so-and-so had to do it his way, she could affirm for herself that she always worked in the ideal place.

By adopting this philosophy she could either help bring out the best qualities in others because they would be responding differently to her inner changes, or she would find herself in another work arena where the conditions would be as she declared.

A man once told me that when he started his job he had all these incredible instincts, and his job was wonderful and sailed along smoothly. He was precise, direct, and satisfied. Suddenly, he began to make mistakes every day. I asked him what he was frightened of? Could it be an old childhood fear that was surfacing? Was there someone at work with whom he was angry, or was he trying to get even with somebody? Did that person remind him of one of his parents? Had this happened in other jobs? It seemed to me that he was creating some chaos at work because of an old belief system. He recognized that it was an old family pattern where he was ridiculed every time he made a mistake. I suggested that he forgive his family and affirm that he now has wonderful, harmonious relationships at work where people totally respect him and appreciate everything he does.

When you think of your co-workers, don't think, "They're so negative." Everybody has every quality in them, so respond to the good qualities that are in them, and respect their peacefulness instead. When you can focus on these qualities, they will rise to the surface. If others are constantly saying negative things, don't pay attention. You want to change *your* consciousness. Since they are reflecting something negative within you, when your consciousness really changes, negative people won't be around very much. Even if you feel frustrated, start affirming what you want to have in your work space. Then accept it with joy and thanksgiving.

One woman had an opportunity at work to do what she loved and to grow from the experience. However, she would constantly get sick and sabotage herself. She recalled that when she was a child she was always getting sick because it was her way of getting love and affection. So she kept recreating the pattern of getting sick as an adult.

What she needed to learn was how to get love and affection in a more positive way. When anything went wrong at work, she went right back to being the five-year-old girl. So when she began to take care of her little inner child she also learned to feel safe, and to accept her own power.

Competition and comparison are two major stumbling blocks to your creativity. Your uniqueness sets you apart from all others. There has never been another person like you since time began, so what is there to compare or compete with? Comparison either makes you feel superior or inferior, which are expressions of your ego, your limited-mind thinking. If you are going to compare to make yourself feel a little bit better, then you are saying somebody else isn't good enough. If you put others down, you may think you will raise yourself up. What you really do is put yourself in a position to be criticized by others. We all do this on some level and its good when we can transcend it. Becoming enlightened is to go within and shine the light on yourself so you can dissolve whatever darkness that is in there.

I want to say, again, that everything changes, and what was perfect for you once, may not be anymore. In order for you to keep changing and growing, you keep going within and listening for that which is right for you in the here and now.

Changing the Way We Do Business

For the past several years, I have owned my own publishing business. My motto has been that we open the mail and answer the phone, and handle what's in front of us, and there is always plenty to do. As we did this day by day, the business grew from a few people to well over 20 employees.

We established our business on spiritual principles, using affirmative mind treatments to open and close meetings. We realized that many other businesses ran on competition, often condemning others, and we did not want to put that energy out to others, knowing that it would come back two-fold.

We decided that if we were going to live by the philosophy, we were not going to operate under the old concepts of doing business. If problems arose, we would spend time affirming what we wanted to change.

We also had a soundproof "*screaming room*," where employees could let off steam without being heard or judged. It was also a place where they could meditate or relax, and we supplied it with plenty of tapes for people to listen to. It became a safe haven in times of difficulty.

I remember a time when we were having many problems with our computer system, and every day something would break down. Because I believe machines reflect our consciousness, I realized that many of us were sending negative energy to the computers and we were *expecting* them to constantly break down. I had an affirmation programmed into the computer, "Good Morning, how are you today? I work well when I am loved. I love you." In the morning when everyone turned on their computers, that message would appear. Its amazing how we had no more problems with our computers.

Sometimes we think of things that happen, especially at work, as "disasters." But we must look at them for what they are—simply life experiences that *always* teach us something. I know that I have never had a "disaster" that did not end up a good learning experience in the end, and it often moved me to a much better level in life.

For instance, recently my company, Hay House, was not doing so well. Like the economy, our sales would go up and down and it appeared that sales were down and staying that way, at least for the moment. However, we did not adjust to that and month after month we were spending more than we took in. Anyone who has owned a business knows that that is not the way to do it. Eventually it looked as if I would lose my business if I didn't take some "drastic measures."

Those "drastic measures" included letting go of over half of my staff. You can imagine how difficult it was for me to do that. I remember walking into the conference room, where all my staff had gathered, to deliver the news. I was in tears, but I knew that it had to be done. As difficult as it was for all of us, I also trusted that my much loved employees would soon find new and better jobs. And almost all of them have! Some of them have even started their own businesses and are very successful. At the darkest time I kept knowing and affirming that this experience would turn out to be for the highest good of all concerned.

Of course, everyone else assumed the worst. Rumors were flying that Hay House was belly up. Not just within the people I knew, but all over the country! Our sales staff were surprised that so many business people even *knew* about our company, let alone its financial condition. I have to admit that we took great joy in proving those forecasts wrong. By tightening our belts tremendously, we didn't go belly up. With our smaller staff, and each of us determined to make it work, we've come through it very well, but most importantly *we have learned a lot.*

In the meantime, Hay House is now doing better than ever. My staff is enjoying their work and I am enjoying my staff. Even though we are all working harder, the interesting thing is that no one feels that they have too much work to do. We are even getting more books out than we ever had and are attracting much more prosperity in all areas of our lives.

I believe that everything does work out for the best in the end, but sometimes it is hard to see that while you are going through the experience. Think of a negative experience that may have happened to you in your work or in you past, in general. Perhaps you were fired or maybe your spouse left you. Now go beyond it and take a look at the big picture. Didn't many good things happen as a result of that experience? I've heard so many times, "Yes, that was a horrible thing that happened to me, but if it hadn't, I never would have met so-and-so . . . or start my own business . . . or admit that I had an addiction . . . or learn to love myself."

By trusting the Divine Intelligence to let us experience life in the way that is best for us, we empower ourselves to actually enjoy *everything* that life has to offer; the good as well as the so-called bad. Try applying this to your work experiences and notice the changes that happen to you.

Those who own or operate businesses can begin to function as an expression of Divine Intelligence. It is important to keep the lines of communication open with employees and allow them to express their feelings about their work in a safe way. Make sure the offices are a neat and clean place to work. Here again, clutter in an office reflects the consciousness of the people working there. With all the physical clutter, how can the mental or intellectual tasks be done well and on time? You could adopt a statement of purpose that reflects the desired philosophy of your business. At Hay House we feel our purpose is: *"Creating a world where it is safe for us to love each other."* When you allow Divine Intelligence to operate in all aspects of business, then everything flows on purpose and according to a divine plan. The most wonderful opportunities will fall in your lap.

I see many businesses beginning to change. There will come a time when business will not be able to survive using the old ways of competition and conflict. One day we will all know that there is plenty for everyone and that we bless and prosper each other. Companies can begin to shift their priorities and make it a great place for their workers to express themselves, and have their products and services benefit the planet in general.

People want to get more out of their work than just a paycheck. They want to contribute to the world and feel fulfilled. In the future, the ability to do good on a global level will overshadow the need for materialism.

Chapter 13

The Totality of Possibilities

*Each one of us is totally linked with
the Universe and with all of life. The
Power is within us to expand the
horizons of our consciousness.*

Now I want you to stretch even further. If you have been
on the pathway and doing work on yourself for some
time, does that mean you have nothing else to do? Are
you really going to sit on your laurels and rest? Or do you
realize that this inner work is a lifetime occupation, and
once you start, you really never stop? You can hit
plateaus and take vacations, but basically it's a lifetime's
worth of work. You may want to ask yourself what areas
you still need to work on and what you need. Are you
healthy? Are you happy? Are you prosperous? Are you
creatively fulfilled? Do you feel safe? Do you feel secure?

Limitations Learned from the Past

There is an expression I like to use a lot—*the totality of
possibilities.* I learned it from one of my early teachers in

New York—Eric Pace. It always gave me such a taking-off place for letting my mind go beyond what I thought possible; far beyond the limited beliefs I grew up with when I was young.

Being a child, I didn't understand that the passing criticisms of grown-ups and friends were just the result of a bad day or a small disappointment and really weren't true. I accepted these thoughts and beliefs about myself willingly, and they became a part of my limitations. I may not have looked awkward, or dumb, or silly, but I sure felt it.

Most of us create the ideas we believe about life by the time we are five years old. We add a little bit more when we are teenagers, and maybe a tiny bit more when we're older, but very little. If I were to ask most people why they believe such and such on any subject, and they trace it back, they would discover that they made a certain decision about the subject by the time they were this young age.

So, we live in the limitations of our five-year-old consciousness. It was something we accepted from our parents, and we still live under the limitations of our parents' consciousness. Even the most wonderful parents in the world didn't know everything and had their own limitations. We say what they said and do what they did: "You can't do that," or "That won't work." However, we don't need limitations, as important as they may seem.

Some of our beliefs may be positive and nourishing. These thoughts served us well all of our lives, such as, "Look both ways before you cross the street," or "Fresh fruits and vegetables are good for your body." Other thoughts may be useful at a young age, but as we grow older, they are no longer appropriate. "Don't trust strangers," for instance, may be good advice for a small child. As adults, to perpetuate this belief only creates isolation and loneliness. The good news in all of this is that we can always make adjustments all the time.

The moment we say "I can't," or "It won't work," or "There's not enough money,"or "What would the neighbors think?" we are limited. This last expression is a significant obstacle for us. "What will the neighbors, or my friends, or my co-workers, or whoever, think?" It's a good excuse—now we don't have to do it, because *they* wouldn't do it, and *they* wouldn't approve. As society changes, what the neighbors think changes, also, so to hold on to this assumption doesn't make sense.

If someone says to you, "Nobody has ever done it this way before," you can say, "So what?" There are hundreds of ways of doing something, so do the way that's right for you. We tell ourselves other absurd messages such as, "I'm not strong enough," or I'm not young enough," or "I'm not old enough," or I'm not tall enough, or "I'm not the right sex."

How often have you used the last one? "Because I'm a woman, I can't do this," or "Because I'm a man, I can't do that." Your soul has no sexuality. I believe you agreed upon your sexuality before you were born to learn a spiritual lesson. To feel inferior because of sexuality is not only a poor excuse but also another way to relinquish your power.

Our limitations often stop us from expressing and experiencing the totality of possibilities. "I don't have the right education." How many of us have let that one stop us? We have to realize that education is something set up by groups of people who say, "You can't do such and such unless you do it our way." We can accept that as a limitation, or we can go beyond it. I accepted it for many, many years because I was a high school drop-out. I used to say, "Oh, I don't have any education. I can't think. I can't get a good job. I can't do anything well."

Then one day I realized that the limitation was all in my mind and had nothing to do with reality. When I dropped my own limiting beliefs, and I allowed myself to move into the totality of possibilities, I discovered that I could think. I discovered that I was very bright, and I could communicate. I discovered all sorts of possibilities, which when viewed from the limitations of the past seemed impossible.

Limiting the Potential Within Us

Then, there are some of you who think you know it all. The trouble with knowing it all is that you don't grow, and nothing new can come in. Do you accept that there is a Power and an Intelligence greater than you, or do you think that you are "it"—you in your physical body? If you think that you're "it," then you will be running scared because of your limited mind. If you realize that there is a Power in this Universe that is far greater and wiser, and you are a part of It, then you can move into the space where the totality of possibilities can operate.

How often do you allow yourself to dwell in the limitations of your present consciousness? Every time you say, "I can't," you are putting a stop sign in front of you. You shut down the door to your own inner wisdom, and you block the flow of energy that is your spiritual knowingness. Are you willing to go beyond what you believe today? You woke up this morning with certain concepts and ideas. You have the ability to move beyond some of them to experience a far greater reality. It is called learning—because you are taking in something new. It may fit in with what is already there, or it may even be better.

Have you ever noticed that when you start rearranging your closet, you discard clothes and odds and ends that you no longer need. You pile up the possessions you are giving away on one side, and throw away the stuff that is no longer usable. Then you begin to put everything back, and in a totally different order. It's easier to find what you're looking for, and at the same time, you made room for new clothes. If you bought a new outfit and put it in the old closet, you may have had to jam it between other paraphernalia. If you clean out your closet and rearrange it, then when you bring in the new outfit, it has room for itself.

We need to do the same routine with our minds. We need to clean out the contents that no longer work so we have room for the new possibilities. Where God is, all things are possible, and God is in each one of us. If we continue with our preconceived ideas, then we are blocked. When someone is ill, do you say, "Oh, poor person, how he or she must be suffering!" Or, do you look

465

at the person and see the absolute truth of being and affirm the health of the Divine Power that is within? Do you see the totality of possibilities and know that miracles can happen?

A man I once met told me very emphatically that it was absolutely impossible for a grown person to change. He was living in the desert and had all sorts of illnesses, and he wanted to sell his property. He didn't want to change his thinking, so he was very rigid when it came time to negotiate with a buyer. It had to be done his way. It was apparent that he would have a very burdensome time trying to sell his property because his belief was that he could never change. All he had to do was open his consciousness to a new way of thinking.

Expanding Our Horizons

How do we keep ourselves from moving into this totality of possibilities? What else limits us? All our fears are limitations. If you are frightened and you say, "I can't; it won't work," what will happen? Fearful experiences will come back. Judgments are limitations. None of us like to be judged, yet how often do we do it? We're encouraging limitations by our judgments. Every time you find yourself judging or criticizing, no matter how small, remind yourself that what goes out comes back. You may want to stop limiting your possibilities and change your thinking to something wonderful.

There is a difference between being judgmental and having an opinion. Many of you are asked for your judgment of something. In actuality, you are really giving your opinion. An opinion is how you feel about something, such as, "I prefer not to do this. I prefer to wear red instead of blue." To say someone else is wrong because she wears blue becomes a judgment. We need to discern between the two. Remember, criticism is always making yourself or someone else wrong. If someone asks your opinion, your preference, don't let it become a judgment or criticism against something else.

Similarly, every time you indulge in guilt, you are setting a limitation. If you hurt someone, say you're sorry, and don't hurt the person anymore. Don't walk around feeling guilty because it keeps you locked out from experiencing your good and has nothing to do with the reality of your true being.

When you are unwilling to forgive, you limit your growth. Forgiveness allows you to right a wrong in your spiritual self, to have understanding instead of resentment, to have compassion instead of hatred.

Look at your problems as opportunities for you to grow. When you have problems, do you see only the restrictions of your limited-mind thinking? Do you think, "Oh, poor me, why did it happen to me?" You don't always have to know how situations are going to work out. You need to trust the Power and Presence within, which is far greater than you are. You need to affirm that all is well and everything is working out for your highest good. If you open yourself to the possibilities when you have problems, you can make changes; changes can happen in incredible ways, perhaps ways you could not even imagine.

We've all been in situations in our lives where we've

said, "I don't know how I'll work this out." It seemed like we were up against a brick wall, and yet we are all here now, and we've worked through whatever it was. Maybe we didn't understand how it happened, yet it did happen. The more we can align ourselves with the cosmic energy, the One Intelligence, the Truth and Power within us, the quicker those wonderful possibilities can be realized.

Group Consciousness

It is essential that we leave our limited thinking and beliefs behind and awaken our consciousness to a more cosmic view of life. The development of higher consciousness on this planet is happening at a rate far faster than ever before. The other day I saw a graph that just fascinated me. It showed the growth of various systems in our history and how they have changed. Agricultural development was overshadowed by industrial growth, and then around 1950, the informational phase took over as communication and computer operation became widespread.

Alongside this informational period, there is also a consciousness-raising movement graph that is shooting far ahead of the informational phase at a unchallenged rate of advancement. Can you imagine what it means? I do a lot of traveling, and wherever I go, I see people who are studying and learning. I've been to Australia, Jerusalem, London, Paris, and Amsterdam, and everywhere I go I meet large groups of people who are searching for ways to expand and enlighten themselves. They are fascinated by how their minds work, and they are using their wisdom to take control of their lives and their experiences.

We are reaching new levels of spirituality. Although religious wars are still being fought, they are becoming less and less prevalent. We are beginning to connect with one another on higher levels of consciousness. The collapse of the Berlin wall and the birth of freedom in Europe are examples of our expanding consciousness, as freedom is our natural birthright. As the consciousness of each person awakens, group consciousness becomes influenced as well.

Every time you use your consciousness in a positive way, you are connecting with other people who are doing the same. Every time you use it in a negative way, you are also connecting to that. Every time you meditate, you are connecting with other people on the planet who are meditating. Every time you visualize good for yourself, you do it for others as well. Every time you visualize the healing of your body, you connect with others who are doing the same thing.

Our goals are to expand our thinking and to go beyond what was, to what might be. Our consciousness can create miracles in the world.

The totality of possibilities connects everything, including our Universe and beyond. What are you connecting with? Prejudice is a form of fear. If you're prejudiced, you are connecting with other prejudiced people. If you open your consciousness and do the best you can to work on a level of unconditional love, then you connect with the curve on the graph that is climbing upwards. Do you want to be left behind? Or do you want to go up with the curve?

Often there is a crisis in the world. How many people send positive energy to the troubled area and do affirmations that everything works out as quickly as possible and that there is a solution for the highest good of all concerned? You need to use your consciousness in a way that will create harmony and plenty for all people. What sort of energy are you sending? Instead of condemning and complaining, you can connect with the Power on the spiritual level and affirm the most positive results imaginable.

How far are you willing to expand the horizons of your thinking? Are you willing to go beyond your neighbors'? If your neighbors are limited, make new friends. How far will you stretch? How willing are you to change *I can't* to *I can*.

Every time you hear that something is incurable, know in your mind that it isn't true. Know that there is a Power greater. "Incurable" to me means that the medical profession simply hasn't yet figured out how to cure that particular illness. It doesn't mean that it's not possible. It means that we go within and find a cure. We can go beyond statistics. We are not numbers on a chart. Those are someone else's projections, somebody's limited-mind thinking. If we don't give ourselves possibilities, we don't give ourselves hope. Dr. Donald M. Pachuta at the National Aids Conference in Washington, D.C., said that "we have never had an epidemic—*ever*—that was 100 percent fatal."

Somewhere on this planet, someone has been healed of every single dis-ease that we have been able to create. If we just accept doom and gloom, we are stuck. We need to take a positive approach so we can find some answers. We need to begin to use the Power within us to heal ourselves.

Our Other Powers

It is said that we use only 10 percent of our brain—only 10 percent! What is the purpose of the other 90 percent? I think having psychic ability, telepathy, clairvoyance, or clairaudience are all normal and natural. It's just that we don't allow ourselves to experience these phenomena. We have all sorts of reasons why we don't, or why we don't believe we can. Little children are often very psychic. Unfortunately, parents immediately say, "Don't say that," or "That's your imagination," or "Don't believe in that foolish nonsense." The child inevitably turns off these abilities.

I think the mind is capable of remarkable things, and I know for certain that I could go from New York to Los Angeles without a plane if I only knew how to dematerialize and rematerialize there. I don't know how yet, but I know it is possible.

I think that we are capable of accomplishing incredible achievements, but we haven't the knowledge yet because we won't use it for our good. We will probably hurt others with the knowledge. We have to get to a point where we really can live in unconditional love, so we can begin using the other 90 percent of our brains.

Fire Walking

How many have heard about fire walking? Whenever I ask this question at seminars, several hands always go up. We all know that it is totally impossible to walk on hot coals, right? Nobody can do it without burning their feet. Yet people have done it, and they aren't extraordinary people; they are people like you and me. They probably learned it in one evening by attending a fire-walking workshop.

I have a friend, Darby Long, who works with Dr. Carl Simonton, the cancer specialist. They do a week-long workshop for people with cancer, and during the week, they have a fire-walking demonstration. Darby has done it herself many times, and has even carried people across the hot coals. I always think how incredible it must be for people with cancer to see and experience such a process. It probably blows a lot of people's minds. Their concepts about limitation would somehow be different afterward.

I believe Anthony Robbins, the young man who started fire walking in this country, is here to do something really extraordinary on the planet. He studied NLP, Neuro-linguistic Programming, a process whereby he could observe someone's patterns of behavior and then repeat that person's responses and cues of behavior to achieve similar results. NLP is based on the hypnotic techniques of Milton Erickson, M.D. which were systematically observed and recorded by John Grinder and Richard Bandler. When Tony heard about fire walking, he wanted to learn it, and, in turn, to teach it to others. He was told by a yogi that it would take years of study and meditation. However, using NLP, Tony learned it within a few hours. He knew that if he could do it, anyone could do it. He has been teaching people how to walk on coals, not because it is a wonderful parlor trick, but because it shows them how to go beyond their limitations and fears.

Everything Is Possible

Repeat with me: *"I live and dwell in the totality of possibilities. Where I am there is all good."* Think about these words for a minute. *All good*. Not some, not a little bit, but *all good*. When you believe that anything is possible, you open yourself up to answers in every area of your life.

Where we are is the totality of possibilities. It is always up to us individually and collectively. We either have walls around us or we take them down and feel safe enough to be totally open to allow all good to come into our lives. Begin to observe yourself objectively. Notice what is going on inside you—how you feel, how you react, what you believe—and allow yourself to observe without comment or judgment. When you can, you will live your life from the totality of possibilities.

PART FIVE

Letting Go of the Past

The planet is becoming conscious as a whole. It is becoming self-conscious.

Chapter 14

Change and Transition

*Some people would rather leave the
planet than change.*

Change is usually what we want the other person to do,
isn't it? When I speak about the other person, I want to
include the government, big business, the boss or co-
worker, the Internal Revenue Service, foreigners; the
school, husband, wife, mother, father, children, et cetera
—anyone other than ourselves. We don't want to change,
but we want everybody else to change so our lives will be
different. And yet, of course, any changes that we are going to make at all have to come from within ourselves.

Change means that we free ourselves from feelings of
isolation, separation, loneliness, anger, fear and pain. We
create lives filled with wonderful peacefulness, where we
can relax and enjoy life as it comes to us—where we
know that everything will be all right. I like to use the
premise that *"Life is wonderful, all is perfect in my world,
and I always move into greater good."* In that way, it
doesn't matter to me which direction my life takes, because I know it's going to be wonderful. Therefore, I can
enjoy all sorts of situations and circumstances.

Someone at one of my lectures was going through a lot of turmoil, and the word *pain* kept coming up in the conversation. She asked if there was another word that she could use. I thought about the time I had smashed my finger by slamming a window on it. I knew if I gave into the pain, I was going to go through a very difficult period. So when it happened, I started to do some mental work right away and referred to my finger as having a lot of *sensation*. By viewing what happened in that particular way, I think it helped to heal the finger much more quickly and to handle what could have been a very unpleasant experience. Sometimes if we can alter our thinking a little bit, we can completely change a situation.

Can you think of change as an internal housecleaning? If you do a little bit at a time, it will eventually all get done. You don't have to do it all, however, before you begin to see results. If you change just a little bit, you'll begin to feel better soon.

I was at the Reverend O.C. Smith's City of Angels Science of Mind Church on New Year's Day, and he said something that made me think. He said:

"It's the new year, but you've got to realize that the new year is not going to change you. Just because it's a new year, it's not going to make any difference in your life. The only way there's going to be a change is if you are willing to go within and make the change."

That's so true. People make all sorts of New Year's resolutions, but because they don't make any internal changes, the resolutions fall away very quickly. "I'm not going to smoke another cigarette," or whatever, someone says. Right away, it's put in a negative phrase rather than one that will tell the subconscious mind what to do. In this situation you could say instead, "All desire for cigarettes has left me and I am free."

Until we make the inner changes, until we are willing to do the mental work, nothing outside of us is going to change. Yet, the inner changes can be so incredibly simple because the only thing we really need to change are our thoughts.

What can you do for yourself this year that you didn't do last year that could be positive? Take a moment and think about this question. What would you like to let go of this year that you clung to so tightly last year? What would you like to change in your life? Are you willing to do it?

There is a lot of information available that will give you ideas once you are willing to change. The moment you are willing to change, it is remarkable how the Universe begins to help you. It brings you what you need. It could be a book, a tape, a teacher or even a friend making a passing remark that suddenly has deep meaning to you.

Sometimes conditions will get worse before they get better, and that's okay because the process is beginning. The old threads are untangling, so flow with it. Don't panic and think its not working. Just keep working with your affirmations and the new beliefs you are planting.

Making Progress

Of course, from the moment you decide to make a change until you get the demonstration, there is a transitional period. You vacillate between the old and the new. You go back and forth between what was and what you would like to be or to have. It is a normal and natural process. Often I hear people saying, "Well, I know all this stuff." My answer is, "Are you doing it?" Knowing what to do and doing it are two separate steps. It takes time until you are strong in the new and have gone the complete shift. Until then, you must be vigilant in your efforts to change.

For instance, many people say their affirmations maybe three times and give up. Then they say that affirmations don't work, or they're silly, or whatever. We have to give ourselves time to practice to make the changes; change requires action. As I said, it's what you do after you say your affirmations that counts the most.

As you go through this transitional phase, remember to praise yourself for each small step forward that you make. If you beat yourself up for the step backward, then change becomes oppressive. Use all the tools available to you as you move from the old to the new. Assure the little child inside that he or she is safe.

Author Gerald Jampolsky says that love is letting go of fear, and that there is either fear or there is love. If we are not coming from the loving space of the heart, then we're in fear, and all those states such as isolation, separation, anger, guilt, and loneliness are part of the fear syndrome. We want to move from fear into love and make love a more permanent position for us.

There are a variety of ways to change. What do you do on a daily basis to make yourself feel good inside? You're not going to do it by blaming other people or by being a victim. So what is it you do? How are you experiencing peace within you and around you? If you are not doing it now, are you willing to begin? Are you willing to start creating inner harmony and peace?

Another question to ask yourself is: Do I really want to change? Do you want to continue to complain about what you don't have in your life? Do you want to really create a much more wonderful life than you have now? If you are willing to change, you can. If you are willing to do the work involved, then you can change your life for the better. I have no power over you, and I can't do it for you. You have the power and you need to keep reminding yourself of that.

Remember, maintaining inner peace will help us connect with like-minded, peaceful people all over the world. Spirituality connects us all over this planet on a soul level, and the sense of cosmic spirituality that we are just beginning to experience is going to change the world for the better.

When I speak of spirituality, I don't necessarily mean

religion. Religions tell us who to love and how to love and who is worthy. To me we are all worthy of love, and we are all lovable. Our spirituality is our direct connection with our higher source, and we don't need a middleman for that. Begin to see that spirituality can connect us all over the planet on a very deep soul level.

Several times during the day, you might stop and ask yourself, *"What kind of people am I connecting with now?"* Ask yourself periodically, *"What do I really believe about this condition or situation?"* And think about it. Ask: *"What do I feel? Do I really want to do what these people are asking me? Why am I doing this?"* Start to examine your thoughts and feelings. Be honest with yourself. Find out what you are thinking and believing. Don't go on automatic pilot, living your life by routine: "This is the way I am, and this is what I do." Why do you do it? If it isn't a positive, nourishing experience, figure out where it came from. When did you first do it? You know what to do now. Connect to the Intelligence within you.

Stress Is Another Word for Fear

We talk a lot about stress these days. Everyone seems to be stressed out about something. Stress seems to be a buzzword and we use it to the point where I think it's a copout. "I'm so stressed," or "This is so stressful," or "All this stress, stress, stress."

Stress, to me, is a fearful reaction to life's constant changes. It is an excuse we use for not taking responsibility for our feelings. If we can equate the word "stress" with the word "fear," then we can begin to eliminate the need for fear in our lives.

The next time you think about how stressed you are, ask yourself what is scaring you. Ask: *"How am I overloading or burdening myself? Why am I giving my power away?"* Find out what you are doing to yourself that is creating this fear within you that keeps you from achieving inner harmony and peace.

Stress is not inner harmony. Inner harmony is being at peace with yourself. It's not possible to have stress and inner harmony at the same time. When you're at peace, you do things one at a time. You don't let things get to you. When you feel stressed, do something to release the fear, so you can move through life feeling safe. Don't use the word "stress" as a copout. Don't give a little word like "stress" a lot of power. Nothing has any power over you.

You Are Always Safe

Life is a series of doors closing and opening. We walk from room to room having different experiences. Many of us would like to close some doors on old negative patterns, old blocks, situations that are no longer nourishing or useful to ourselves. Many of us are in the process of opening new doors and finding wonderful new experiences.

I think that we come to this planet many, many times, and we come to learn different lessons. It's like coming to school. Before we incarnate at any particular time on the planet, we decide the lesson we are going to learn so that we can evolve spiritually. Once we choose our lesson, we choose all the circumstances and situations that will enable us to learn the lesson, including our parents, sexuality, place of birth, and race. If you've gotten this far in your life, believe me, you've made all the right choices.

As you go through life, it is essential to remind yourself that you are safe. It is only change. Trust your Higher Self to lead you and guide you in ways that are best for your spiritual growth. As Joseph Campbell once said, "Follow your bliss."

See yourself opening doors to joy, peace, healing, prosperity, and love; doors to understanding, compassion, forgiveness and freedom; doors to self-worth, self-esteem and self-love. You are eternal. You will go on forever from experience to experience. Even when you pass through the last doorway on this planet, it is not the end. It is the beginning of another new adventure.

Ultimately, you cannot force anyone to change. You can offer them a positive mental atmosphere where they have the possibility to change if they wish. However, you cannot do it for or to other people. Each person is here to work out his or her own lessons, and if you fix it for them, then they will eventually do it again because they haven't learned for themselves. They haven't worked out what they needed to do.

Love your sisters and brothers. Allow them to be who they are. Know that the truth is always within them, and they can change at any moment that they want.

Chapter 15

A World Where It's Safe to Love Each Other

We can either destroy the planet or we can heal it. Send some loving, healing energy to the planet every day. What we do with our minds makes a difference.

The planet is very much in a period of change and transition. We're going from an old order to a new order, and some people say it began with the Aquarian Age—at least the astrologers like to describe it in that way. To me, astrology, numerology, palmistry, and all those methods of psychic phenomena are merely ways of describing life. They explain life to us slightly differently.

So the astrologers say that we are moving out of the Piscean Age into the Aquarian Age. During the Piscean Age, we looked to other people to save us. We looked for other people to do it for us. In the Aquarian Age, which we are now entering, people are beginning to go within, acknowledging that they have the ability to save themselves.

Isn't it wonderfully liberating to change what we don't like? Actually, I'm not so sure that the planet is changing, as much as we are becoming more conscious and aware. Conditions that were brewing for a long time are coming to the surface, such as family dysfunction, child abuse, and our endangered planet.

As with everything else, first we must become aware in order to make changes. In the same way that we do our mental housecleaning so that we can change, we are doing the same thing with Mother Earth.

We are beginning to see our earth as a whole, living, breathing organism, an entity, a being unto itself. It breathes. It has a heartbeat. It takes care of its children. It provides everything here that we could possibly need. It's totally balanced. If you spend a day in the forest or somewhere in nature, you can see how all the systems on the planet work perfectly. It's set up to live out its existence in absolute, perfect equilibrium and harmony.

So here we are, great mankind who knows so much, and we are doing our very best to destroy the planet by disrupting this balance and harmony. Our greed gets in the way to an enormous extent. We think we know best, and through ignorance and greed we are destroying the living, breathing organism of which we are a part. If we destroy earth, where are we going to live?

I know that when I talk to people about caring more for the planet, they become overwhelmed by the problems we are encountering now. It seems that just one person doing something will not affect anything in the entire scheme of things. But that is not so. If everyone did a little it would wind up being a lot. You may not be able to see the effects right in front of you, but believe me, Mother Earth feels it collectively.

We have a little table set up to sell books at my aids support group. Recently we ran out of bags to put products in, so I thought I would start saving the bags I received when I was out shopping. At first, I thought, "Oh, you won't have that many bags by the end of the week," but boy, was I mistaken! I had bags coming out of my ears! One of my workers experienced the same thing. He said he had no idea how many bags a week he used until he started saving them. And when you put that in terms of Mother Earth, that's quite a few trees we're cutting down just to use for one or two hours, because we usually end up throwing the bags away. If you don't believe me, just try it for one week: save all the bags you receive and just be aware of how many you use.

Now I have a cloth shopping bag that I use and if I am shopping and have forgotten to bring it, I ask for a big bag and as I shop at other stores, I put my merchandise in one bag instead of collecting several. No one has ever looked at me twice for doing it. It just seems so sensible.

In Europe they have been using cloth shopping bags for a long time. A friend of mine from England visited and loved to go shopping at the supermarkets here because he wanted to carry the paper bags home. He thought they were very American and very chic. It may be a cute tradition, but the truth is we have to start thinking globally and consider the effects that these little traditions have on our environment.

American's particularly have a thing about the packaging of products. When I was in Mexico a few years ago, I visited a traditional market place and was fascinated by the unvarnished fruits and vegetables that were laid out. They certainly weren't as pretty as the ones we have in the states, but they looked natural and healthy to me, however some of the people I was with thought they looked terrible and unappealing.

In another part of the market there were open bins with powdered spices in it. Again it fascinated me because all the bins next to each other looked so bright and colorful. My friends said that they would never buy any spices from an open bin like that and I asked, "Why?" They said because it wasn't clean. When I asked why again, the answer came back that it was because it wasn't in a package. I had to laugh. Where did they think the spices were before they were put in a package? We have become so used to having things presented to us in a certain way that it's hard to accept it if we don't have all the frills and pretty packaging attached to it.

Let's be willing to see where we can make small adjustments for the sake of the environment. Even if all you do is buy a cloth shopping bag, or turn the water tap off while you brush your teeth, you have contributed a great deal by doing it.

At my office, we conserve as much as possible. There's a maintenance man in our building who picks up our recyclable copy paper every week and takes it to the recycling plant. We reuse padded envelopes. We use recycled paper in our books whenever possible, even though it costs a little more. Sometimes, it isn't possible to get, but we always ask for it anyway as we realize that if we continue to ask for it, eventually enough printers will have it available. It works that way in all areas of conservation. By creating a demand for something, we can help heal the planet in different ways as a collective power.

At home I am an organic gardener and make compost for the garden. Every piece of used vegetation goes into that compost pile. Not a lettuce leaf nor a leaf from a tree leaves my property. I believe in returning to the land what is taken away. I have a few friends who even save their vegetable trimmings for me. They put them into a bag in the freezer and when they visit they put their collection into my compost bin. What goes in as trash, comes out as rich earth filled with nourishment for plants. Because of my recycling practices, my garden produces lavishly for all my needs and is beautiful too.

Eat Nourishing Foods

Our planet is designed to give us every single thing we need to take care of ourselves. It has all the food we need. If we eat the foods of the planet, we're going to be healthy because it is part of the natural design. However, we, in our great intelligence, have designed foods such as Twinkies, and we wonder why our health isn't so good. A lot of us give lip service to diets. We say, "Yes, we know," as we reach for one sugar-filled treat after another. Two generations ago when Betty Crocker or Clarence Birdseye or whomever, came out with the first convenience-type food, we said, "Oh, isn't this wonderful!" Then came another and another and another, until generations later, there are people in this country who have never tasted real food. Everything is canned, processed, frozen, chemicalized, and, ultimately, microwaved.

I recently read that the young people in the military today do not have the healthy immune systems that youths had 20 years ago. If we don't give our body natural foods, which it needs to build and repair itself, how can we expect it to last a lifetime? Add to this: drugs, cigarettes, and alcohol abuse, a dose of self-hatred, and you have the perfect climate for dis-ease to flourish.

I had a very interesting experience recently. I took something called a "Responsible Driver's Course." It was filled with people over 55 years of age who were there ostensibly to get 5 to 10 percent off their auto insurance. I really found it fascinating that we spent the whole morning talking about illness—all the illnesses we could look forward to as we grow older. We talked about dis-eases of the eyes and everything that could go wrong with our ears and our hearts. When lunchtime came, 90 percent of these same people ran across the street to the nearest fast-food restaurant.

I thought to myself, we still don't get it, do we? One thousand people a day die from smoking. That's 365,000 people a year. I understand that over 500,000 people die from cancer each year. A million people die from heart attacks every year. A million people! Knowing this, why do we still run out to fast-food restaurants and pay so little attention to our bodies?

Healing Ourselves and Our Planet

Part of the catalyst for this transitional period is the crisis of aids. The aids crisis is showing how unloving and prejudiced we are toward one another. We treat people with aids with such little compassion. One of the things that I would really like to see happen on this planet, and I want to help create this, is a world where it is safe for us to love each other.

When we were little, we wanted to be loved for who we were, even if we were too skinny or too fat, too ugly, or too shy. We come to this planet to learn unconditional love—first to have it for ourselves, and then to give the same unconditional love to other people. We need to get rid of this idea of *them and us*. There is no *them and us*; there is only us. There are no groups that are expendable or *less than*.

Every one of us has a list of *those* people *over there*. We can't really be spiritual as long as there is one person *over there*. Many of us grew up in families where prejudice was normal and natural. This group or that group was not good enough. In order to make ourselves feel better, we would put the other group down. However, as long as we are saying that someone else isn't good enough, what we're really reflecting is that *we're* not good enough. Remember, we're all mirrors of each other.

I remember when I was invited to *The Oprah Winfrey Show*. I appeared on TV with five people with aids who were doing quite well. The six of us had met the evening before for dinner, and it was such an incredibly powerful gathering. When we sat down to have dinner, the energy was extraordinary. I started to cry because this was something I had been striving for for several years— to get a positive message out to the American public that there is hope. These people were healing themselves, and it wasn't easy. The medical community told them that they were going to die. They had to experiment with many different methods by trial and error, and they were willing to expand and go beyond their own limitations.

We taped the next day, and it was a beautiful show. I was pleased that women with aids were also represented on the show. I wanted Middle America to open their hearts and to realize that aids doesn't affect a group that they don't care about. It affects everybody. When I came out, Oprah said to me off-camera, "Louise, Louise, Louise," and came up to me and gave me a big hug.

I believe we relayed the message of hope that day. I've heard Dr. Bernie Siegel say that there is someone who has healed his or herself of every form of cancer. So there is always hope, and hope gives us possibilities. There is something to work towards instead of throwing up our hands and saying there's nothing that can be done.

The aids virus is just doing its thing—being what it is. It breaks my heart to realize that there will be more and more heterosexual people who are going to die from aids because the government and the medical profession are not moving fast enough. As long as aids is perceived as a "gay" dis-ease, it will not receive the attention it urgently needs, so how many "straight" people will have to die before it's considered a legitimate illness?

I think the faster we all put away our prejudices and work for a positive solution to this crisis, the faster the whole planet will heal. However, we can't heal the planet if we allow people to suffer. To me, aids is very much a part of the pollution of the planet. Do you realize that dolphins off the coast of California are dying of immune deficiency dis-eases? I don't believe it's because of their sexual practices. We've been polluting our lands so that a lot of the vegetation is unfit to eat. We are killing the fish in our waters. We are polluting our air, so now there is acid rain and a hole in the ozone layer. And we continue polluting our bodies.

Aids is a terrible, terrible dis-ease, yet the numbers of people who are dying from aids are far fewer than those who are dying from cancer, smoking, and heart dis-ease. We search for ever-more potent poisons to kill the dis-eases we create, yet we don't want to change our lifestyles and diets. We either want some drug to suppress our illness, or we want to surgically remove it, rather than heal it. The more we suppress, the more that problems manifest in other ways. It's even more incredible to learn that medicine and surgery only take care of 10 percent of all dis-ease. That's right. Even with all the money we spend on chemicals, radiation, and surgery, they only help 10 percent of our dis-eases!

I read an article that said that the dis-eases in the next century will be caused by new strains of bacteria that will affect our weakened immune systems. These bacteria strains have begun to mutate, so that the drugs we have now will have no effect upon them. Obviously, the more we build up our immune systems, the quicker we are going to heal ourselves and the planet. And I'm not only referring to our physical immune systems; I mean our mental and emotional immune systems as well.

To me, healing and curing bring about two different results. I think healing needs to be a team effort. If you expect your doctor to fix you, he or she may take care of the symptoms; however, that doesn't heal the problem. Healing is making yourself whole. To be healed, you must be a part of the team, you and your doctor or health care professional. There are many holistic M.D.'s who not only treat you physically, but who see you as a whole person.

We have been living with erroneous belief systems, not only individual ones, but societal ones as well. There are people who say that earaches run in their family. Others believe that when they go out in the rain, they catch cold, or they get three colds every winter. Or, when someone catches a cold in the office, everyone gets a cold because it's contagious. "Contagious" is an idea, and the idea is contagious.

A lot of people talk about dis-ease being hereditary. I don't think that's necessarily so. I think that what we pick up are the mental patterns of our parents. Children are very aware. They begin to imitate their parents, even their illnesses. If a father tightens his colon every time he feels angry, the child picks up on that. It's no wonder that when the father gets colitis years later, the child get colitis, too. Everyone knows that cancer is not contagious, yet why does it run in families? Because the patterns of resentment run in families. Resentment builds and builds until finally there is cancer.

We must allow ourselves to be aware of everything so that we can make conscious, intelligent choices. Some things may horrify us (which is part of the awakening process), but then we can do something about them. Everything in the Universe from child abuse and aids, to the homeless situation and starvation, needs our love. A tiny child who is loved and appreciated will become a strong, self-assured adult. The planet, which has everything here for us and all of life, if we allow it to be itself, will take care of us always. Let's not think about our past limitations.

Let's open ourselves to the potential of this incredible decade. We can make these final 10 years of the century a time of healing. We have the Power within us to clean up—clean our bodies, our emotions, and all the various messes we have made. We can look around and see what needs care. The way each of us chooses to live will have a tremendous impact on our future and on our world.

For the Highest Good of All

You can take this time to apply your personal growth methods to the entire planet. If you just do things for the planet and not for yourself, then you're not in balance. If you only work for yourself and stop there, then that's not balanced either.

So let's see how we can begin to balance ourselves *and* the environment. We know that our thoughts shape and create our lives. We don't always live the philosophy totally; nonetheless, we've accepted the basic premise. If we want to change our immediate world, we must change our thinking. If we want to change the greater world around us, we need to change our thinking about it, not viewing it as *them and us.*

If all the effort you put out in complaining about what's wrong with the world is applied to positive affirmations and visualizations of the world, you could begin to turn things around. Remember, every time you use your mind, you are connecting to like-minded people. If you inflict judgment, criticism, and prejudice on others, you are connecting to all the other people who are doing the same. However, if you are meditating, visualizing peace, loving yourself, and loving the planet, you are connecting with these kinds of people. You could be at home, bed-ridden, and still help to heal the planet by the way you use your mind—by practicing inner peace. I heard Robert Schuller of the United Nations once say, *"The human species needs to know that we deserve to have peace."* How true those words are.

If we can make our young people aware of what is happening in the world and give them options as to what they can do about it, then we can really begin to see a shift in consciousness. Teaching our children early about conservation efforts is one way to reassure them that important work is being done. Even though some adults still won't take responsibility for what is going on in the world around them, we can assure our children that more and more people throughout the world are becoming aware of the long-term effects of global pollution and are striving to change the situation. Becoming involved as a family in an ecological foundation such as *Greenpeace* or *Earthsave* is wonderful, as it is never too soon to impress upon children that we all have to accept responsibility for the good of our planet.

I recommend that you read John Robbins' book, *Diet For A New America*. I find it so interesting that John Robbins, heir to the Baskin-Robbins ice cream business, is doing his best to help create a holistic and peaceful planet. It's wonderful to know that some of the children of people who exploit the health of the nation turn around and do things to help the planet.

Volunteer groups are also helping to take over where the government is falling short. If the government won't help heal our environment, we can't sit around and wait. We have to get together on a grass roots level and take care of it. We can all do our part. Start to find out where you can help. Volunteer where you can. Give one hour a month if you can't do anything else.

We are definitely on the cutting edge of the forces that are going to help heal this planet. We are at a point right now where we can all go down the tubes or we can heal the planet. It isn't up to *them*, it's up to us, individually and collectively.

I see more opportunities for a blending of the scientific technologies of the past and the future with the spiritual truths of yesterday, today, and tomorrow. It is time that these elements come together. By understanding that acts of violence come from a person who is a traumatized child, we could combine our knowledge and technologies to help them change. We don't perpetuate violence by starting wars or throwing people in prisons and forgetting them. Instead, we encourage self-awareness, self-esteem, and self-love. The tools for transformation are available; we just have to use them.

Lazaris has a wonderful exercise that I would like to share with you. Pick a spot on the planet. It could be anywhere—very far away or just around the corner—some place on the planet that you would like to help heal. Envision that place as peaceful, with people well fed and clothed and living in safety and peace. Take a moment every day and envision it.

Put your love to work to help heal the planet. You are important. By sharing your love and all the magnificent gifts within you will begin to change the energy on this beautiful, blue-green, fragile planet that we call our home.

And so it is!

Afterword

I remember when I couldn't sing very well at all. I still don't sing very well, but I am much more brave. I lead people in song at the end of my workshops and support groups. Perhaps one day, I will take some lessons and learn; however, I haven't gotten around to it yet.

At one event I began to lead everyone in song, and the man in charge of the sound system turned off my microphone. Joseph Vattimo, my assistant, said, "What are you doing?" The other man said, "She's singing off key!" It was so terribly embarrassing. Now, it really doesn't matter anymore. I just sing my heart out, and it seems to open up just a little bit more.

I've had some extraordinary experiences in my life, and the one that has opened my heart on a very deep level has been working with people with aids. I can hug people now who, three years ago, I couldn't even look at. I've gone beyond a lot of my own personal limitations. In reward for that, I have found so much love—wherever I go, people give me tremendous amounts of love.

In October 1987, Joseph and I went to Washington, D.C., to march for governmental help for aids. I don't know how many are aware of the *aids quilt*. It's rather incredible. Many, many people from around the country got together and made quilt patches to commemorate someone who has died from aids. These patches are made with so much love and put together with patches from all over the world to make an enormous quilt.

When we were in Washington, the patches were put into sections and displayed between the Washington and Lincoln monuments. At six o'clock in the morning, we began to read the names of the people on the quilt. As we did, people would unfold the patch and put it in place next to the others. It was a very emotional time, as you can imagine. People were crying everywhere.

I was standing with my list, waiting to read, when I felt this tap on my shoulder. I could hear someone say, "Could I ask you a question, please?" I turned around, and the young man standing behind me looked at the badge with my name on it, and shouted, "Louise Hay! Oh my God," and he went into absolute hysteria and flung himself in my arms. We held each other, and he just sobbed and sobbed. Finally, when he could contain himself, he told me that his lover had read my book many times, and when he was about to leave the planet, his lover asked him to read a treatment from my book. He read it slowly, as his lover read the lines with him. The very last words his lover said were, "All is well," and he died.

So here I was, right in front of him. He was extremely touched. When he could compose himself enough, I said, "But what did you want to ask me?" It seemed that he had not been able to complete his lover's patch on time, and he wanted me to add his lover's name to my list. He just happened to pick me. I remember this moment very well, because it showed me that life is really simple and the things that are important are also simple.

I want to share a quote with you from Emmett Fox. If you don't know Emmett Fox, he was a very popular teacher in the '40s, '50s, and early '60s and one of the clearest teachers I know. He has written some beautiful books, and these are some of my favorite words of his:

"There is no difficulty that enough love will not conquer. There is no disease that enough love will not heal. No door that enough love will not open. No gulf that enough love will not bridge. No wall that enough love will not throw down. And no sin that enough love will not redeem. It makes no difference how deeply seated may be the trouble. How hopeless the outlook. How muddled the tangle. How great the mistake. A sufficient realization of love will dissolve it all. And if you could love enough you would be the happiest and most powerful person in the world."

It's true, you know. It sounds wonderful and it is true. What do you need to do to get to that space where you could be the happiest and most powerful person in the world? I think inner space travel is just beginning. We are just beginning to learn about the Power that we have inside us. We're not going to find it if we contract. The more we can open to ourselves, the more we are going to find the Universal energies available to assist us. There are incredible accomplishments that we are capable of.

Take a few breaths. Open your chest and give your heart room to expand. Keep practicing, and sooner or later the barriers will begin to drop. Today is your beginning point.

I love you,

Louise L. Hay

Meditations for Personal and Planetary Healing

Acknowledge yourself for being centered when there is incredible chaos around you. Acknowledge yourself for being courageous and for doing so much more than you thought you could.

The healing work we do at the end of our workshops and support groups is very powerful. We usually break into groups of three and do a form of laying-on-of-hands for each other. It is a wonderful way to accept energy and also share energy with many people who are reluctant in one way or another to ask for help. Often, profound experiences occur.

I would like to share some of the meditations we do at our healing circles. It would be wonderful if we all did them on an ongoing basis either by ourselves or in groups.

Touching Your Inner Child

See your inner child in any way that you can and notice how it looks and feels. Comfort your child. Apologize to it. Tell it how sorry you are for forsaking it. You have been away for so long, and you are now willing to make it up. Promise this little child that you will never ever leave her or him again. Anytime it wants, it can reach out and touch you, and you will be there. If it is scared, you will hold it. If it is angry, it is okay to express the anger. Tell it you love it very much.

You have the power to help create the kind of world that you want you and your child to live in. You have the power of your mind and your thoughts. See yourself creating a wonderful world. See your child relaxed and safe, peaceful, laughing, happy, playing with friends. Running free. Touching a flower. Hugging a tree. Picking an apple from the tree, and eating it with delight. Playing with a puppy or a kitten. Swinging high above the trees. Laughing with joy and running up to you and giving you a big hug.

See the two of you healthy and living in a beautiful, safe place. Having wonderful relationships with your parents, friends and co-workers. Being greeted with joy wherever you go. Having a special kind of love. See where you want to live and what you want to work at. And see yourselves as healthy. Very healthy. Joyous. And free. And so it is.

A Healthy World

Envision the world as a great place to live in. See all the sick being made well and the homeless being cared for. See dis-ease become a thing of the past, and all the hospitals now apartment buildings. See prison inmates being taught how to love themselves and being released as responsible citizens. See churches remove sin and guilt from their teachings. See governments really taking care of people.

Go outside and feel the clean rain falling. As the rain stops, see a beautiful rainbow appear. Notice the sun shining, and the air is clean and clear. Smell its freshness. See the water glisten and sparkle in our rivers, streams, and lakes. And notice the lush vegetation. Forests filled with trees. Flowers, fruits, and vegetables abundant and available everywhere. See people being healed of dis-ease, so that illness becomes a memory.

Go to other countries and see peace and plenty for all. See harmony between all people as we lay down our guns. Judgment, criticism, and prejudice become archaic and fade away. See borders crumbling and separateness disappearing. See all of us becoming one. See our Mother Earth, the planet, healed and whole.

You are creating this new world now, just by using your mind to envision a new world. You are powerful. You are important, and you do count. Live your vision. Go out and do what you can to make this vision come true. God bless us all. And so it is.

Your Healing Light

Look deep within the center of your heart and find that tiny little pinpoint of brilliantly colored light. It is such a beautiful color. It is the very center of your love and healing energy. Watch the little pinpoint of light begin to pulsate, and as it pulsates, it grows until it fills your heart. See this light move through your body from the top of your head to the tip of your toes and the tip of your fingers. You are absolutely glowing with this beautiful colored light. It is your love and your healing energy. Let your whole body vibrate with this light. You can say to yourself, *"With every breath I take, I am getting healthier and healthier."*

Feel this light cleansing your body of dis-ease and allowing normal health to return to you. Let this light begin to radiate out from you in all directions, touching the people around you. Let your healing energy touch everyone whom you know who needs it. What a privilege it is to share your love and light and healing energy with those who are in need of healing. Let your light move into hospitals and nursing homes and orphanages and prisons, mental hospitals, and other institutions of despair. Let it bring hope and enlightenment and peace.

Let it move into every home in the city in which you live where there is pain and suffering. Let your love and light and healing energy bring comfort to those in need. Let it move into the churches and soften the hearts of those involved, so that they truly operate with unconditional love. Let the beautiful light that comes from your heart move into the Capitol and government buildings, bringing enlightenment and the message of truth. Let it move into every capital in every government. Select one place on the planet as a place that you would like to help heal. Concentrate your light on that place. It may be very far away or it may be around the corner. Concentrate your love and light and your healing energy on this place and see it come into balance and harmony. See it whole. Take a moment every day to send your love and light and healing energy to this particular place on the planet. We are the people. We are the children. We are the world. We are the future. What we give out comes back to us multiplied. And so it is.

Receiving Prosperity

Let's realize some positive qualities for ourselves. We are open and receptive to wonderful new ideas. We allow prosperity to enter into our lives on a level that it has never entered before. We deserve the best. We are willing to accept the best. Our income is constantly increasing. We move away from poverty thinking into prosperity thinking. We love ourselves. We rejoice in who we are and we know that life is here for us and will supply us with everything that we need. We move from success to success, from joy to joy, and from abundance to abundance. We are one with the Power that created us. We express for ourselves the greatness that we are. We are divine, magnificent expressions of Life, and we are open and receptive to all good. And so it is.

Welcome the Child

Put your hand over your heart. Close your eyes. Allow yourself not only to see your inner child but to be that child. Let your own voice speak for your parents as they welcome you into the world and into their lives. Hear them say:

We're so glad you came. We've been waiting for you. We wanted you so much to be part of our family. You're so important to us. We're so glad you are a little boy. We're so glad you are a little girl. We love your uniqueness and your specialness. The family wouldn't be the same without you. We love you. We want to hold you. We want to help you grow up to be all that you can be. You don't have to be like us. You can be yourself. You're so beautiful. You're so bright. You're so creative. It gives us such pleasure to have you here. We love you more than anything in the whole world. We thank you for choosing our family. We know you're blessed. You have blessed us by coming. We love you. We really love you.

Let your little child make these words true for it. Be aware that every day you can hold yourself and say these words. You can look in the mirror and say these words. You can hold a friend and say these words.

Tell yourself all the things you wanted your parents to tell you. Your little child needs to feel wanted and loved. Give that to your child. No matter how old you are or how sick, or how scared, your little child needs to be wanted and loved. Keep telling your child, "I want you and I love you." It is the truth for you. The Universe wants you here, and that's why you are here. You've always been loved and will always be loved throughout eternity. You can live happily ever after. And so it is.

Love is Healing

Love is the most powerful healing force there is. I open myself to love. I am willing to love and be loved. I see myself prosper. I see myself healthy. I see myself creatively fulfilled. I live in peace and safety.

Send everyone you know thoughts of comfort and acceptance and support and love. Be aware that as you send these thoughts out, you also receive them back.

Envelop your family in a circle of love, whether they are living or not. Include your friends, the people at work, and everyone from your past, and all the people you would like to forgive, but don't know how.

Send love to everyone with aids and cancer, and to the friends and lovers, hospice workers, doctors, nurses, alternative therapists, and caretakers. Let's see an end to aids and cancer. In your mind's eye, see a headline that reads, "Cure for cancer found. Cure for aids found."

Put yourself in this circle of love. Forgive yourself. Affirm that you have wonderful, harmonious relationships with your parents, where there is mutual respect and caring on both sides.

Let the circle of love envelop the entire planet, and let your heart open so you can find that space within you where there is unconditional love. See everyone living with dignity and in peace and joy.

You are worth loving. You are beautiful. You are powerful. You open yourself to all good. And so it is.

We Are Free to be Ourselves

In order to be whole, we must accept all of ourselves. So let your heart open and make plenty of room in there for all the parts of yourself. The parts you are proud of and the part that embarrass you. The parts you reject and the parts you love. They are all of you. You are beautiful. We all are. When your heart is full of love for yourself, then you have so much to share with others.

Let this love now fill your room and permeate out to all the people that you know. Put the people you want in the center of your room so that they can receive the love from your overflowing heart. From your child to theirs. Now see all the children in all the people dancing as children dance, skipping and shouting and turning somersaults and cartwheels, filled with exuberant joy. Expressing all the best of the child within.

Let your child go and play with the other children. Let your child dance. Let your child feel safe and free. Let your child be all that it ever wanted to be. You are perfect, whole, and complete, and all is well in your wonderful world. And so it is.

Sharing Healing Energy

Shake your hands and then rub them together. Then share the energy in your hands with the beautiful being before you. It is such an honor and privilege to share healing energy with another human being. It is such a simple thing to do.

Whenever you are with friends, you can spend a little time sharing healing energy. We need to give to each other and receive from each other in simple, meaningful ways. The touch that says *I care*. We may not be able to fix anything, but we care. *I'm here for you and I love you.* Together we can find the answers.

All dis-ease comes to an end. All crises come to an end. Feel the healing energies. Let that energy, that intelligence, that knowledge be awakened in us. We deserve to heal. We deserve to be whole. We deserve to know and love who we are. Divine love has always met and always will meet every human need. And so it is.

A Circle of Love

See yourself standing in a very safe space. Release your burdens and pains and fears. Old negative addictions and patterns. See them falling away from you. Then see yourself standing in your safe place with your arms wide open, saying "I am open and receptive to_____." Declaring for yourself what it is you want. Not what you don't want, but what you do want. And know that it is possible. See yourself whole and healthy. At peace. See yourself filled with love.

All we need is one idea to change our lives. On this planet we can be in a circle of hate or we can be in a circle of love and healing. I choose to be in a circle of love. I realize that everyone wants the same things that I want.

We want to express ourselves creatively in ways that are fulfilling. We want to be peaceful and safe.

And in this space, feel your connection with other people in the world. Let the love in you go from heart to heart. And as your love goes out, know that it comes back to you multiplied. *"I send comforting thoughts to everyone and know that these thoughts are returning to me."* See the world becoming an incredible circle of light. And so it is.

You Deserve Love

We don't have to believe everything. In the perfect time-space sequence, that which you need will rise to the surface. Each one of us has the ability to love ourselves more. Each one of us deserves to be loved. We deserve to live well, to be healthy, to be loved and loving, to prosper, and the little child deserves to grow up to have a wonderful, wonderful life.

See yourself surrounded by love. See yourself happy and healthy and whole. See yourself as you would like your life to be. Put in all the details. Know that you deserve it. Then take the love from your heart and let it begin to flow, filling your body with healing energies.

Let your love begin to flow around the room and around your home until you are in an absolutely enormous circle of love. Feel the love circulating, so as it goes out from you, it returns to you. The most powerful healing force is love. Let it circulate over and over again. Let it wash through your body. You are love. And so it is.

A New Decade

See a new door opening to a decade of great healing. Healing that we have not understood in the past. We are in the process of learning the incredible abilities that we have within ourselves. And we are learning to get in touch with those parts of ourselves that have the answers and are there to lead us and guide us in ways that are for our highest good.

So let's see this new door opening wide and ourselves stepping through it to find healing in many, many different forms. For healing means different things to different people. Many of us have bodies that need healing. Some of us have hearts that need healing, or minds that need healing. So we are open and receptive to the healing that we each need individually. We open the door wide for personal growth, and we move through this doorway, knowing we are safe. It is only change. And so it is.

Spirit Am I

We are the only ones who can save the world. As we band together with a common cause, we find the answers. We must always remember that there is a part of us that is far more than our bodies, far more than our personalities, far more than our dis-eases, and more than our past. There is a part of us that is more than our relationships. The very central core of us is pure spirit. Eternal. Always has been and always will be.

We are here to love ourselves. And to love each other.

By doing this, we will find the answers so that we can heal ourselves and the planet. We are going through extraordinary times. All sorts of things are changing. We may not even know the depth of the problems. Yet, we are swimming as best as we can. This, too, shall pass, and we will find solutions.

We are spirit. And we are free. We connect on a spiritual level, for we know that level can never be taken from us. And on the level of spirit, we are all one. We are free. And so it is.

A World That Is Safe

You might like to hold a hand on either side of you. We've touched on many things, and each of us has something we relate to. We've talked about negative things and positive things. We've talked about fears and frustrations, and how scary it is to go up to somebody and just say, "Hello." Many of us still do not trust ourselves to take care of ourselves. And we feel lost and lonely.

Yet we have been working on ourselves for some time and have noticed that our lives are changing. Lots of problems in the past aren't problems anymore. It doesn't change overnight, but if we are persistent and consistent, positive things do happen.

So let's share the energy we have and the love we have with people on either side of us. Know that as we give from our hearts, we are also receiving from other hearts. Let's open our hearts so that we can take in everyone in the room with love, support, and caring. Let's move that love to people in the street who have no homes and no place to go. Let's share our love with those who are angry, frightened or in pain. Every person. And all those in denial. Those who are in the process of leaving the planet, and those who have already left.

Let's share our love with everybody, whether they accept it or not. There is no way we can be hurt if our love is rejected. Let's hold the entire planet in our hearts, the animals, fish, the birds, the vegetation, and all the people. All the people we are angry at, or frustrated with. Those who are not doing it our way, and those who are expressing so-called evil. Let's take them into our hearts, too. So that out of the feeling of safety, they can begin to recognize who they really are.

See peace breaking out all over the planet. Know that you are contributing to peace right now. Rejoice that you have the ability to do something. You are a beautiful, person. Acknowledge yourself for how wonderful you are. Know that it is the truth for you. And so it is.

Loving All The Parts of Ourselves

I would like you to go back in time to when you were five years old and see yourself as clearly as you can. Look at that little child, and with your arms outstretched, say to that child: *"I am your future and I have come to love you."* Embrace the child and bring it forward with you to present time. Now both of you stand in front of a mirror so you can look at each other with love.

You see that there are a few parts of you that are missing. Once again go back in time to the moment you were first born. You were wet and felt the cold air on your body. You had just come through a difficult journey. The lights were bright, and the umbilical cord was still attached, and you were scared. Yet here you were ready to start life on this planet. Love the little baby.

Move to the time when you were just learning to walk. You stood up and fell down and stood up and fell down once again. Suddenly you took your first step, and then another step and another. You were so proud of yourself. Love the little child.

Move forward to your first day of school. You didn't want to leave your mother. You were brave to step across the threshold of a new period of time in your life. You did the very best you could with the whole situation. Love the little child.

Now you are ten years old. You remember what was going on. It may have been wonderful or frightful. You were doing the very best to survive. Love the ten-year-old child.

Go forward to when you just entered puberty and were a teenager. It may have been exciting because you were finally growing up. It may have been frightening because there was a lot of peer pressure to look right and act the right way. You handled it the best you could. Love the teenager.

Now you are graduating high school. You knew more than your parents. You were ready to begin your life now the way you wanted. You were brave and scared all at the same time. Love that young adult.

Now remember your first day at work. The first time

you earned money and you were so proud. You wanted to do well. There was so much to learn. You did the best you knew how. Love that person.

Think of another milestone in your life. A marriage. Your own child. A new home. It may have been a dreadful experience or a wonderful one. Somehow you handled it. You survived in the best way you could. Love the person you are.

Now bring all these parts of yourself forward, and stand in front of the mirror so you can look at each of them with love. Coming towards you is yet another part. Your future stands with arms outstretched and says, *"I am here to love you."* And so it is.

Feel Your Power

Feel your power. Feel the power of your breath. Feel the power of your sound. Feel the power of your love. Feel the power of your forgiveness. Feel the power of your willingness to change. Feel your power. You are beautiful. You are a divine, magnificent being. You deserve all good, not just some, but *all* good. Feel your power. Be at peace with it, for you are safe. Welcome this new day with open arms and with love. And so it is.

The Light Has Come

Sit opposite your partner and hold your partner's hands. Look into each other's eyes. Take a nice deep breath and release any fear that you may have. Take another deep breath and release your judgment and allow yourself to be with this person. What you see in them is a reflection of you, a reflection of what is in you.

It's all right. We are all one. We breathe the same air. We drink the same water. We eat the foods of the earth. We have the same desires and needs. We all want to be healthy. We all want to love and be loved. We all want to live comfortably and peacefully, and we all want to prosper. We all want to live our lives with fulfillment.

Allow yourself to look at this person with love, and be willing to receive the love back. Know that you are safe. As you look at your partners, affirm for them the perfect health. Affirm for them loving relationships, so that they are surrounded by loving people wherever they may be. Affirm for them prosperity so that they live comfortably. Affirm for them comfort and safety and know that what you give out returns to you multiplied. So affirm the very best of everything, and know that they deserve it and see them willing to accept it. And so it is.

SELF-HELP RESOURCES

The following list of resources can be used to access information on a variety of issues. The addresses and telephone numbers listed are for the national headquarters; look in your local yellow pages under "Community Services" for resources closer to your area.

In addition to the following groups, other self-help organizations may be available in your area to assist your healing and recovery for a particular life crisis not listed here. Consult your telephone directory, call a counseling center or help line near you, or contact:

AIDS

CBC National AIDS Hotline
(800) 342-2437

Children with AIDS (CWA)
Project of America
(800) 866-AIDS (24-hour hotline)

The Names Project—
AIDS Quilt
(800) 872-6263

Project Inform
19655 Market St., Ste. 220
San Francisco, CA 94103
(415) 558-8669

PWA Coalition
50 W. 17th St.
New York, NY 10011

Spanish HIV/STD/AIDS Hotline
(800) 344-7432

TTY (Hearing Impaired) AIDS Hotline
(CDC National HIV/AIDS)
(800) 243-7889

ALCOHOL ABUSE

Al-Anon Family Headquarters
1600 Corporate Landing Parkway
Virginia Beach, VA 23454-5617
(800) 4AL-ANON

Alcoholics Anonymous (AA)
General Service Office
475 Riverside Dr.
New York, NY 10115
(212) 870-3400

Children of Alcoholics Foundation
164 W. 74th St.
New York, NY 10023
(800) 359-COAF

Meridian Council, Inc.
Administrative Offices
4 Elmcrest Terrace
Norwalk, CT 06850

Mothers Against Drunk Driving
(MADD)
(254) 690-6233

National Association of Children
of Alcoholics (NACOA)
11426 Rockville Pike, Ste. 100
Rockville, MD 20852
(301) 468-0985
(888) 554-2627

National Clearinghouse for Alcohol
and Drug Information (NCADI)
P.O. Box 234
Rockville, MD 20852
(301) 468-2600

National Council on Alcoholism and
Drug Dependence (NCADD)
12 West 21st St.
New York, NY 10010
(212) 206-6770
(800) 475-HOPE

Women for Sobriety
(800) 333-1606

ALZHEIMER'S DISEASE

Alzheimer's Association
919 N. Michigan Ave., Ste. 1100
Chicago, IL 60611
(800) 621-0379
www.alz.org

Alzheimer's Disease Education
and Referral Center
P.O. Box 8250
Silver Spring, MD 20907
(800) 438-4380
adear@alzheimers.org

Eldercare Locator
927 15th St. NW, 6th Fl.
Washington, DC 20005
(800) 677-1116

CANCER

National Cancer Institute
(800) 4-CANCER

CHILDREN'S ISSUES

Child Molestation

Child Help USA/Child Abuse Hotline
232 East Gish Rd.
San Jose, CA 95112
(800) 422-4453

Prevent Child Abuse America
200 South Michigan Ave., Ste. 17
Chicago, IL 60604
(312) 663-3520

Crisis Intervention

Boy's Town National Hotline
(800) 448-3000

Children of the Night
P.O. Box 4343
Hollywood, CA 90078
(800) 551-1300

Covenant House Hotline
(800) 999-9999

Kid Save Line
(800) 543-7283

Youth Nineline
(referrals for parents/teens about drugs,
homelessness, runaways)
(800) 999-9999

Missing Children

Missing Children...HELP Center
410 Ware Blvd., Ste. 710
Tampa, FL 33619
(800) USA-KIDS

**National Center for Missing
and Exploited Children**
699 Prince St.
Alexandria, VA 22314
(800) 843-5678

Children with Serious Illnesses
(fulfilling wishes):

Brass Ring Society
National Headquarters
213 N. Washington St.
Snow Hill, MD 21863
(410) 632-4700
(800) 666-WISH

Make-a-Wish Foundation
(800) 332-9474

CO-DEPENDENCY

Co-Dependents Anonymous
(602) 277-7991

DEATH/GRIEVING/SUICIDE

Grief Recovery Institute
P.O. Box 461659
Los Angeles, CA 90046-1659
(323) 650-1234
www/grief-recovery.com

**National Hospice and
Palliative Care Organization**
1700 Diagonal Rd., Ste. 300
Alexandria, VA 22314
(703) 243-5900
www.nhpco.org

**SIDS (Sudden Infant Death Syndrome)
Alliance**
1314 Bedford Ave., Ste. 210
Baltimore, MD 21208

Parents of Murdered Children
(recovering from violent death
of friend or family member)
100 E 8th St., Ste. B41
Cincinnati, OH 45202
(513) 721-5683

Survivors of Suicide
Call your local Mental Health Association
for the branch nearest you.

AARP Grief and Loss Programs
(202) 434-2260
(800) 424-3410 ext. 2260

DEBTS

Credit Referral
(information on local credit
counseling services)
(800) 388-CCCS

Debtors Anonymous
General Service Board
P.O. Box 888
Needham, MA 02492-0009
(781) 453-2743
www.debtorsanonymous.org

DIABETES

American Diabetes Association
(800) 232-3472

DOMESTIC VIOLENCE

National Coalition Against
Domestic Violence
P.O. Box 34103
Washington, DC 20043-4103
(202) 745-1211

National Domestic Violence Hotline
P.O. Box 161810
Austin, TX 78716
(800) 799-SAFE

DRUG ABUSE

Cocaine Anonymous
National Referral Line
(800) 347-8998

National Helpline of Phoenix House
(cocaine abuse hotline)
(800) 262-2463
(800) COCAINE
www.drughelp.org

National Institute of Drug Abuse (NIDA)
6001 Executive Blvd., Rm. 5213
Bethesda, MD 20892-9561
Parklawn Building
(301) 443-6245 (for information)
(800) 662-4357 (for help)

World Service Office, Inc. (CA)
3740 Overland Ave., Ste. C
Los Angeles, CA 90034-6337
(310) 559-5833
(800) 347-8998 (to leave message)

EATING DISORDERS

Overeaters Anonymous
National Office
P.O. Box 44020
Rio Rancho, NM 87174-4020
(505) 891-2664

GAMBLING

Gamblers Anonymous
New York Intergroup
P.O. Box 7
New York, NY 10116-0007
(212) 903-4400

HEALTH ISSUES

Alzheimer's Association
919 N. Michigan Ave., Ste. 1100
Chicago, IL 60611-1676
(800) 621-0379

American Chronic Pain Association
P.O. Box 850
Rocklin, CA 95677
(916) 632-0922
www.theacpa.org

American Foundation
of Traditional Chinese Medicine
P.O. Box 330267
San Francisco, CA 94133
(415) 392-7002

American Holistic Health Association
P.O. Box 17400
Anaheim, CA 92817
(714) 779-6152
e-mail: ahha.org
www.ahha@healthy.net

Office of Deepak Chopra
The Chopra Center at
La Costa Resort and Spa
2013 Costa Del Mar
Carlsbad, CA 92009
(760) 494-1600
www.chopra.com

The Fetzer Institute
9292 West KL Ave.
Kalamazoo, MI 49009
(616) 375-2000

Hippocrates Health Institute
1443 Palmdale Court
West Palm Beach, FL 33411

Hospicelink
190 Westbrook Rd.
Essex, CN 06426
(800) 331-1620

Institute for Noetic Sciences
P.O. Box 909
Sausalito, CA 94966
(415) 331-5650

The Mind-Body Medical Institute
110 Francis St., Ste. 1A
Boston, MA 02215
(617) 632-9525

National Health Information Center
P.O. Box 1133
Washington, DC 20013-1133
(800) 336-4797

Optimum Health Care Institute
6970 Central Ave.
Lemon Grove, CA 91945
(619) 464-3346

Preventive Medicine Research Institute
Dean Ornish, M.D.
900 Bridgeway, Ste. 2
Sausalito, CA 94965
(415) 332-2525

HOUSING RESOURCES

Acorn
(nonprofit network of low-
and moderate-income housing)
739 8th St., S.E.
Washington, DC 20003
(202) 547-9292

IMPOTENCE

Impotence Institute of America
P.O. Box 410
Bowie, MD 20718-0410
(800) 669-1603
www.impotenceworld.org

MENTAL HEALTH

**American Psychiatric
Association of America**
www.psych.org

**Anxiety Disorders Association
of America**
www.adaa.org

**The Help Center of the American
Psychological Association**
www.helping.apa.org

**The International Society
for Mental Health Online**
www.ismho.org

Knowledge Exchange Network
www.mentalhealth.org

National Center for PTSD
www.dartmouth.edu/dms/ptsd

National Alliance for the Mentally Ill
www.nami.org

**National Depressive
and Manic-Depressive Association**
www.ndmda.org

National Institute of Mental Health
www.nimh.nih.gov

PET BEREAVEMENT

Bide-A-Wee Foundation
410 E. 38th St.
New York, NY 10016
(212) 532-6395

Holistic Animal Consulting Centre
29 Lyman Ave.
Staten Island, NY 10305
(718) 720-5548

RAPE/SEXUAL ISSUES

**Rape, Abuse, and
Incest National Network**
(800) 656-4673

Safe Place
P.O. Box 19454
Austin, TX 78760
(512) 440-7273

**National Council on
Sexual Addictions and Compulsivity**
1090 S. Northchase Parkway, Ste. 200
South Marietta, GA 30067
(770) 989-9754

Sexually Transmitted Disease Referral
(800) 227-8922

SMOKING

Nicotine Anonymous
P.O. Box 126338
Harrisburg, PA 17112
(415) 750-0328
www.nicotine-anonymous.org

STRESS REDUCTION

**The Biofeedback & Psychophysiology
Clinic The Menninger Clinic**
P.O. Box 829
Topeka, KS 66601-0829
(913) 350-5000

**New York Open Center
(In-depth workshops
to invigorate the spirit)**
83 Spring St.
New York, NY 10012
(212) 219-2527

**Omega Institute
(a healing, spiritual retreat community)**
150 Lake Dr.
Rhinebeck, NY 12572-3212
(845) 266-4444 (info)
(800) 944-1001 (to enroll)

**The Stress Reduction
Clinic Center for Mindfulness
University of Massachusetts
Medical Center**
55 Lake Ave. North
Worcester, MA 01655
(508) 856-1616 • (508) 856-2656

TEEN HELP

ADOL: Adolescent Directory Online
Includes information on eating disorders,
depression, and teen pregnancy.
www.education.indiana.edu/cas/adol/adol.html

Al-Anon/Alateen
1600 Corporate Landing Parkway
Virginia Beach, VA 23454-5617
(888) 425-2666
(888) 4AL-ANON
www.al-anon.org

**Focus Adolescent Services:
Eating Disorders**
www.focusas.com/EatingDisorders.html

Future Point
A nonprofit organization that offers message boards and chat rooms to empower

teens in the academic world and beyond.
www.futurepoint.org

Kids in Trouble Help Page
Child abuse, depression, suicide,
and runaway resources,
with links and hotline numbers.
www.geocities.com/EnchantedForest/2910

Planned Parenthood
810 Seventh Ave.
New York, NY 10019
(212) 541-7800
www.plannedparenthood.org

SafeTeens.com
Provides lessons on online safety and pri-
vacy; also has resources for homework and
fun on the web.
www.safeteens.com

TeenCentral.net
This site is written by and about teens.
Includes celebrity stories, real-teen tales,
an anonymous help-line, and crisis
counseling.
www.teencentral.net

TeenOutReach.com
Includes all kinds of information geared at
teens, from sports to entertainment to help
with drugs and eating disorders.
www.teenoutreach.com

Hotlines for Teenagers

Boys Town National Hotline
(800) 448-3000

**Childhelp National Child Abuse Hotline/
Voices for Children**
(800) 422-4453
(800) 4ACHILD

Just for Kids Hotline
(888) 594-5437
(888) 594-KIDS

National Child Abuse Hotline
(800) 792-5200

National Runaway Hotline
(800) 621-4000

National Youth Crisis Hotline
(800) 442-4673
(800) 442-HOPE

Suicide Prevention Hotline
(800) 827-7571

RECOMMENDED READING

Ageless Body, Timeless Mind—Deepak Chopra, M.D.

Aging Parents & You—Eugenia Anderson-Ellis

Alternative Medicine, the Definitive Guide—The Burton Goldberg Group

As Someone Dies—Elizabeth A. Johnson

Autobiography of a Yogi—Paramahansa Yogananda

Between Parent and Child—Hiam Ginott

The Body Knows—Caroline Sutherland, Medical Intuitive

The Canary and Chronic Fatigue—Majid Ali, M.D.

The Celestine Prophecy—James Redfield

The Complete Book of Essential Oils & Aromatherapy—Valerie Ann Worwood

Constant Craving: What Your Food Cravings Mean and How to Overcome Them—Doreen Virtue, Ph.D.

Cooking for Healthy Healing—Linda G. Rector-Page, N.D., Ph.D.

The Course in Miracles—Foundation for Inner Peace

Creative Visualization—Shakti Gawain

Diet for a New America—John Robbins

Discovering the Child Within—John Bradshaw

Do What You Love, the Money Will Follow—Marsha Sinetar

Everyday Wisdom—Dr. Wayne W. Dyer

Feel the Fear and Do It Anyway—Susan Jeffers, Ph.D.

Fire in the Soul—Joan Borysenko, Ph.D.

Fit for Life—Harvey and Marilyn Diamond

The Fountain of Age—Betty Friedan

Great American Cookbook—Marilyn Diamond

Handbook to Higher Consciousness—Ken Keyes

Healthy Healing, An Alternative Healing Reference—Linda G. Rector-Page, N.D., Ph.D.

How to Meditate—Lawrence LeShan

Instead of Therapy: Help Yourself Change and Change the Help You're Getting—Tom Rusk, M.D.

Learning to Love Yourself—Sharon Wegscheider-Cruse

Life After Life—Raymond Moody, M.D.

Lifegoals—Amy E. Dean

Life! You Wanna Make Something of It?—Tom Costa, M.D.

Losing Your Pounds of Pain: Breaking the Link Between Abuse, Stress, and Overeating—Doreen Virtue, Ph.D.

Love Is Letting Go of Fear—Gerald Jampolsky, M.D.

Love, Medicine, and Miracles—Bernie Siegel, M.D.

Man's Search for Meaning—Viktor Frankl

Many Lives, Many Masters—Brian Weiss, M.D.

The Menopause Industry: How the Medical Establishment Exploits Women—Sandra Coney

Menopause Made Easy—Carolle Jean-Murat, M.D.

Minding the Body, Mending the Mind—Joan Borysenko, Ph.D.

Mutant Message, Down Under—Marlo Morgan

My Mother Made Me Do It—Nan Kathryn Fuchs

The Nature of Personal Reality—Jane Roberts

Opening Our Hearts to Men—Susan Jeffers, Ph.D.

Parents' Nutrition Bible—Dr. Earl Mindell, R.Ph., Ph.D.

Passages—Gail Sheehy

Peace, Love, and Healing—Bernie Siegel, M.D.

The Power of the Mind to Heal—Joan and Miroslav Borysenko, Ph.D.'s

The Power of Touch—Phyllis K. Davis

Prescription for Nutritional Healing—James F. Balch, M.D., and Phyllis A. Balch, C.N.C.

Real Magic—Dr. Wayne W. Dyer

The Reconnection—Dr. Eric Pearl

The Relaxation Response—Benson and Klipper

A Return to Love—Marianne Williamson

Revolution from Within—Gloria Steinem

The Road Less Traveled—M. Scott Peck, M.D.

Saved by the Light—Dannion Brinkley

The Science of Mind—Ernest Holmes

Self-Parenting—John Pollard III

Staying on the Path—Dr. Wayne W. Dyer

Super Nutrition Gardening—Dr. William S. Peavy and Warren Peary

Thoughts of Power and Love—Susan Jeffers, Ph.D.

The Tibetan Book of Living and Dying—Sogyal Rinpoche

What Do You Really Want for Your Children?—Dr. Wayne W. Dyer

What Every Woman Needs to Know Before (and After) She Gets Involved with Men and Money—Judge Lois Forer

When 9 to 5 Isn't Enough—Marcia Perkins-Reed

Woman Heal Thyself: An Ancient Healing System for Contemporary Woman—Jeanne Elizabeth Blum

A Woman's Worth—Marianne Williamson

Women Alone: Creating a Joyous and Fulfilling Life—Julie Keene and Ione Jenson

Women Who Love Too Much—Robin Norwood

Your Sacred Self—Dr. Wayne W. Dyer

❀ Any book by Emmett Fox or Dr. John MacDonald

❀ Also, the audiocassette program, *Making Relationships Work*, by Barbara De Angelis, Ph.D.

ABOUT THE AUTHOR

Louise Hay is a metaphysical lecturer, teacher, and best-selling author with more than 50 million books sold worldwide.

For more than 30 years, Louise has helped people throughout the world discover and implement the full potential of their own creative powers for personal growth and self-healing. Louise is the founder and chairman of Hay House, Inc., which disseminates books, CDs, DVDs, and other products that contribute to the healing of the planet.

Please visit: www.LouiseHay.com® and www.HealYour Life.com®, and Louise's Facebook page: www.facebook.com/ LouiseLHay

Hay House Titles of Related Interest

YOU CAN HEAL YOUR LIFE, the movie,
starring Louise L. Hay & Friends
(available as a 1-DVD program and an expanded 2-DVD set)
Watch the trailer at: www.LouiseHayMovie.com

THE SHIFT, the movie,
starring Dr. Wayne W. Dyer
(available as a 1-DVD program and an expanded 2-DVD set)
Watch the trailer at: www.DyerMovie.com

▲▼▲

THE ESSENTIAL DOREEN VIRTUE COLLECTION, by Doreen Virtue

THE ESSENTIAL LAW OF ATTRACTION COLLECTION,
by Esther and Jerry Hicks (The Teachings of Abraham®)

THE ESSENTIAL WAYNE DYER COLLECTION, by Dr. Wayne W. Dyer

All of the above are available at your local bookstore,
or may be ordered by contacting Hay House (see next page).

▲▼▲

We hope you enjoyed this Hay House book. If you'd like to receive
our online catalog featuring additional information on Hay House books
and products, or if you'd like to find out more about the
Hay Foundation, please contact:

Hay House, Inc., P.O. Box 5100, Carlsbad, CA 92018-5100
(760) 431-7695 or (800) 654-5126
(760) 431-6948 (fax) or (800) 650-5115 (fax)
www.hayhouse.com® • www.hayfoundation.org

▲▼▲

Published and distributed in Australia by: Hay House Australia Pty. Ltd., 18/36
Ralph St., Alexandria NSW 2015 • *Phone:* 612-9669-4299
Fax: 612-9669-4144 • www.hayhouse.com.au

Published and distributed in the United Kingdom by: Hay House UK, Ltd., Astley
House, 33 Notting Hill Gate, London W11 3JQ • *Phone:* 44-20-3675-2450
Fax: 44-20-3675-2451 • www.hayhouse.co.uk

Published and distributed in the Republic of South Africa by: Hay House SA
(Pty), Ltd., P.O. Box 990, Witkoppen 2068 • *Phone/Fax:* 27-11-467-8904
www.hayhouse.co.za

Published in India by: Hay House Publishers India, Muskaan Complex, Plot No.
3, B-2, Vasant Kunj, New Delhi 110 070 • *Phone:* 91-11-4176-1620
Fax: 91-11-4176-1630 • www.hayhouse.co.in

Distributed in Canada by: Raincoast, 9050 Shaughnessy St.,
Vancouver, B.C. V6P 6E5 • *Phone:* (604) 323-7100 • *Fax:* (604) 323-2600
www.raincoast.com

▲▼▲

Take Your Soul on a Vacation

Visit www.HealYourLife.com® to regroup, recharge,
and reconnect with your own magnificence.
Featuring blogs, mind-body-spirit news, and
life-changing wisdom from Louise Hay and friends.

Visit www.HealYourLife.com today!

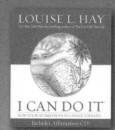

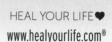